An Unplanned Life

An Unplanned Life

A Memoir

Franklin A. Thomas

NEW YORK
LONDON

Requests for permission to reproduce selections from this book should be made
through our website: https://thenewpress.com/contact.

Published in the United States by The New Press, New York, 2022
Distributed by Two Rivers Distribution

ISBN 978-1-62097-757-6 (hc)
ISBN 978-1-62097-773-6 (ebook)
CIP data is available

The New Press publishes books that promote and enrich public discussion and
understanding of the issues vital to our democracy and to a more equitable world.
These books are made possible by the enthusiasm of our readers; the support of a
committed group of donors, large and small; the collaboration of our many partners
in the independent media and the not-for-profit sector; booksellers, who often
hand-sell New Press books; librarians; and above all by our authors.

www.thenewpress.com

Composition by Westchester Publishing Services
This book was set in Adobe Caslon Pro

Printed in the United States of America

2   4   6   8   10   9   7   5   3   1

Contents

Foreword

One of my great privileges was visiting regularly with Frank Thomas in his modest office in the Chanin Building, on East 42nd Street. I would walk the few blocks from the Ford Foundation, an institution that Frank stewarded and brought back from the brink—excited to see him, grateful for the gift of our friendship. I relished our time together. I luxuriated in these opportunities to bask in his glow, to wallow in his wisdom. He gave me the gift of clarity but also confidence.

Through the years, Frank counseled me on dealing with difficult foundation staff who resisted change, on how to build a successful engagement with the Ford trustees, and later, joining boards myself. Frank challenged my thinking, sharpened my ideas, warned me against the arrogance and ego that naturally accrete in any high office, especially in the hallowed halls of large foundations. Even now, I marvel at his discretion, his humility, his equanimity in all things. His wisdom.

He could pull me back, or lift me up, or keep me on track—knowing always what I needed to hear, even if I didn't want to hear it. Frank believed in the human capacity to transform, evolve, and build bridges across lines of ideology and difference.

Of course, we also swapped personal stories—the latest updates from Vernon Jordan were always at the top of our list.

His pride when he talked about his beloved Kate was especially palpable. And he fully embraced me, a gay man, and my partner David, for the people we were and the life we had made together over twenty-six years. When David died suddenly, Frank was one of the first people to reach me.

In short, Frank made an indelible impact on my life. He changed its trajectory. And in this regard, I am hardly alone.

Countless individuals and institutions, even nations, owe a debt to Frank Thomas.

At home:
- The United States Attorney's Office for the Southern District of New York;
- The New York City Police Department;
- The Bedford Stuyvesant Restoration Corporation, the granddaddy of the community-development movement;
- The September 11th Fund.

Across the nation:
- Early in his career, at the agency that later became the Department of Housing and Urban Development;
- The Local Initiatives Support Corporation—LISC—which he helped create;
- And later, on the boards of companies and universities.

And around the world:
- Where Frank's partnership with Nelson Mandela modeled the power of truth and reconciliation;
- Where Frank championed the rule of law and values of democracy in South Africa's new constitution;
- And, of course, through the Ford Foundation—which he boldly served and strengthened. Dare I say . . . No Frank? No Ford.

So, what are we to make of a world without Frank, now that he has left us? How are we to inhabit this world that he shaped and improved for us, knowing we feel his absence and miss his voice?

It is difficult to consider our own mortality—our finite, limited time on this earth. We humans tend to have a problem with contemplating such things. But we learn from Frank that the measure of our lives is not how big we are, but how big-hearted we are.

That significance, meaning, comes from how we love, not just what we lead. For each of us, if we had only one wish, if only one of our prayers was answered, would it not be to live well, and fully, with joy, and purpose, and grace? Would it not be to live—to leave a legacy—like Frank's?

Let us resolve, then, to continue as Frank did: To know love and be generous. To be righteous in our cause, but never self-righteous in our character. To advance the slow and steady march of progress. To bend the arc of the moral universe, with our own hands, in our own way, toward justice.

Darren Walker
January 2022

An Unplanned Life

1

Growing Up in Bedford-Stuyvesant

When I was growing up in the Bedford-Stuyvesant section of Brooklyn, New York, there were two public figures whose pictures were prominently displayed on the walls of our home: my namesake, Franklin D. Roosevelt, and the Queen of England.

FDR was much respected by my family. We would gather in the living room regularly to listen to his radio broadcasts. I was the one who delivered word of his death to my mother after hearing it from a neighbor in April of 1945. The grief in our household was considerable.

The Queen of England was important to us, and to all Barbadians, because Barbados was part of the Commonwealth. I remember a Barbadian telling me that when the Queen was crowned in the early 1950s, someone who'd been to London for the coronation came back and described it to a local Barbadian, who replied, "Oh, they had a celebration there too?" Some say Barbados sees itself as the healthy center of the world, and it is certainly true that a robust self-confidence and proud commitment to education, democracy, and independence are palpable in the country and its people.

I was born in Brooklyn on May 27, 1934, the youngest child of immigrant parents. My father, James Thomas, was born in Antigua and came to the States as part of the group recruited from the Caribbean to help dig the Panama Canal. My mother,

Viola Atherley, made her way directly from Barbados at age sixteen.

They met in New York, married, and had six children, two boys and four girls. The oldest, my brother, was born in 1918. When I was three years old my parents separated, but they reconnected some seven years later when my father suffered a stroke and came back to live with us. He died when I was eleven. Not long after, my brother died of pneumonia. From that point forward I was the sole male in our six-member household.

My mother was a strong and capable woman. Nothing seemed beyond her ability to address. She had all kinds of jobs, but she mainly worked as a housekeeper for families in Brooklyn until the war years, when, in addition to handling her daily workload, she went to New York Technical College at night, became a lathe operator, and was hired by the American Can Company in Long Island City to replace the men who had been drafted during World War II. When the war ended in 1945, and the company fired most of the women to provide opportunities for returning veterans and to get back to a more traditional way of operating, my mother resumed work as a housekeeper. She didn't express bitterness about it. She just did what she had to do, and that's pretty much how she ran her life, and our lives too.

I was taught that if you were smart, had good values, and worked hard, there were no limits to what you could do, even though I was growing up in a period of intense racial segregation in many parts of the United States. In our family, education was paramount and teachers were revered. They were viewed as the people who could most help you realize your potential. As a result, no complaints about homework or much else were allowed. During my elementary school years a teacher once slapped my hand. I wasn't sure why and reported the incident to my mother that evening. "Did she slap anyone else?" she asked.

"No," I replied. "Then just let me know if it happens again." Not many words were spoken but the message was clear. Maybe I'd been daydreaming or in some way had inadvertently earned the teacher's punishment, but if for some reason I was being mistreated, I could count on my mother to handle it. She would protect me, but with that protection came responsibility.

Inside the gate of our front yard on Putnam Avenue I felt secure as a child, even when the nearby high school had just let out and the boisterous teens were walking by on their way home. Unpleasant encounters beyond that safe space puzzled me but were usually absorbed only after they'd been astutely interpreted by my mother. I recall an instance when I was quite young, maybe six years old, playing with a neighborhood friend, a white boy, on the sidewalks near our houses. He wanted to go into his apartment for something. "Come on," he said, matter-of-factly. I followed up the stairs, standing near him as he knocked on the door. A woman opened it, motioned for him to come in, and made it clear that I should not. I had no idea why I was denied entry but went back to my own house, around the corner, and told my mother what happened. "Don't worry about that," she said. "They're just prejudiced." Clueless as to the meaning of that word, I thought that meant they were sick. Whatever the definition, my mother's messaging was plain. There wasn't anything wrong with me. It was their problem, their disadvantage. I somehow was able to walk away from that situation without feeling rejected and with my self-esteem intact.

My sense of security and overall confidence were further bolstered by my four older sisters, all incredibly smart and competent. When I was very young and had trouble sleeping, one or another of them wouldn't hesitate to take me out for a trolley ride to make me sleepy. As I grew, they'd let me stick around when they had their friends over to listen to music on the radio. That's how I learned to dance. They were generous

with their support, and they were infinitely more knowledgeable and experienced than I was. I took their investment seriously, although all of them wanted desperately for me to
become a doctor, and since I hated the sight of blood, I knew
that possibility was highly unlikely.

My sisters attended Girls Commercial High School and entered the workforce upon graduating. The oldest went to work
for the War Department in Washington, DC, during World
War II. My mother and I visited her when she lived there, and I
remember encountering racial segregation that was unlike anything I'd experienced in New York City. You couldn't go to the
movies and sit where you chose, you couldn't do many things
freely. The trip made a strong impression on me. We were a
family that was content in our own skin, taught to believe that
if you could imagine it, you could accomplish it, and that obstacles were just part of life. The obstacles on clear display in
our nation's capital were different from any I'd faced thus far,
even though I'd grown up in Bedford-Stuyvesant during the
era of the fighting street gangs. They all had their turfs marked
out, and even a short trip from one location to another required
strategy and careful navigation in order to avoid trouble. I realize that my mother had been preparing me to overcome obstacles of all kinds since I was a little boy.

Going to church every Sunday was required. Our primary
church was the African Orthodox, whose liturgy resembled that
of the Church of England. Baptism and service as an altar
boy were part of the obligatory ritual, and I complied. When I
developed an interest in the Boy Scouts and their marching
bands, I sought out a church that sponsored a troop with a drum
and bugle corps, and that ultimately led me to Concord Baptist
Church, some distance from where we lived.

I transferred from my local troop to Concord Troop 198 at
the age of eleven, and I remained a member until I left for col-

lege at seventeen. Twice a week I attended meetings to advance up the scout ladder, and to learn to play the bugle and later the drums so I could join the troop's drum and bugle corps. The corps marched in parades throughout Brooklyn and Manhattan, and it was the lure of those parades that motivated me to practice the horn until my lips were swollen. By age sixteen, I was proud to lead that marching band of one hundred members.

My first bicycle, which I had been given at the age of ten, had greatly expanded my world. It helped me get to Boy Scout meetings, basketball games, and even to scout retreats in Alpine, New Jersey. To this day I remember the leg pains from peddling a three-gear Columbia bike, fully loaded with equipment, across the George Washington Bridge to the Palisades Parkway, up the hills of 9W to Alpine Boy Scout Camp, and the sense of satisfaction that ensued.

From the time I was a very young boy and had to jog to keep pace with my older brother, whose job was to walk me there each morning, I always found school an enjoyable place to be, both academically and socially. It was always clear to me that part of the responsibility for making that experience good and worthwhile was mine. The public schools I attended up until high school were in various parts of Bedford-Stuyvesant, depending on the neighborhood we lived in at the time. There was only one situation in which I distinctly remember feeling unwelcome. It was toward the end of my elementary school years, after a move and a mid-year school transfer into a classroom in which the teacher let it be known that it was a big imposition for her to have to incorporate me into her already established learning environment. This classroom and the school more generally were much less diverse than the one I had just left. I seem to recall maybe one other African American student in the room. I sensed the teacher's resistance right away, but as time passed, and I proved myself to be a good student, her attitude toward me improved.

By junior high school I qualified for the Rapid Advance program, which at the time was reserved for the most motivated and academically gifted students. This designation put me on track for an earlier graduation than my peers. I used the percussion skills I developed with the Boy Scouts to play drums in the junior high school band, and I was also appointed "Captain of the Guards" to keep order in the schoolyard during recess. The position involved regular meetings with the teachers and administrators to discuss school issues.

During one recess, a boy was being aggressive toward other students, and as I attempted to subdue him, he pulled out a knife. I continued to go toward him, not backing off. My hand was cut in the process, which actually caused him to retreat and apologize. I still have that scar. Looking back, I don't remember feeling any fear at the time. I just knew it was my job to keep the others safe.

More than forty years later, during my tenure at the Ford Foundation, one of my classmates from junior high managed to track me down and pay a visit because she wanted to thank me for coming to her rescue one day in the schoolyard when I intervened on her behalf. I had no recollection of the incident, but my actions were meaningful to her, as her visit was to me.

I'd grown tall early, and my physical presence was certainly an asset in my "guard" duties, as it was on the basketball court. I played as much as I could and was known to be strong off the backboards and a very solid defender. Around the Brooklyn playgrounds I was called a "horse."

Basketball was an important part of my life, and that continued throughout my high school years at Franklin K. Lane High School in Queens. I captained the basketball team there and excelled as both a student and an athlete. Gil Scott, one of my high school classmates and basketball teammates, says I was the only person who had books on the table during lunch. We had a very good team at Franklin Lane, and to this day my teammates chide me about graduating early, in January instead of June of 1952, and missing the citywide championship, which they felt we could have won had I played.

While I was at Franklin Lane, a citywide basketball coaches' strike shut down high school basketball for a year. I, along with many other players throughout the city, headed to the local YMCAs and other facilities to play. I joined the team of the Carleton YMCA in Bedford-Stuyvesant, and it was one of the most exciting years of basketball I'd ever played. Some of the most talented players in the city were on the Carleton Y team, and big crowds filled the stands for our intense games.

I'd been offered athletic scholarships for college, but my extraordinary basketball coach at Franklin Lane advised me against accepting any of them, worried that were I to be injured, I might lose the scholarship and my ticket to college. He told me that my grades were strong enough to get me into a good college and I could apply for financial aid once accepted. My mother and sisters were also against me attending college on an athletic scholarship, fearful that I would be pegged only as an athlete.

I'd heard about Columbia University and its reputation, and when I visited I met Lou Rossini, the basketball coach, who encouraged me to apply. I liked a lot of things I observed during my tour of the place, and as things turned out, I did apply and was admitted. I was also offered a scholarship. Columbia didn't officially have athletic scholarships, but I would be playing basketball there in addition to pursuing an academic degree. At the time I wasn't sure exactly what I wanted to study, but I was very excited about the wide range of courses open to me.

Early graduation meant I had half a year before college be-gan, and I would fill that time with a full-time job. I was no stranger to work. I'd had odd jobs since I was a small boy. The first, on my own initiative, was when I was six or seven. I started to shine shoes for money on Fulton Street—that is, until my mother found out and put an end to it, feeling I was much too young to be engaged in such an activity on my own. At home my job was to shovel coal into the furnace in the basement, and also to check the truck when the coal was delivered to ensure they dumped the proper amount into the chute and we weren't being shorted. I also worked for our neighbors across the street, the Allens, cleaning the hallways of a building they owned, and I regularly worked on weekends with my uncle, who was a car-penter and taught me carpentry. He was strong in mind and body; he played the organ in church, didn't talk much, and he rarely laughed. But when we went to the movies, usually a triple bill including the feature and the serials on a Saturday after-noon, he would excitedly talk out loud to the characters on the screen. "Look out," he would call to the hero, "he's behind you!"

In the nine months leading up to my freshman year at Co-lumbia, I was an office boy at Farkas & Barron, a structural en-gineering firm at 150 Broadway in Manhattan. I liked the job but hated answering the phones every day when the secretary was at lunch. It was interesting being around the engineers, and I even thought about what it would be like to study engineer-ing. Once, I recognized an unusual shape in one of the projects being worked on and I blurted out the name. Surprised, the engineer turned and said, "You're right." I was eager where learning was concerned and not shy about expressing it.

Even though I could get there on the subway, in many ways, when I entered college in the fall of 1952, there was a great distance between my childhood home in Bedford-Stuyvesant and Columbia University in Morningside Heights.

2

A Higher Education

Columbia was a revelation for me. My mind and imagination were stimulated in ways they hadn't been up to that point. When I arrived, along with 693 other young men, I was eager to immerse myself in the new surroundings and experiences.

Everyone basically took the same courses for the first two years—a core curriculum that wasn't designed to answer questions, but instead to raise them, and to give you the tools and the desire to delve more deeply into subjects and ideas. This felt like manna from heaven, and I embraced all the knowledge I could. On a few occasions, though, my eagerness may have overshadowed my sounder judgment.

This was the case when I enrolled in Jacques Barzun's cultural history of Europe, a class taught in French, despite the fact that I had very little foreign language training in high school. It was a great course, one of the most talked about at Columbia, and Barzun was a legendary professor and a gifted teacher. I, however, was in school six days a week (we did our labs on Saturdays), working (an obligation as part of my scholarship), and on the basketball team, so translating the textbook and other readings from French into English on a nightly basis and keeping up with the lectures became impossible. I still have the book from that class, clearly marked with my struggled translations.

Another early elective that damaged the pride I had in my mastery of high school academics was a specialized mathematics course I took in vector analysis. It was a small class, maybe eight students, all already focused on math as a primary area of study. It was a challenge for me from the beginning, and when I started doing poorly on exams it came as a shock. I'd always excelled at math and didn't even contemplate there were aspects that might be beyond me. When it became clear that my grade could be low enough to put my scholarship in jeopardy, I had serious consultations with my professor about whether dropping the class might be the best option. Instead, I persevered and picked up a summer class to offset my less than stellar result. It was a powerful experience, and an important life lesson. I'd gone from being completely sure that there was almost nothing I couldn't manage, to realizing that no matter how good I was at some things, there were others that would be much more challenging for me.

Basketball was something that remained a constant for me. I had been enthusiastic about playing for Lou Rossini since meeting him, and I was on the team for four years. In my senior season I was named captain by my teammates, making me the first African American to earn the honor at Columbia, or at any Ivy League institution. We had a 15–9 record that year and I was named most valuable player. I was the only African American player on the team, and although my teammates didn't exhibit racist attitudes or behavior, there were times during our travel when they were forced to confront it directly, because they were with me. On more than one occasion, while playing teams in the South, I was denied entry to eating establishments. In those instances the entire team would leave and find another place to eat. They wouldn't consider going in without me.

I finished my career as a Lion as the single season and career rebounding record holder, with 1,022 rebounds, a record that still stands. We had a very competitive team, and basketball was an important part of my college life, as it had been up until then. Teamwork, leadership, learning to take blows—these are all things I think I first learned with a basketball in my hand, and at Columbia I took them to a new level. My mother was always supportive of me, but she only came to one game during those years. I think she wanted to be clear that in her mind basketball wasn't the reason I was at college. I visited her in Bedford-Stuyvesant, though, as much as my schedule allowed, often bringing new friends along with me who she was always happy to feed and welcome into our family home.

Those of us on scholarship had work obligations to fulfill in addition to our academic and athletic requirements, and during football season one of my assignments was "serving training table" for the football team. This meant taking the food from where it was prepared to where it was being consumed. I was able to meet other athletes while doing this work, including George Patterson, a football player who would become a lifelong friend. George was in his second year at Columbia and was also African American. "When I saw this very tall Black guy at the training table, I thought, 'I've got to talk to him,'" George later recounted. In a school of more than two thousand young men with perhaps four or five men of color per class, getting to know one another was something that was not only beneficial, but important. During off-season I was assigned other tasks. I became adept at managing a full load of responsibilities without much support, and knew I couldn't take anything for granted. It was clear that a door had been opened for me, but it could just as easily close and then I'd be standing outside.

Columbia was alive with student energy and activity in the early 1950s. The school was admitting very few students of color at the time; there were maybe five other African American students in the freshman class when I started, though no official records were kept to corroborate that number. But there was an NAACP chapter on campus, as well as a vigorous effort to break down racial segregation in housing in the adjacent neighborhoods in which I became involved. We would identify rooms that were being rented and have a person of color respond to the ad. Inevitably, that person would be told that the room had already been rented. We'd then send a white student who would be told otherwise and shown around. We wanted to build enough evidence to take a case to the administration that would force them to ensure that only those who agreed not to discriminate could list rooms and apartments with the university's off-campus registry. The administration tried to be accommodating yet also not take responsibility, and the struggle between the student activists and the university was intense. The leaders of the effort were a few years older than I was, and although the group was racially diverse, it was an environment in which I was able to connect with other African American students on campus.

It was impactful for me to be spending time with other African American students, some who had completed their undergraduate degrees and were studying in the Graduate School of Architecture and others who were undergraduates preparing to study medicine and law. There were others who were successfully influencing Columbia's organizations in significant ways. One in particular, Victor Crichton, was the chairman of the Student Board, at the time a powerful position for a young man of color to hold at the college. He was a couple of years older than I was, and I have a vivid memory of him preparing for an interview of some sort, perhaps upon graduation, and a group of us pridefully accompanying him to Brooks Brothers to help him choose a suit. There may have only been a very small number of us in proportion to the total student body, but that only seemed to sharpen our focus and ambition.

ROTC was a requirement back then, and when it was time for me to spend a summer engaged in training in South Carolina, as one of three Columbia students, and the only African American in a group of 250 ROTC Air Force cadets, I'd already been living away from my family and childhood friends for a few years. Since I'd left my Brooklyn home, I'd learned a great deal about myself, as one does when transplanted to new and unfamiliar surroundings, but the South and the military would take this to a new level.

I was already accustomed to a structured and disciplined lifestyle, so that aspect of the military didn't require too much adjustment. As the only Black cadet, however, my mere existence created complications for the Air Force. The officers consistently attributed any problems to local tradition, and seemed completely uninterested and unwilling to push against the status quo in any way.

On one occasion I was surprised to be called into a meeting with one of my commanders only to find out I was there to discuss an upcoming ball to be held for the cadets. The officer described the event in great detail. All 250 cadets would be in attendance, along with officers, and the local debutantes from the area and their families. It was a "tap" ball, meaning that couples danced together and changed partners by tapping another person on the shoulder. I soon realized that I, the only African American cadet, was called into this special meeting to be asked, politely, to refrain from interracial dancing. I knew I was in the American South, and I understood that attitudes and behaviors with respect to race were different from what I was accustomed to in New York City, but I was there, officially, as part of the military, working on behalf of the U.S. government, and I questioned why such conduct was permitted to seep into that domain. The ball was, after all, an Air Force–promoted and sponsored event, taking place on U.S. government property. I did pose that question and was assured that the Air Force didn't condone that kind of thinking, but considered itself a guest of the local people, and as such, was respectful of their traditions. I was determined not to let that response go unchallenged and pushed the commander to articulate exactly what was being suggested and what role the Air Force was playing in upholding this practice. A great deal of effort and planning were devoted to maintaining racial separation at this ball, and I, the sole Black cadet, was the focus.

When the evening arrived, the arrangement was that I would be seated at a table with two African American officers and their wives, the only other people of color in the very large room. It was a festive atmosphere and very soon after the music began, people headed to the dance floor in pairs. The wife of one of the officers I was sitting with asked me to dance and we made our way onto the crowded floor. Before I had the chance to think about what might or might not happen next, one of us was tapped, and we were now both dancing with white partners. Just like that, all of the planning, and instruction, and tradition were tossed aside and, interestingly, no one in the immediate vicinity seemed to care, or at least said anything about it. The whole experience was an instructive one, however, not least because of the role the Air Force leadership played in trying to enforce segregation in our social activities, though not being overtly in support of it. In my mind, as long as they were asking us to silently maintain the status quo, for the sake of being good neighbors, they, too, were promoting the conduct. I drove back from South Carolina that summer with my two white classmates, who were equally disturbed by the Air Force's handling of the situation. We spent time expressing our views on the subject both during our time in South Carolina and on the way back, and we hoped we'd made a dent, even a small one, in the way things might be handled in the future.

The Air Force became a part of my life in a much more significant way upon my graduation from Columbia in 1956.

Military service was required at the time, and my only real choice was whether I would commit to the Navy or the Air Force. I chose the Air Force, and Texas was the first of a very long list of places around the country and the world I would see during the next four years of my life. After my initial engagement, where my basic skills and areas of interest were evaluated, I was moved from one base in Texas to another, in San Antonio, which is where I spent the better part of the next year learning navigation skills. I was then assigned to the Strategic Air Command, during the era of General Curtis LeMay, who had already gained a reputation as a strategist and tactician during World War II. I flew missions for the Strategic Reconnaissance Wing as a senior navigator and learned about the Cold War firsthand (and the ways in which we and the Soviets gathered strategic information about one another).

I loved learning navigation. I had to know everything about the universe and the stars. It required the kind of precision that came naturally to me and a sense of calm and steadiness that I also possessed, although I'm not sure I knew it at the time. It was the kind of work you can do when you're in your early twenties, because at that age you think you're invincible. I mean, the whole notion of being up beyond the magnetic North Pole, flying radio silent for hours, not being able to use a magnetic compass because you've already passed magnetic north, so you disable the magnetic sensors and fly with a gyrocompass, requires a certain amount of fearlessness. You rely on the loran system and the stars to guide you to your destination and then back to your base.

I traveled much of the world, including three months in Thule, Greenland, during the winter. The Air Force moved us around to different places on very short notice, and we wouldn't know where we were going or how long we might be there. While I was flying Strategic Reconnaissance, our crew was responsible for offloading fuel midair to aircraft that were flying at much higher altitudes than we were. These aircraft would come down in groups of five or six, and they had to be able to swoop in, refuel, and move out in synchronicity. Everything was radio silent, so you had to be in a certain place at a certain time and they had to be able to find you. As the sole navigator on these missions, the pressure was considerable.

As a senior navigator I was also given assignments in which I was asked to oversee other navigators who had not passed recent evaluations. On one such mission I was flying with a navigator who had flown in World War II, an older man who was quite experienced, but not up to date with current systems and methods. Things were proceeding smoothly but at some point, after I'd stepped away, I was called back in by the co-pilot, who said it was just about time for the aircraft to report in, but the navigator could not determine location. I found him with his charts out, perspiration pouring down his face, and the pilots waiting for instruction. I calmly tried to determine the last location we could be certain of, what speed we were going, what the headings had been since then, and finally, what I could see in the sky. We were then able to determine where we were, report our location, and land safely and as planned. It was also my job to then write an evaluation of the navigator whose work I was observing.

I rose to the position of captain during my time in the Air Force. It was a fascinating learning experience, great for building self-confidence and conquering fears, and could have been the foundation for a long career in the military. As my mandatory duty was coming to an end, three of my senior officers had a very serious conversation with me about that possibility. They knew I'd been considering law school but they tried to persuade me that very good things would come to me if I stayed on the military path. "Why are you going to leave?

You've got a great career opportunity here," they said. "You're going to spend what little money you've saved while you've been here, and go into debt. When you come out of law school, if you're successful, you'll make less money in that first job than you're making right now, and you'll be three years older." All of this was, in fact, true and I didn't have any substantive rebuttals.

But there was one extraordinary commander whom I'd met, who was very much like a few of the best teachers and coaches I'd had in high school and college. He said, "Everything they tell you is true about the great career opportunities you have in the service. But if you want the fruits of life, you have to be willing to go out on a limb, because that's where all the fruit is. If all you want to do is hold on and be safe and secure, the fruits of life are going to elude you." And it was such a wonderful thing to say—not just the idea, but the powerful imagery it evoked. So I left with the intent of pursuing a law degree, seeking the fruit that had been dangled before me.

3

Choosing Law

I first thought about being a lawyer at a very young age. When I was about nine years old, my mother was the victim of a bad real estate deal. She'd managed to save enough money to put a down payment on a house, which was no small feat for a single mother who'd raised six children on her own. The transaction was handled improperly or she was simply taken advantage of, but either way she lost her money and the house. Even her tremendous strength and smarts weren't able to remedy this injustice, and she didn't have a lawyer, or the means to hire one. It may have been the first time I saw my mother in a position of weakness. I wanted desperately to help, but there was nothing I could do. It was at that moment I decided I wanted to know everything I could about the law and the ways it could be used to protect people. I was fairly confident that law school was in my future.

When I left the Air Force and moved back to New York to live and attend Columbia Law School, I quickly learned that my four years away from academic studies had taken a toll. I'd gotten married while I was in the Air Force to a woman who was also from Brooklyn, and our son Keith was born in 1958. I had a job and family responsibilities, was older than most of my classmates, and traveled more than two hours a day on the subway from Bedford-Stuyvesant, where we rented a house, to

Morningside Heights to get to my classes. All of this tested my mettle.

In spite of the considerable demands, I took to law school immediately. It felt right for me even though I was being pounded with material and putting in twelve-hour days trying to keep up. I was older than most of my cohort—students who had come directly from receiving their undergraduate degrees—but I quickly bonded with two other atypical students, who were also older and had other commitments in their lives. The three of us relied on one another a great deal throughout those years. One of them was a police officer; the other was Kay McDonald, who became a dear friend, and at the time was head of labor relations and personnel at the Helena Rubinstein Corporation, where she was negotiating labor contracts with powerful unions including the Teamsters. Kay was married, had a young daughter, and was one of eight women in our class of 250. I, of course, was one of only a few African Americans. We were certainly not part of the mainstream in terms of Columbia law students, and I'm sure that served to strengthen our bond. The frequent study groups Kay hosted at her home were a source of motivation and camaraderie, which were especially helpful when I had to plow my way through some of the more tedious requirements. Mostly, though, I loved law school, and felt that all of my brain cells were working, despite a few sputters from time to time. I was especially engaged by civil procedure classes, and moot court, when we tested our lawyering skills in front of practicing attorneys, who were there to make determinations about our abilities. I discovered that I had a talent for arguing cases, and when I graduated from Columbia Law School in 1963 I did so with moot court honors.

I had my sights set high, and along with countless other eager law school graduates I'd hoped to land a position at the U.S.

attorney's office for the Southern District of New York, which was led by Robert Morgenthau and thought to be the best legal office in the country. Everyone knew there was no better place to work if you wanted to be a lawyer, so not only were the openings few and far between, but the number of people vying for them was sizable. I was interviewed and led to believe that when a job became available, I might be contacted. In the meantime I took a position with the Manhattan office of the Federal Housing and Home Finance Agency (which is now the Department of Housing and Urban Development, or HUD). There were approximately twenty lawyers in the group, and I was fortunate that the head of the legal department, who was a high-profile attorney, assigned me to several important tasks that I found fulfilling. I spent much of my time visiting cities in the Northeast, determining whether they were eligible for federal financing for housing and development and then assisting them in securing it. The work honed my skills in real estate, housing, and community development—both the financial side and working with the people who were in need of support during the process. Little did I know at the time how useful this would be later in my career.

After about a year and a half with the agency, the U.S. attorney's office kept their word and offered me a job in the criminal division. This position brought me into a completely different kind of legal operation. I was a novice except for what I'd learned in law school, and eager for the invaluable experience I knew the office could provide.

The two newest assistants always shared an office, and when I started, I took over the second desk in a space that was occupied by Pierre Leval, who'd arrived a few months earlier. Pierre was a brilliant young lawyer, and later an outstanding federal district and appellate court judge; at that point he'd just spent a year clerking for Henry Friendly, a prominent federal judge. We hit it off right away, which turned out to be a good thing since before long we found ourselves spending very long days and nights together.

It was 1965 and the criminal division was just handed a very high-profile case. Three American men and a Canadian woman were arrested in connection with a plot to blow up the Statue of Liberty, the Liberty Bell, and the Washington Monument. The three men, who were Black, were affiliated with the Black Liberation Front, and the woman, a white Canadian who provided the dynamite, was part of the Quebecois separatist movement. The assistant chief of the Criminal Division, Stephen Kaufman, was in charge of the case and for some reason, he chose Pierre and me, the two newest guys in the office, to work with him. When asked about it later, he said, "I've never made a better decision," but at the time neither of us had much experience: we never tried a case or questioned a witness, and we certainly hadn't been involved in the kind of extensive investigation the situation involved. Yet there we were, working on a case of great importance for the attorney's office and handed an enormous amount of responsibility for the investigation and the trial.

We were able to gain a conviction of the three men after gathering evidence that persuaded the Canadian defendant, Michelle Duclos, to testify against them. We came by that evidence in the most unlikely way. Pierre and I had made a trip to Canada in the hope of finding family members or friends of Duclos who might convince her to become a witness for the U.S. government. We were not successful, but at some point during the investigation we learned that shortly before Duclos left Canada to drive to the U.S. with the dynamite to be used for the explosion, she was seen having difficulty starting her car and enlisted the help of a man wearing a gas station attendant uniform. We had a few hours to spare before our flight back to New York, and as a last resort, I convinced Pierre that we should blindly visit gas stations to see if we might get lucky and find that man. Understandably, Pierre was skeptical and became more so as our wild goose chase continued and our flight time drew closer. Canadian Mounties escorted us from station to station, and we showed the attendants the photograph of Duclos. None of them recognized her, until, against all odds, and as we were running out of time, we showed the photo to a gas station attendant who looked at it for a long time and said, "We need to talk." That man not only knew her but was aware of the fact that she had an interest in procuring explosives. The information he gave us was invaluable, and not long after that Duclos became the key government witness in the case.

We worked on the investigation and trial day and night for nine months, and the bond forged between Stephen, Pierre, and me remains very strong to this day. I was fortunate to have been given that opportunity so early in my career. I was doing things I'd never done before, and doing them in a high-profile case that was one of the biggest the office ever had. I was also working in an environment created by Bob Morgenthau, one of the legal greats.

Vincent Broderick was the chief assistant U.S. attorney in Morgenthau's office at the time, and I was assigned to work on the appeal of a conviction he had gotten in an espionage case. While reviewing the record of the trial and the defendant's appeal, I spent a lot of time with Broderick getting his feedback and advice. We wrote the brief together and submitted it to the Second Circuit, and then, to my surprise, the office asked me to argue the case before a three-judge panel. The appeal was denied, and more than one of the judges told Morgenthau what they thought of my performance. He, in turn, shared that praise with me.

Soon after, in May of 1965, Broderick was named police commissioner of New York City by Mayor Robert Wagner and began serving during what the *New York Times* called "a tumultuous period of transition." In his first eight months on the job, he would lead the police force through the biggest transit strike in the city's history, the first visit to New York by a pope, a major blackout that affected the entire Northeast, and a conflict with Mayor John V. Lindsay, who succeeded Wagner, over the creation of a new civilian board to monitor complaints about the police.

What I didn't realize at the time of Broderick's departure was that he would soon ask me to follow him to the police department to be one of his five deputies, in a position he'd held some years earlier, the deputy commissioner for legal matters. I would be just the fourth Black man to be appointed deputy police commissioner of this overwhelmingly white police force. I was thirty-one at the time, I wasn't looking for a new job, and was still very engaged in my work at the U.S. attorney's office. But it was a fascinating time in New York City. There was a great deal of pressure about creating an effective civilian complaint review board (CCRB) to get at issues of police brutality. Yet there was also a need, coming from the communities, for more, and more effective, policing. So both tensions were at work. One was the appeal to limit police authority by making it more accountable to the public, the other was the call for more police presence in communities where people were feeling threatened. My respect for Broderick and the relationship I'd developed with him, as well as the fact that I was driven by the challenge of this new job, kept pushing me in its direction. I did think the CCRB was a good thing for the city, and I knew my experience at the U.S. attorney's office would give me the capacity and reputation to tackle it effectively when navigating a police department that was not sympathetic to this initiative. My colleagues, however, advised me not to take the job.

The timing was less than perfect. I would be stepping into the position in the early fall, and if John Lindsay won the mayoral election in November, it was very likely that Broderick would be out as police commissioner by the end of the year. Generally, the five deputies who work with a commissioner are expected to submit resignations when he departs.

Responding to the opportunity, or maybe the challenge, I followed Broderick to the department in October of 1965 and three months later, in January 1966, there was a new mayor and Broderick was out of a job.

Upon becoming mayor, Lindsay went outside the city to choose his new police commissioner, bringing in Howard Leary from Philadelphia. Leary wasn't known to us, but he did have a reputation for having worked amicably with a civilian board in Philadelphia, a priority for the new mayor who was preparing to do battle with the police department. Although a CCRB did exist in New York City, it was an organization operated completely within the police department; all investigations were handled by police officers and discipline recommendations were made by police commissioners. Lindsay, and many others in the city, believed strongly that the New York City Police Department needed a check on its power and that unbiased people outside the department must be added to the CCRB. The reaction from police was tremendously negative. At a City Council hearing that summer, more than five thousand officers protested at City Hall. This was all happening in the throes of the civil rights movement and during a time when police were clashing with African Americans across the nation. The racial component was evident in the New York CCRB controversy as well.

The president of the Patrolmen's Benevolent Association, John Cassese, was quoted saying, "I am sick and tired of giving in to minority groups, with their whims and their gripes and shouting. Any review board with civilians on it is detrimental to the operations of the police department." Representing the other side of the issue, a *New York Times* article during the height of the battle quoted State Senator Basil A. Paterson, a pillar of Harlem politics, who commented that if the CCRB were defeated, the people of Harlem would be confirmed in their belief that the city does not care about them. "The words are different but the message is the same. If you're black, get back," he stated.

Leary was sworn in on February 21, 1966, and shortly thereafter, along with the other deputies, I tendered my resignation to him, after five months on the job. To my surprise, he had another plan in mind.

4

Policing in Mayor Lindsay's New York

Howard Leary was brand new to a city and department that were already bristling at the reforms that Mayor Lindsay was determined to implement. The situation would only intensify as the mayor moved ahead with his campaign promise to add civilian members, and thus outside control, to the existing police department review board. Leary knew he had a lot to learn about New York City, and when I submitted my resignation, he told me that he'd been inquiring about me and was advised by Lindsay's people and others that he would be wise to ask me to stay on, which he did.

Although I hadn't been in the position long and had made peace with the fact that I would likely have to find a new job when Broderick left, I was glad to be given the opportunity to stay. It was clear that there was important work to be done. However, the difference in working for Leary and Broderick was dramatic.

When I took something to Broderick for signature or approval, we'd discuss and review it, carefully examining all aspects, as two lawyers are wont to do. I'd then make corrections and bring it back to him for action. The first time I brought something to Leary for signing, after a brief discussion, he took his pen out and signed it. It scared the life out of me. In that moment I realized that professionally the buck stopped with me. Everything I brought to the commissioner had to be 100 percent ready. It was not being taken there for editing or for review; it was being taken for action. I was the final decision-maker. That mini-epiphany greatly affected my early professional life.

As I moved forward in my role as deputy commissioner for legal matters, I did so with expanded authority, and in a relatively unique position. I was working for a police commissioner with a subdued public style, who still had a great deal to learn about the complex and at the time volatile city of New York, and a new mayor who came into office with soaring ambition and a long list of reforms, many of which involved the NYPD. It was a chance to deepen my own knowledge and understanding (the people who worked around Lindsay were very savvy), and at the same time, help get the police department to comport with the expectations that the people of the city had for those enforcing the law. It was absolutely fascinating work but was sure to be an uphill battle, not the least because Lindsay had already challenged the white establishment in the top levels of the NYPD as well as the rank-and-file. In addition to his strong commitment to add civilian members to the CCRB, the mayor wanted a more intensive recruitment campaign among minorities in the city, and he questioned why such low numbers of minorities managed to make their way up to higher positions. According to a 1966 report, only one in seventy-nine precinct commanders and three out of four hundred police captains were African American.

As an African American in the top levels of the department hierarchy, I'm sure I faced resistance, but interestingly, my basketball history, which was known and, it seemed, respected by the people I was working with, made a difference to many who were deciding whether they were going to cooperate and assist me, or stonewall me every step of the way.

When I was growing up in Bedford-Stuyvesant, many in my community feared the police, but my mother had a somewhat different view. She didn't deny that some members of the force abused their power, but she also believed in the good of others who she felt put their lives on the line for their work. She recognized, quite realistically, that as humans, police officers could be protectors or villains. That recognition, and trying to navigate the reality of it, was the way I approached law enforcement, and now, my job. Additionally, I had a responsibility to serve both the department and the community, and I took that seriously.

Lindsay, following through on his campaign promise and strongly held belief, quickly created the new CCRB, which would now have seven members instead of five, and for the first time, four of them would be civilians. The police and their union, the Patrolmen's Benevolent Association (PBA), fought hard, unsuccessfully, to block the formation of the new board, and when it began operating in July of 1966, they did everything in their power to shut it down including lobbying for the introduction of a bill to the state legislature, which failed. Their last hope was an Election Day referendum that would allow the citizens of New York City to vote directly on whether Mayor Lindsay's new CCRB should remain intact. Few issues were as hotly contested in the city that year. Democratic senator Robert Kennedy and Republican senator Jacob Javits both campaigned in support of the new CCRB, as did Franklin D. Roosevelt Jr. (the then Liberal Party candidate for governor). But when the electorate voted on November 9, the vote was overwhelmingly against Lindsay's CCRB, even though many believed it had already begun to create closer ties with communities of people throughout the city who had previously felt marginalized.

Commissioner Leary had the unenviable position of dismantling Mayor Lindsay's CCRB and creating a new one, once again from within the ranks of the police department. Regardless of the referendum vote, he knew he had to reestablish goodwill and reopen communication between those on opposing sides of this divisive debate. According to reports, those opposing Lindsay's CCRB spent somewhere between $500,000 and $1 million to defeat it, and after the decisive vote, those who supported the board quickly and strongly addressed the pervasive message of fear that influenced white voters. Shortly after Election Day, Aryeh Neier, executive director of the American Civil Liberties Union, attributed the massive vote against the board to "fear, or hate, or ignorance, or a combination of all three." And State Senator Basil Paterson, a Harlem Democrat and former president of the New York NAACP, worried that "all the good that Leary and Chief Inspector Sanford D. Garelik have accomplished may have been in a large part undone by the P.B.A. campaign. The people voted against the board on an emotional and racial basis and this vote was complete confirmation in the minds of many people in the Negro community that the White community has been—will always be—against it." Even though those most opposed to Lindsay's CCRB within the police department would never admit it, it is hard to believe that during the long struggle they did not come to realize that there were some actors within the NYPD whose behavior did warrant correction.

Upon the naming of the new board, which reverted to comprising five members, Leary went as far as he could in actually ensuring civilian representation from within the police department. Three of the men were civilian employees of the department and two were commissioners, of which I was one. I'd been a member of the prior CCRB as well. None of us had ever been a line police officer, and all of us were lawyers. The board was assisted by forty-five members of the force, organized into three advisory panels, and one in five of this group was African American or Puerto Rican. Leary tried to reassure the public that the new board would continue the inroads that

Lindsay's CCRB had already made in reducing racial tensions, and it was also resolved that the CCRB would continue to utilize the "conciliation" technique that Lindsay's board had used during its four-month existence.

In spite of the outcome of the referendum, and the reestablishment of a five-member CCRB that did not include civilian members from outside the police department, it was not business as usual when the CCRB resumed its work. Both sides had made accommodations, and as a result, the public's confidence in the board began to grow. In 1968 the CCRB reported that in the first six months of the year, 900 complaints were filed, which was an increase of 325 over the same period the year before (1967), and 500 more than in the first half of 1966.

During this time, we also had somewhat of a breakthrough in our communication and negotiations within the department that I believe contributed to the overall consciousness about matters of protection. This resulted when we created a bill of rights for police officers after many conversations with the leadership of the PBA and officers themselves about their grievances with the department. These generally involved officers accused of inappropriate behavior who felt vilified, belittled, and generally unprotected before they had been proven guilty of any wrongdoing. Some even described being dragged out of their homes by force.

These legitimate complaints prompted a whole series of conversations that led to the establishment of a bill of rights providing law enforcement officers with protection from unfair, sometimes extreme, behavior from the department.

This bill of rights for the first time guaranteed a policeman the right to be informed of the nature of the complaint against him as well as the name of the complainant. Previously, it was standard procedure to interrogate an officer who was suspected of an infraction without informing him why he was under investigation or who had filed a complaint. The bill also allowed for an officer being questioned to have a lawyer present.

We'd hoped that once a cadre of police officers understood the importance of this kind of protection, they would be more understanding about the rights of citizens to have similar protection, and the strong feelings that surrounded the CCRB reforms. It also allowed us to be more demanding of them than had been the case before, when in their minds they were the victims. I felt good at the time about my ability to access the department and to elevate people who recognized the department's responsibility to the public. I was also glad that the department would now respect the rights of officers themselves to fair and impartial treatment when they faced accusations. In my mind, our ability to constrain the department in its enforcement of its rules and regulations against officers was an integral part of getting some results with regard to respecting the rights of the public. It was an important milestone, as well, in opening a pathway to talking to the leadership of the police department's different units.

This communication was especially useful because in June of 1966 the Supreme Court had handed down the landmark *Miranda v. Arizona* decision, which essentially requires arresting police officers to inform suspects of their constitutional rights to remain silent and obtain an attorney before being questioned. Because the *Miranda* decision required new procedures, as well as widespread training efforts to implement them, it created a stir in policing throughout the country. There was a good deal of resistance and suspicion among law enforcement officials, including the 28,000 policemen in New York City at the time, who felt that the new procedures would make them less effective and lead to fewer crimes being solved and prosecuted.

Officers were trained in procedures for notifying suspects of their rights immediately upon apprehension, and by December of 1966 my staff and I had drafted a new interrogation report form, to comply with the Supreme Court ruling, that would furnish proof that suspects in police custody had been informed of their legal rights. This would ensure that proper police questioning could stand up as evidence in court. It also provided a place for a suspect to sign if they chose to do so, to "knowingly and intelligently waive" their safeguards against self-incrimination after these had been explained. A few months later, posters in Spanish and English informing suspects of their rights under the law had been put up in all seventy-nine of the city's precinct stations.

Mayor Lindsay forged ahead with his agenda, although his relationship with the police department never seemed to advance to one of mutual respect and trust. He wanted change, a lot of it, and he wanted it to happen quickly. Those who were suspicious of his ideas felt threatened and resisted. I was comfortable walking the tightrope between the opposing factions, and I did my best to build bridges that would lead to positive change.

While I was busy with the NYPD, Senator Robert Kennedy was becoming increasingly concerned with the plight of American cities, and disillusioned with President Lyndon B. Johnson's War on Poverty. His commitment to addressing what he viewed as an urban crisis only intensified after the Watts Riots raged in South Los Angeles for six days in August of 1965. Kennedy believed strongly that in order to effectively fight urban poverty, the affected communities, and the people within them, needed to have a stake in the decisions that would impact their daily lives. Kennedy's vision included government, but it also harnessed the power of the community and its residents. And finally, he believed that the private sector had to be engaged in any such effort. In early 1966, Kennedy was ready to put a plan into action. The only question that remained was where.

5

A Call to Come Home

When Senator Kennedy paid his first visit to Bedford-Stuyvesant in February of 1966, my mother and sister still lived there, and I was living just a few blocks outside the neighborhood with my wife and son. I was deeply connected to that part of Central Brooklyn, which would always feel like home to me. Kennedy and his staff had made it fairly clear that they were serious about initiating their broad-based development program in New York City, and Harlem and Bedford-Stuyvesant were the two neighborhoods that they were exploring.

Until the beginning of the 1950s, Bedford-Stuyvesant was a racially and economically mixed community, and one that I knew well. I had been born and raised there; played punchball in the streets, basketball in the playgrounds; and attended neighborhood public schools from first grade through junior high school. By 1960, the community had grown to the size of a small city, and its population of more than four hundred thousand people had shifted from 75 percent white to 85 percent African American and Latino.

When the racial balance changed from predominantly white to predominantly people of color, it became increasingly difficult for local residents and businesses to get credit. Most banks stopped making loans or granting mortgages to African American residents, which meant they were forced to pay exorbitant rates to mortgage brokers and as often as not to take out a second mortgage. At the same time, real estate speculators frightened many white families into selling their houses at fire-sale prices, houses they then resold or rented to African American buyers at spectacular profits to themselves. The new owners had to then turn to the mortgage brokers, and became trapped in the credit cycle.

Unable to get affordable credit, existing homeowners were hard pressed to keep up with necessary maintenance and repairs to their properties. Many let out rooms to help cover mortgage payments and other basic expenses, a practice which led to severe overcrowding. Conditions in the neighborhood deteriorated, exacerbated by a decline in public services—garbage collection, police, education, health care. By 1960, incomes had fallen, unemployment was high, and so was the teenage high school dropout rate.

Following serious riots in Harlem and Bedford-Stuyvesant in July of 1964, the Central Brooklyn Coordinating Council (CBCC), a robust network of civic groups and political organizations, commissioned the Pratt Institute's Planning Department to survey the area's problems and possibilities and come up with a plan for rehabilitation. The Pratt study described 10.5 percent of the housing units in the twelve-block survey area as "in a dilapidated condition," and another 28.5 percent as "seriously deteriorating" and in need of "immediate attention." The study also found a high rate of owner-occupancy—22.5 percent of the buildings were owner-occupied and another 9.7 percent were owned by individuals who lived "in close proximity"—and identified that homeowners lived in the area an average of fifteen years. This suggested the existence of a stable, middle-class base in the community that could potentially provide leadership for reform.

When Senator Kennedy arrived in Bedford-Stuyvesant on that winter afternoon in February, his visit was big news, but he was greeted by community leaders who were cynical at best. The politics at work were complicated and the key players were opinionated and tenacious—with good reason. Kennedy wasn't the first to show interest in Bedford-Stuyvesant. Others had taken notice of the community and vowed to help, but there was little to show for it.

The *New York Times* story reporting his February 5th visit was titled "Brooklyn Negroes Harass Kennedy," and it reported that the senator "toured dilapidated Bedford-Stuyvesant buildings yesterday and found himself the focus of wrathful comments by leaders of the heavily Negro Brooklyn section." In addition to describing the various stops made and the contentious meeting that took place at the Bedford Avenue YMCA to conclude the visit, the piece detailed the skepticism, even anger, of the community activists, most of whom were leaders in the CBCC. It quoted Ruth Goring, who was assistant to Brooklyn Borough president Abe Stark, as saying, "You know what, I'm tired, Mr. Kennedy. We've got to have something concrete now, not tomorrow, yesterday." Even Elsie Richardson, another strong, strategic organizer active in the CBCC at the time, who led the tour as chairwoman of the Urban Planning Committee, admitted that she'd almost withdrawn the invitation. "What another tour?" she told the senator's office. "Are we to be punished by being forced again to look at what we look at all the time? We've been studied to death."

Hundreds showed up to the YMCA to hear Kennedy and to express their strongly held views. They were open to his good intentions, but had been disappointed by woefully inadequate anti-poverty initiatives too many times to stay silent. Also, the situation was more urgent than ever, with crime, poverty, and unemployment at their highest rates and growing.

It was a tense meeting for the senator by all accounts, and perhaps he underestimated the strong reaction he would receive.

One of his biographers quotes him as telling an aide the next day, "I don't have to take that shit. I could be smoking a cigar in Palm Beach." But the senator wasn't put off. He left Brooklyn feeling challenged and inspired and soon announced that Bedford-Stuyvesant would be the home of his revitalization initiative.

Tom Johnston, executive assistant to Senator Kennedy, later explained why Kennedy and his team chose Bedford-Stuyvesant.* To begin with, he said, the second largest concentration of Black people in the country was in Central Brooklyn. Only the South Side of Chicago was bigger. "But beyond that," Johnston said, "we found that the community people we were working with were . . . much more interested, it seemed to us, and much more willing to work together for the community, than say, people in Harlem, to take the other example." Johnston also referred to the neighborhood's better housing stock as playing an important role in fostering a greater sense of community. The community leaders whom Kennedy and his team met, and tousled with, may have been frustrated, but they were also passionate and committed, and it was clear they would be fierce allies in the fight for urban renewal.

From the beginning, Kennedy and the team he assembled were committed to addressing the underlying problems in urban centers from a development focus. They wanted to look at the community as a whole—its jobs, its housing, its education system, its arts, its culture, and its recreation—and combine community action with the private enterprise system to make change. Kennedy was interested in working with the commu-

---

* Thomas M.C. Johnston was executive assistant to Senator Kennedy in charge of his New York City office from 1965 to 1968. He was Kennedy's representative on the Bedford Stuyvesant project. His papers, which deal with the origins and early development of the project (1966–69), are housed in the John F. Kennedy Presidential Library and Museum.

nity to put together a comprehensive plan, and he was willing and able to enlist the brightest business minds around to help. It would be a social mission that would use the best business practices to accomplish its goals. The result was the establishment of the first community development corporation in the country.

I was still working for the NYPD when I'd first heard about Kennedy's efforts in Bedford-Stuyvesant. I believe it was an article in the *Amsterdam News* in December of 1966 that alerted me to the fact that Kennedy had come to Bedford-Stuyvesant, along with Senator Jacob Javits, New York City mayor John Lindsay, and Under Secretary of the Department of Housing and Urban Development Robert Wood, to announce the formation of a new development corporation created to revitalize Bedford-Stuyvesant. It was actually two corporations—one representing the community and made up of community leaders, to facilitate housing rehabilitation projects, job training, education, health services, and education; and the other made up of prominent business leaders, to provide fiscal and managerial leadership and attract capital and businesses to the area.

Kennedy made his announcement to a crowd of about a thousand people during a CBCC community development conference, held at P.S. 305 on Monroe Street. He was adamant that the success of the initiative depended on it having roots in the community, and he was critical of programs that were imposed from the outside, where members of the community did not have a stake. He also acknowledged that he sounded like a Republican since he was advocating for private assistance, rather than governmental action, but he defended his approach, which he said was a very sensible way to rehabilitate poverty-stricken neighborhoods. And Kennedy had managed to gain support for the effort from Republicans, many of whom were not big fans of the Kennedys and were not necessarily people who might have imagined themselves leading efforts to fight urban poverty.

When the initial announcement was made on December 10, Kennedy had already recruited Thomas Jones, a civil court judge with a history of political involvement in Bedford-Stuyvesant, to lead the board of the community corporation, which would be called the Bedford Stuyvesant Renewal and Rehabilitation Corporation (R&R, for short), as well as a group of active community leaders, including Elsie Richardson, Lucille Rose, Oliver Ramsey, and Don Benjamin, who very much wanted this new initiative to succeed. Kennedy had also assembled an impressive group of leaders for the business corporation, which would be called the Development and Services Corporation (D&S), including former secretary of the treasury C. Douglas Dillon, William Paley of CBS, Andre Meyer of Lazard Freres & Co., and Thomas Watson of IBM. He had also managed to get a significant investment, $750,000, from the Ford Foundation. Within a few months, Benno Schmidt of J.H. Whitney & Co. and George Moore of First National City Bank would also join. The senator had for the first time, as he'd hoped, brought together a city government, private foundations, the federal government, the private sector, and a community to work together on a groundbreaking urban revitalization project during a time when cities across the U.S. were struggling.

I was intrigued by Kennedy's innovative idea that you could bring the most successful for-profit thinkers into an arena with community people to collaborate about how best to address major societal issues, and he was doing it in my own backyard. Here you had a man who many thought was next in line for the presidency of the United States, choosing to focus on Bedford-Stuyvesant as a place where he could make a necessary and demonstrable difference. Kennedy's association with Bedford-Stuyvesant made people pay attention to it in a way they hadn't before. He'd already built an unlikely coalition of major business leaders and seasoned political activists, and started to raise capital.

That was the extent of my knowledge and interest when my phone rang a few weeks later and Earl Graves was on the other end. Graves, who went on to do many things, including becoming an extremely successful media entrepreneur, at the time was the only African American on Kennedy's staff, and also a Bedford-Stuyvesant native. Earl and I had grown up together in Bedford-Stuyvesant. We'd played together when we were kids of eleven or twelve years old, and he was a member of the Boy Scouts' drum and bugle corps when I'd led it. He'd called to invite me to come and meet with Senator Kennedy, whom I'd met once before, very briefly—basically a hello and a handshake—during an official police department ceremony at the Statue of Liberty. Earl also spent some time trying to persuade me to take an active interest in the Bedford-Stuyvesant project.

I was immersed in my work when Kennedy's people came calling. It was a fascinating, but tense, time in New York and my position as deputy commissioner for the NYPD, which I'd had for a little over a year, kept me busy and challenged. The idea of a new job was the farthest thing from my mind, but I was fascinated by Kennedy's initiative, and I feared Bedford-Stuyvesant was in danger of self-destructing if something constructive wasn't put into place soon. I agreed to meet with the senator.

Kennedy's Manhattan apartment, where we met, overlooked the United Nations. When I walked in and was introduced, it seemed like there was a long period of silence, but the senator then quickly got right to the heart of the matter telling me that he was undertaking an important effort in Bedford-Stuyvesant. He talked about his vision and how important he thought it

would be not only for the community but for the country. He
also talked about giving people more say in what was happening to them. "Have you read about it?" he asked. I said that I
had. "I've been told," he replied, "and I agree, that we need you
to work with us on it." He then asked if I'd be willing to meet
with Tom Jones, the chairman designate of R&R, who he said
was personally interested in the project succeeding and personally interested in having me involved.

It was a brief meeting as meetings go, but he was serious in
his purpose, and it was clear pretty quickly that we had a point
of connection, in the way that you just do with some people.
It was flattering to have him tell me that I had something he felt
could be important to the success of the Bedford-Stuyvesant
project. A specific job hadn't been named, but it was implicit
that they were looking for an operating head, and although I
wasn't looking for a new job, I remained intrigued enough to
meet with Tom Jones a couple of days later.

Jones had apparently been briefed pretty well—by Earl
Graves, I assume—and he, like Graves and Kennedy, emphasized what a tremendous opportunity this initiative represented
for Bedford-Stuyvesant and how much was riding on its success. We talked at great length about my background and
what I'd been doing, and he stressed that it would take a very
serious—or as he called it, professional—person to realize the
potential of this position, and that he was determined to hold
out for the right person, no matter what pressure might be ex-
erted from others in the organization. He also indicated that,
from everything he'd heard and seen on paper, he thought
I was that kind of person.

When Jones asked if I'd meet with his personnel committee,
I agreed, but I wasn't sure I'd be willing to take on the job were
it offered. For one thing, once I'd had the chance to learn more
about the basic design of the program, which at that point was

still pretty thin, I worried that it was high on purpose and objectives, but awfully short on methodology and resources. I wasn't certain that it would turn out to be anything more than a great announcement that died, not for lack of motive or intent, but for lack of deep and cohesive support. Jones also expressed some concern about the personnel committee having other candidates, and his particular unease about their top candidate's ability to carry out the job.

Tensions were running high within R&R at the time, and that was no surprise. There were strong factions forming within the organization, struggles over the appointment of an executive director, and an uneasy alliance with D&S, the business corporation, who the community group already felt was acting without input from them.

My meeting with the personnel committee was scheduled to take place in a small storefront office on Fulton Street between Nostrand and Bedford Avenues. In those days when you worked in the police department, they both protected and controlled you to such an extent that drivers were assigned to you twenty-four hours a day and you had to fight to get away from them. Some people look at a car and driver as a great benefit. To me, it often felt like a burden as it required constant communication and a significant compromise in independence. In any event, as I was driven to Bedford-Stuyvesant that day, I remember driving past the boarded-up, abandoned buildings on Fulton Street, surveying the vast landscape of urban decay, and thinking how much improvement was necessary, and would be possible, with a serious and well-supported renewal effort.

I arrived about ten minutes before the scheduled meeting time and waited for an hour for the committee to assemble.

6

A Battle in Bed-Stuy

"What makes you think you're qualified for this job?" Elsie Richardson asked at the beginning of the meeting, and we were off. It was interesting for me because I wasn't there soliciting a job, and wasn't even sure I'd want the job in question if it was officially offered to me. Yet, I was being challenged in such a way that my competitive instincts were aroused, and before I knew it I was deeply immersed in the discussion.

It was actually a wonderful question, because it was the assertion of Richardson and the other leaders that it was their community and their organization to protect, so they had an understandable degree of skepticism. Why would I, having gone through college and law school, and now having a good and reasonably prominent job, want to leave that position to come back to the place I was born and raised to head this new initiative? What was in it for me? What were my motives? Would I be accountable to them in the way they would have desired, or did I have other masters on whose behalf I was being asked to come back into the community? They asked many tough questions, the kind that make the hair rise on the back of your neck and allow you to learn a little more about yourself in the process of answering them. The business board that had been created, which consisted of some of the titans of American financial life, evoked the establishment in the minds of these community leaders, and they were justifiably concerned that the whole project could be a vehicle for exploitation on the part of Senators Kennedy and Javits to further their political aspirations.

Richardson, at the time, was one of the most visible and powerful community leaders in Central Brooklyn. Her years of activism and community organizing with the Central Brooklyn Coordinating Council (CBCC) had paved the way for Bedford-Stuyvesant to become the home for Kennedy's community development corporation, and she, along with the other "matriarchs" of the community, as they were called by some, were not willing to cede control. They were also not pleased that Judge Tom Jones now had more direct access to Kennedy than they did.

In addition to Richardson, Lucille Rose, Constance Mc-Queen, and Shirley Chisholm (who would soon become a national politician) all had a stake in the new organization. For years, these smart and able women, with deep roots in the community, were at the heart of CBCC organizing. From the beginning, Kennedy and his aides were unaccustomed to being dealt with in the forthright manner in which these women treated them, and Jones himself was having difficulty working with them, especially when it came to the question of who should lead the Bedford Stuyvesant Renewal and Rehabilitation Corporation (R&R).

The community leaders wanted Donald Benjamin to head up R&R. Benjamin, a former social worker, had been the executive director of CBCC until he'd recently stepped down to lead the newly formed Brooklyn Small Business Development Opportunities Corporation. Since he'd emerged from their own ranks, it was clear their loyalty and trust were with him. I didn't know at the time whom they were supporting, but I certainly knew it wasn't me.

Richardson, Oliver Ramsey—who represented Bedford-Stuyvesant on the citywide Council Against Poverty—and the others who were there were relentless in their questioning. "How many community meetings have you been to? How would you select staff? How would you feel about having a committee approve staff selections?" I told them that the purpose of having a chief executive officer is being able to hold that person accountable for the performance of the entire organization. If you were at a point where you didn't feel confident enough to allow your chief officer to choose the people who were going to work with him or her, it probably meant there was something fundamentally wrong with your relationship with that person. By the end of that meeting, we definitely weren't friends, but there was a sense of what our positions and our respective strengths were. It was also clear to me that whoever took that job was in for a bumpy road, not only trying to produce results with resources that might or might not be available, but just trying to survive in that climate.

When it was over I was honest with Jones. "I think you've got a hell of a problem getting someone who has something to lose to take this on given the kind of hostility that's there," I said. "If the job were offered to me now, my answer would be no."

Jones was quick to reply, "Don't give me an answer yet. Just hold on to it." I agreed not to officially withdraw my name.

Around this time, at the urging of Jones and Kennedy, I spent more time with the R&R folks. I even accompanied them on a trip to New Haven to look at some of the development work that had been done by Ed Logue when he was the city's urban renewal chief. Logue had gained notoriety for his planning work in New Haven and Boston, and Kennedy had decided to bring him on to take a major role in the Bedford-Stuyvesant development effort. During that time, I continued to be questioned by the Bedford-Stuyvesant leaders, and the more I talked to them, the more convinced I became that the very structure of the new entity was problematic. "Where would the power actually lodge?" "Would it be with the community board or the business board?" The Bedford-Stuyvesant community group wanted to know if the person who took the reins of R&R would be responsive to them or to the white business powerhouses that sat on the D&S board. To have two separate entities—a Manhattan-based business group and a Brooklyn-based community group—coming together as partners, while conceptually fine, was probably, in human emotional terms, not the most desirable situation. I was in close touch with Jones as well as with Tom Johnston, Kennedy's executive assistant, and for a mix of reasons I continued to believe that I wasn't the right person for the job. "I don't think my candidacy is going to fly with the local group," I told them. "Even if you persuade them the right choice is not the person they are proposing, it will be a constant battle, and I don't think that will help the overall effort."

When I delivered the news to Kennedy, he was furious. He'd had his own run-ins with the group and he knew firsthand what I encountered. He immediately got on the phone to Jones. "You've got to control them," he said. "You're not going to get anyone to take this job in that climate." I expressed my concerns about the dual structure, about the parallel staffs, about the tensions between the community group and Judge Jones. My concerns seemed to reinforce his interest in me rather than diminish it and he, again, asked me not to step completely away.

Tom Johnston really got into it at that point, I assume on mandate from Senator Kennedy. We had several meetings, some at my home, and we even spent an entire day together talking through the issues. At the end of it all he said, "Now what's your answer?" I told him I'd be happy to work with him in a board capacity, in any other capacity—but I didn't see myself leading this organization. He, too, asked me to hold off on giving a final public answer, so they would have a chance to come up with other candidates and find someone acceptable to both boards.

Meanwhile, tensions were brewing throughout the organization. The work Ed Logue had been doing and his approach to the development of Bedford-Stuyvesant was the source of much resentment and controversy. He'd put together a powerful team that included the modernist architect I.M. Pei and George Raymond, the director of the Pratt Center for Community Improvement and a former CBCC consultant, but Logue's grandiose plan was met with hostility by the R&R community leaders, who felt it had little to do with the actual needs of the Bedford-Stuyvesant community. It didn't help that Logue had little patience for, or interest in, working with the community group, and Jones himself, as chairman of R&R, was feeling excluded from meetings and decisions that were taking place between Logue's people, Kennedy and his staff, and the D&S board. Additionally, the D&S board wasn't pleased with Logue's proposal, finding the plans lacking when it came to short-term results and viable projects.

It was early 1967, and by then I'd had talks with people in every part of the operation. I'd spent time with members of the D&S board, particularly Benno Schmidt, who understood that I was interested in seeing the initiative move forward successfully, but not looking for a job. I had an immediate positive reaction to Schmidt. A partner in J.H. Whitney & Co., Schmidt had been asked to join that venture capital firm by Jock Whitney when it was a new business in 1945. Fundamentally smart, a straight shooter, and a pleasure to be around, Schmidt, who I always said talked in full paragraphs, made it clear that the business group was 100 percent behind my recruitment. However, for the time being, he, along with the senator, and the judge, seemed satisfied with my decision to stay on the sidelines.

As the weeks and months passed, frustrations mounted within R&R. No staff had been hired. There were bitter arguments about whether to expand the board and there was an impasse about who should be appointed president. The community leaders were increasingly at odds with Judge Jones, who felt disrespected, bringing out a side of his personality that did not lend itself to constructive negotiation. At the height of these tensions, Tom Johnston observed that it had almost reached the point of civil war and that "unless something happened . . . it would fall apart."

Around the middle of March, in an interesting turn of events, I began to get calls from Elsie Richardson asking me if I'd made a decision about the position. I got the feeling that if I wanted the job, despite their early objections, the community people would be fine with it, but if I didn't, then they wanted their person. I wasn't their first choice, but they seemed to have decided I would be an acceptable one, and it had become apparent that I was the first choice of the business group. I was the only candidate both boards could agree on. When I was officially asked to consider the job again, I was told, "If you don't agree to lead this effort, it's just not going to happen."

There was still a major battle taking place among the R&R ranks, however, which came to a head at a meeting on March 31, 1967. Much of it revolved around the expansion of the board, something that Jones and the community leaders, particularly the women, had been sparring about for some time. The plan had always been to add members to make the board more representative of the community, but Jones faced resistance at every turn, and he walked into the meeting on that particular Friday night determined to force the issue. He demanded votes on several resolutions having to do with expanding the R&R board and made it clear that if the resolutions weren't supported, he would resign. The debates that ensued were intense and, as always, tempers flared. The board then proceeded to vote down every single resolution, and Jones dramatically stormed out of the room, cutting his ties with R&R.

There had been a tremendous amount of pressure on Jones to get the cooperation of the board, and it was proving an impossible task. The theatrics at the meeting, however, were actually part of a well-executed plan, as I learned during a meeting I was asked to attend the morning after Jones's very public resignation. It couldn't have been more than twelve hours later, but Judge Jones announced the formation of a new corporation at that morning meeting, to be called the Bedford-Stuyvesant Restoration Corporation. He had incorporation papers ready to go, as well as telegrams of support from Senators Kennedy and Javits, and an assurance from Kennedy's office that this new organization would now be the official channel for the senator's work in Bedford-Stuyvesant. As the *New York Times* reported, "The announcement of the new corporation appeared to leave the original group with little but a name."

Jones said the board of the new corporation would expand immediately to fifty members and that it would be representative of the community, which was meant as a direct criticism of R&R and what many felt was its exclusion of the younger and more radical voices of Bedford-Stuyvesant. Five or six people from the R&R board decided to join the new venture right away, and I was among the twelve new board members announced on that Saturday morning.

There was another meeting very soon after that one, to finalize some of the details and also to be sure that everyone in R&R who wanted to be involved in the new group understood that they were invited. It was a repeat of the Friday meeting. Tempers exploding, the judge losing control of himself, and vicious, hostile words going back and forth. When the newspapers reported the story, the animosity between the factions was clear.

Sybil Holmes, one of the R&R activists and a CBCC member, said, "We know [Senator Kennedy's] been having secret meetings with Judge Jones. If he had any complaints he should have brought them before the whole board. That's the democratic process."

Telegrams were flying all over the country—to Washington, DC, to the D&S board members, to the Ford Foundation— and the R&R group was trying to mobilize support, claiming themselves as the real representatives of Bedford-Stuyvesant. It was really a mess. An announcement called an emergency meeting of the D&S people, and I went at the request of Tom Jones to bring Benno Schmidt, Senator Kennedy, and the others up to date. We were sitting in a small conference room in Benno's office, and I was describing what was happening and how I saw it, from my perspective, which sounded like that of someone who was invested in the success of the new group that was being formed. Benno immediately picked up on that and began talking in a way that made it clear to everyone in the room that the most desirable thing that could come out of the meeting was getting a commitment out of me to run the new entity. It was a defining moment, and that, as well as a conversation with Mitch Sviridoff, Mayor Lindsay's human resources administrator, made me finally decide to take the job, although there was a long list of items I wanted addressed before I made it official.

Though I hadn't examined it very closely, and though it was completely unplanned, returning to Bedford-Stuyvesant to work was actually a latent fantasy of sorts. I think throughout my time in the Air Force and in law school, there was a part of me that believed I would be in a position to take my knowledge and training back to Brooklyn, to my community, and achieve things on behalf of that community that otherwise wouldn't be achieved. I don't want to overplay it, but there was a sense of destiny at the time. I was at home in Bedford-Stuyvesant; I respected the people, even those I disagreed with and who disagreed with me. I had the sense that if I could do it here, what an extraordinary place to do it, where I would know every street and building and so many of the people. Part of me also genuinely believed that the community might self-destruct if someone didn't get in there and find a way to help these different factions, at a minimum, respect each other, and ideally, collaborate in a constructive way. It was a challenge that appealed to me and there was a definite sense of urgency about it. The summers of '65 and '66 had seen substantial violence, burning, and looting, and further erosion of the cohesion and asset base of the community.

There was an argument afloat that is also worth recalling. Some people who were part of the struggle for political freedom and civil rights believed that things had to get much worse before fundamental, sustainable change could occur in places like Bedford-Stuyvesant. To some extent, the effort I was going to lead could be seen as counterrevolutionary in their eyes, because by bringing development capacity and empowering the community to seize the channels of opportunity that existed, some of the anger fueling their struggle might be diffused.

Whether people in Bedford-Stuyvesant believed in the development effort or not, it was clear that we would be navigating hostile territory, and one of our first, and biggest, challenges would be earning the trust and respect of the community.

My resignation as deputy police commissioner and my appointment as executive director of the Bedford Stuyvesant Restoration Corporation was announced by Mayor Lindsay at a City Hall news conference on May 9. Lindsay stated that my move to Bedford-Stuyvesant signaled "the administration's commitment to put our very best talent to work at the key job of rehabilitating and upgrading the city's neglected neighborhoods."

I was definitely walking into a war room situation, and a period of maximum stress and maximum challenge. It would be more exhilarating than I could ever have imagined.

7

Restoration

Before I committed myself fully, I asked for assurances that I would have the authority to do what was needed to put the organization together, gain the trust of the community, and take the action necessary to show everyone involved that we were moving forward with a viable, innovative, and promising initiative. Having some sense of control was important to me. I'd just given up my job, my wife was pregnant with our second child, the corporation still didn't have any real money behind it, and the community had splintered into several warring factions. Senator Kennedy agreed I should take the lead and let me know he'd be available whenever I needed him. He was usually in New York once a week, and the Bedford-Stuyvesant project was a priority.

I immediately went to work to prove that I was the cohesive force that could put all the pieces together and move ahead, and by that point, there were more pieces than ever. The Brooklyn groups who had been competing for control of Bedford-Stuyvesant were still reeling over the abrupt walkout of Judge Jones, the subsequent creation of a new corporation (the Bedford Stuyvesant Restoration Corporation—Restoration, for short), and the fact that Kennedy's support followed Jones. More than eight hundred people rallied at P.S. 305 after the split in early April to demand a say in who was appointed to the board of directors of any corporation working to redevelop their community. However, when CBCC activist and original R&R board member Elsie Richardson addressed the audience, she was interrupted by young men from the Brooklyn chapter of the Congress of Racial Equality (CORE) and Youth in Action (YIA), who said they were not consulted in the creation of either corporation or board and that Mrs. Richardson did not speak for them. Vitriol was hurled at Judge Jones, members of YIA and the CBCC tousled, and the mayor's spokesperson was sent packing. There was also general confusion on the part of many who didn't appear to understand the difference between the two corporations. The mayhem of the evening was not lost on the local media. "Bed-Stuy Blight Bedlam" was the headline the *Amsterdam News* used to describe what took place that night.

Those gathered at P.S. 305 were many of the same people who had been there when Kennedy first came in December. They did not want to give up control of their community, our community. It was my job to demonstrate that something different, something important, something new and exciting was going to take place as a result of this partnership. And the people of Bedford-Stuyvesant, themselves, would be an integral part, not only in conceiving what would happen, but in the actual implementation of those ideas. I also believed we could have a board that was representative of the various segments of the Bedford-Stuyvesant community, and I was determined to figure out a way to work together.

I stepped directly into the community meetings, battles, and actions, and asked that Judge Jones step back. I believed it was better for everyone if he took a less visible role at that stage. I quickly and assuredly presented myself and the vision of Restoration to the community and to the local media. I knew that gaining and building the trust of the community stakeholders would be a crucial and ongoing building block to our success.

From the beginning I understood that the resistance was less a personal issue than it was an issue of power and a sense of opportunity lost. Community leaders had seen a unique opportunity to gain access to foundations, government, and the larger business establishment on behalf of Bedford-Stuyvesant, but it was now unfairly slipping out of their hands after they'd been working on community problems and issues for years. They feared they were losing control, both to a board that would not represent their needs and to a CEO—me—who was from the community, but hadn't been a member of the CBCC or any other existing Bedford-Stuyvesant community group.

The attacks, bomb blasts, skepticism, and anger were directed at me and would be for a long time. My seven-day-a-week job began early in the morning and lasted well into the evening, since it often included community meetings and hearings, which were almost always at night, and I was the principal witness/spokesperson for the corporation. Sam Jackson, former director of the NAACP, then a member of the U.S. Equal Employment Opportunity Commission, was a carefully chosen mediator in the Bedford-Stuyvesant disputes who chaired one set of these contentious hearings during which the community expressed their reservations about Restoration. The legitimacy of our enterprise was constantly being challenged by very vocal community groups, and if we showed any impatience in that process, it was just further evidence that we weren't adequately respecting their views and claims. Fortunately, these exhausting battles were offset by my belief that we were on the verge of laying the foundation for the community to seize effective control of itself and better understand how to make the system work for it.

I was willing to endure the slings, arrows, bricks, and bats that were being hurled because I knew the project we would be implementing was radical in the context of Bedford-

Stuyvesant. Not only were these highly organized community groups livid about the possibility of their power being usurped, it was the late 1960s, when the Black Power Movement and the pressures to separate and exclude were almost at their peak. And with Restoration, I was representing a vision that was quite consciously, openly, and aggressively asserting that the future for development and a healthy community, and through it a healthy society, was a future that involved Black and white people working together.

We needed to mend fences but also to build a board that included a broad spectrum of community leaders. This included CBCC veterans who had fought Jones so determinedly, as well as representatives of CORE, YIA, and Brooklyn's Black Nationalist groups. I was willing to take whatever steps were necessary to achieve this, and I remained calm, steady, and firm through the months of relentless pounding.

I was also negotiating the place of Restoration within the city. Although Mayor Lindsay had publicly pledged his support of my move from the NYPD to Restoration, there were moments when it wasn't at all clear that Lindsay would stand behind Kennedy's initiative. There were issues of political control at stake. Some heard that major money would be flowing into the city for development efforts but not through the citywide Council Against Poverty. Lindsay was also being told that by helping Restoration, he was in fact helping Kennedy and his aspirations for higher office, while simultaneously alienating the anti-poverty structure in New York and jeopardizing his own political future. On the other side, he was getting advice from Benno Schmidt, on the D&S board, and from Mitch Sviridoff, his own human resources administrator, explaining that it was a unique opportunity in the history of urban development, and he should assist in its success regardless of who gets credit for it.

We also needed Lindsay's help early on because we were seeking a major grant from the federal government, which would be made possible through the Labor Department's Special Impact Program. In order for the grant to come directly to us and not to the city of New York, we needed Lindsay to send a letter with our application saying that he explicitly agreed the money could flow directly to Restoration. That was a huge hurdle and there was trepidation that he'd never sign such a letter. That concern remained up until the very day I went over to get his signature, with Benno standing by the phone in case I needed reinforcement. We'd made our case to Lindsay previously, but knew he still had concerns. When I arrived, he asked a few questions and then said, "If we're going to join hands, let's join all the way." Then, he signed. The whole thing didn't take longer than ten minutes.

Lindsay's people at the staff level were not enthusiastic about my move to Restoration, because to them it appeared that I was somehow choosing Kennedy over Lindsay. There was pressure from some of his staff to treat my resignation from the NYPD casually and not acknowledge it, just let me drift off. But John, to his credit and to his character, said, "The hell with it, I know Frank, we've worked together and I think this is the right thing for Bedford-Stuyvesant," and that is the stand he took publicly. He, in effect, was showing his commitment to the project by "giving" me over to Restoration.

During that time an informal understanding evolved between Bob and myself—and John to some extent—that I really needed both of them, and that political advantage was not my concern. It also was made clear that there were times when I would want both of them to appear for announcements, and there were times when I wouldn't want either one of them to appear. There would be times when I might want one and not the other, which would be rare. But if having one and not the other was going to jeopardize support of the project, then I wanted to be able to say no to either one of them. This didn't require any great discussion. Bob knew it was the right approach. He had always been clear that he didn't expect any help from me with his campaign work. Making Bedford-Stuyvesant a success should be my priority. For the next year, until the senator's death actually, I walked this great tightrope on the publicity front, between Lindsay and Kennedy and to some extent with Senator Javits as well, who was a supporter of the program but certainly not our most ardent one.

In addition to the significant attention I was giving to the community and the time I was spending navigating city politics, I was firmly establishing myself in the organization, taking my place within the dual structure that I'd viewed as flawed from the moment I learned about it. I believed it would be a source of enormous difficulty and I let that be known in my earliest conversations about the program. While I understood the thinking behind the separate roles for the two boards—with the D&S board focused on raising capital and finding private-sector grants to fund development projects, and the original R&R board, now the Restoration board, overseeing programs and implementation—the parallel staffs, and especially having two executive directors, didn't make sense. In fact, it was a big factor in my initial refusal of the job. What made the job interesting, personally, in addition to coming back into the community in which I'd grown up, hopefully with resources that would improve it, was being able to work with the senator, the business group, and the community. When you put a layer between me and the D&S group through the board structure, and the second executive director, the prospect was much less appealing. The resources, as I saw it, were the members of the

board, not the operating head of the group, and I wanted to re-
late directly to them. It was also difficult to understand the roles
of the parallel staffs.

A single corporation, composed of community and business
leaders who sat around the same table and argued about the
same things to reach decisions, always made sense to me. However, it's very likely that some in the business group were made
nervous by the prospect of direct engagement with the unknown element that was the community. To put it bluntly, I
think essentially the dual board structure was to ensure that at
the first meeting, if somebody said "motherfucker," the white
guys wouldn't all get up and run. There was a fear that you
couldn't put a Sonny Carson (from CORE) and a William Paley
(from CBS) in the same room and expect anything to come out
of it; that somehow you needed to insulate the board people
from one another. The decision to have two separate staffs
flowed naturally from that.

The D&S board would be tapping corporations, foundations,
and sources that wouldn't be readily available to the people of
Bedford-Stuyvesant. The person who was the director of that
group would essentially be doing the legwork of following up
with those contacts and finalizing commitments. Also implicit
in the arrangement was the notion that those pursuits, given the
state of the U.S. in 1967, would probably be better received if
carried out by a white person employed by a group of corporate
businessmen than by a person who had operational responsibility in Bedford-Stuyvesant.

On a practical level, I also believe there was very little confidence that we would be able to find qualified people to work on
the operational, community-based side. It was never spoken, but
I had a sense that I was viewed as "different." I think the pow-
ers that be had the utmost confidence in me and my abilities
but thought it likely that they wouldn't get more people like me

to come work at Restoration, because there weren't many Black guys around who would be as qualified. No one said this out loud, but I'm not sure they thought we would be able to put together the kind of staff that we in fact put together. Instead, they expected I would come to rely on the dual structure, and realize that it was a necessary support.

The entire operation was almost completely segregated—the D&S side was white and Manhattan-based and the R&R side was Black and based in Brooklyn. I'd written a letter to the D&S board in January, shortly after I was first contacted about the position, stating my discomfort with the twin structure, in practice and how it would be understood. "A cynic might well say," I wrote, "that the Negro community has a Negro board with a Negro executive director and no money, while the actual work, power and authority lie outside the community."

At the time, Eli Jacobs, an investment banker, was acting as the director of the business group. He was set up in an office on Madison Avenue in Manhattan, and I was working out of the Granada Hotel in downtown Brooklyn, furiously trying to hire a few anchors—people both knowledgeable about and known to the local community—for my staff. I was seeking a diversity of talent—housing, development, organizational, and management—and I also was interested in hiring a staff of women and men that was racially integrated. I wanted my staff to make a statement that the two boards, by their formal structure, were not making.

We didn't have a fiscal department in the early months, and Jacobs was parceling out funds, and signing all checks, while we were establishing ourselves in Brooklyn. When the arrangement was sorted out in early summer, it was decided that we would be separate fiscal entities, each signing our own checks, with grants made to D&S and Restoration jointly (as opposed to being made to D&S who would then sub-grant the funds to Restoration). Nothing, however, evolved naturally in the transfer of power, and at times the process was quite difficult. Even afterward, it sometimes seemed as if Restoration were being treated as the junior, less experienced half of the project.

Jacobs was cautious by nature, especially when it came to expenditures for Restoration, which created an interesting dilemma since I'm not so sure he was equally cautious with regard to expenditures for D&S. We had joint authority and responsibility, so Restoration could have chosen to fight back by asserting the same level of questioning in return, but that would only have compounded the difficulty. I knew at that stage that Jacobs was in the position temporarily. More importantly, it was essential that things moved along swiftly in those early months since we had to get the programs off the ground. I chose my battles carefully.

I'd gone through an accelerated process with Kennedy's people, the business group, and Jacobs, and had worked out a compromise. Restoration and D&S, in addition to both being signatories to any application for financial support to the feds or any foundation, would remain separate legal entities and the operational/implementation dimensions would be lodged with my staff at Restoration. Also, any meetings of either group would be attended by the president and CEO of the other group. I wasn't wholly satisfied with the arrangement and was never on board with the dual structure, but I was ready to move ahead.

I wanted to focus on programming as quickly as possible, and to do that I had to deal immediately with the plans that had previously been drafted by Ed Logue's team. Logue, who had been hired by Kennedy and had been working with an impressive group, had already created tension. Many thought his initial plans were too grand for the Bedford-Stuyvesant initiative and not in line with the philosophy of the community devel-

opment approach because they left the community completely
out of the process.

We held a couple of all-day Saturday sessions to get caught
up. Logue and his group made their presentations so we could
consider where they were in the process and how to proceed.
I felt they had assessed the present conditions in Bedford-
Stuyvesant and identified one or two targets of opportunity. It
seemed like a logical point for them to stop, so I asked them
not to do anything else and let us digest what they'd done. I
don't think this came as a big surprise, but there was definitely
pushback. However, it was clear to me that this approach was
not the right one for Bedford-Stuyvesant.

It was a difficult launch, with many hurt feelings, fires to be
put out, and relationships to be repaired. It required a great deal
of patience, which was challenging. I'd said I would do the job
for two years, but I was starting to realize how much I wanted
to accomplish, and how long it would take to get things done,
since we were breaking new ground by creating a completely
new model for community development.

8

A New Approach to
Community Development

"If I understand what young people are saying today, it is that institutions don't matter unless we can take part in them." That statement, and others like it, were spoken by Labor Secretary W. Willard Wirtz when he came to Bedford-Stuyvesant on June 24, 1967, for an event to officially announce the $7 million federal Labor Department grant that was being given to the community to create jobs, train local youth, and help attract industry to the area. Also present at the public ceremony were Mayor Lindsay and Senators Kennedy and Javits, and there was no shortage of remarks, my own included, to confidently signal the financial and programming launch of the community development corporation Bobby Kennedy had conceived six months earlier when he toured the dilapidated neighborhoods of Bedford-Stuyvesant. Much had happened in that time, some of it so explosive it seemed the initiative might blow apart, but here we all stood in the Sheffield Farms building, a former dairy processing plant at the corner of Fulton Street and Marcy Avenue that would be renovated as our headquarters, to show the public that we were moving ahead.

The Sheffield Farms building had been abandoned for ten or fifteen years and symbolized the decline of that part of Fulton Street. When I was a kid, one of the stops that almost every schoolchild made regularly was the Sheffield Farms bottling plant, where you could actually see the milk being bottled through huge plate glass windows housed in white marble walls. There was other symbolism associated with the building that I didn't fully appreciate at the time. In the 1930s and '40s it was known as a business that wouldn't hire Black people, and there was at least one member of the Restoration board, Charlie Owens, who recalled that he and his uncles tried, unsuccessfully, to get hired at Sheffield. Choosing the Sheffield building to rehabilitate and use as our headquarters would give us a presence in the heart of Bedford-Stuyvesant, and it would also embody what our whole project was about.

On that day we also announced our $750,000 grant from the Ford Foundation and financing from the federal Office of Economic Opportunity that would fund two neighborhood health centers. We revealed plans to persuade the city's major banks to form a mortgage pool for homeowners, and to negotiate with several companies to come to the area. We also announced the possible construction of a shopping center. An education initiative was in the works as well, and William Birenbaum, former provost of the Brooklyn Center of Long Island University, would join us to draft plans for it. Additionally, a $1 million grant from the Vincent Astor Foundation was being used to design two "superblocks." An idea that had originally emerged from Ed Logue's planning effort, the superblocks would be blocks closed to traffic and converted into green spaces. Homes and community facilities in those areas would also be restored. The architect I.M. Pei, who had been chosen to design the John F. Kennedy Library, would be responsible for them.

The mood in the room was upbeat, but even as we delivered the news I knew that it would mean little to the residents of Bedford-Stuyvesant until there were some tangible results. Promises had been made before, and they'd been disappointed. Even now, many of our plans involved projects with three- to four-year lead times. These had to be pursued, obviously, but I also knew they wouldn't be adequate to meet the community's immediate needs or to lift its spirit.

In order to do something relatively quickly that would have a meaningful impact, we conceptualized a home improvement program as one of our first initiatives. Essentially, it was an exterior renovation program that engaged hundreds of young people in the community and taught them basic skills: how to fix a broken sidewalk—clean it out, prepare it, mix the sand and mortar, float it; how a welder's torch can be used to repair the iron fences and gates that were on the front of many of the houses; how to fix the masonry steps; how to clean and repair the deteriorated facades of the buildings and paint the brownstones. We would offer all of that work to young men and women, and we would train them to do it well, while wearing visually distinctive clothing. Simultaneously, we would visit blocks in the neighborhood to see if we could get them to organize their associations or create new ones that would agree to let this work take place. We wanted to get at least 60 percent of the owners on each block to participate. We would charge a nominal amount for it, $25 or so, and exact from them a written pledge stating that they would spend an amount of money equal to what we were saving them to do work on the inside of their homes, and use local labor to do it.

Additionally, because trash collection was so erratic and inadequate in the community, we would give each household two trash cans per family. We would paint the cans green and they would each have a big "R" on them for Restoration. You can immediately and dramatically improve the appearance and cleanliness of the community by having the trash inside the cans with a lid on it, rather than spilling out on the street. It was pretty basic stuff.

Many of the sophisticates said, "Why are you doing this? People don't live on the outside. They live on the inside of their homes. This is all cosmetic." And therefore not important. No doubt many thought it was superficial and didn't get at the core issue of how you renovate and build new housing units, and how you attract the capital necessary to do that. I suspect they were thinking that this was a temporary diversion, just one notch above traditional anti-poverty work. These were all perfectly legitimate arguments. But those making them failed to see the power of the organizing principle around which this was all based: the pride it would engender, the determination it would inspire to do more.

We went to community meetings, we visited with block associations, we made call after call. The basic response we'd hear time and again was, "Our blocks look like hell now, but how are they going to look when you guys finish with them?" We argued it was a chance worth taking for the minimal investment of $25.

We finally got the residents of one block to sign up: Halsey Street between Throop and Sumner. Montier Easton, the head of their block association, wrote to me and said, "I think we ought to go for this," and he persuaded his neighbors. This was the block on which we launched the program.

We trained our young workers in old warehouses and wherever we could rig scaffolds, since they would be using them to do the facade work. We required them to have physical exams, and discovered many of them had never had them before. These were arranged through Dr. Vernal Cave, who was a physician and a member of the Restoration board. We impressed upon them that they were a select group of community builders who had to prove to a skeptical audience how talented they were. The youth got out there and started working to ever-increasing

audiences of local residents and visitors from other blocks. Then
we signed up a second block, and then a third.

Pretty dramatic things started to happen. First, the blocks began to show improvement. Cornices and window frames were
replaced, iron railings, stoops and sidewalks were repaired, and
there was new address lettering and landscaping, in addition to
new receptacles now containing the trash. One of the block
association presidents even called it "a miracle." We also started
to get reports that the kids were coming back to the blocks on
the weekends to show their parents and friends the work they'd
done. We began to hear from the trainers who were working
with the youth that for many of the youngsters, it was their
first successful work experience.

We knew we were on to something when the kids started getting excited about it, and more and more signed up and went
through the training. The biggest battle we had with them was
insisting they wear hard hats and safety belts while they were
on the scaffolds. It became a kind of marker of courage and self-
confidence not to wear them. But we wouldn't allow them to
stay in the program unless they honored the safety code, so they
complied. Before long we began to see them wearing their hard
hats, with the big Restoration "R" on them, around the neighborhood on weekends. It had become a badge of pride.

By September of 1967 we had three active blocks and 272
young men and women employed in our work-training program
who were recruited through community agencies, churches, and
local groups. We also employed thirty-four previously unemployed craftsmen who were paid union scale to train the young
men. A cadre of local home improvement companies was formed
by then as well, led—and in some instances staffed—by people
who were trainers in the program, and some others who were
particularly skilled and had come through it. The goal was to
make the trainees employable. Training without employment or

marketable skills upon completion only leads to the frustration of an already frustrated people. The restoration of Bedford-Stuyvesant had to, in the final analysis, mean job opportunities and an informed and involved people. If not, the deeply rooted conditions that had rendered it a ghetto would remain untouched.

George Romney, secretary of the U.S. Department of Housing and Urban Development, came to Bedford-Stuyvesant during that time and visited the blocks where the work was being done. Wonderful photos were taken of him painting a facade with the kids. He was captivated by the power of the idea, and the fact that the work was being done by young people whom many had viewed as frightening. The youngsters themselves, who may have been perceived as a menace in the past, particularly to older residents, were suddenly the heroes, and they were immersed in, and growing from, the experience.

By the second year, we had so many blocks organized and wanting to join that we had to hold a community lottery to pick the ten or twelve blocks that could participate. We also had additional funding for the program from both the federal government and the Rockefeller Foundation.

This massive community organizing effort was very powerful, but there were critics who were still skeptical, waiting for the bigger efforts to take hold. The program was, however, having the results I'd hoped, and it only marked the beginning of our work. There was a sense of community pride and agency, and the Bedford Stuyvesant Restoration Corporation was beginning to be viewed as a partner in the redevelopment efforts, and maybe one the people could trust.

Once that program was running successfully, it seemed like a perfect time to pursue the superblock idea. We had to find the right blocks for this treatment, which would be closed to traffic and converted into urban parks designed by I.M. Pei. They had to have a natural dead end, and parallel streets on either side that could handle the diverted traffic. Once again, we met with local people to help make our decisions.

The pivotal moments in those meetings were not when we described the superblocks and displayed the elaborate models and charts, but when neighborhood people said, "If you're powerful enough to pull off something like this, then you ought to be able to get those vacant buildings across the street boarded up. They are being used by winos and drug addicts, they're a fire hazard and an eyesore, and we haven't been able to get the owner or the city to seal them. That should be a manageable task for you. Do that first." People are smart, and so practical. And we did it. Then the people were ready to talk.

The Astor Foundation was putting up the bulk of the money for the planning and the building of the superblocks. To Brooke Astor and her foundation's credit, when the first set of blocks was selected, she came to the community meetings, many of which took place in the homes of people in the immediate area. Her presence reinforced the power of the idea.

Early progress was steady, but slow. As I said to Steven Roberts, the *New York Times* reporter who covered Bedford-Stuyvesant, at the end of 1967, "It is so difficult to deliver. We've been through a period of real struggle out here. We're going slower than I would have desired, but we're beginning to make steady progress in the right direction." And I believed that, while knowing that we faced hurdles at every turn, and that we'd only scratched the surface of the work to be done.

In the midst of the demanding Restoration launch that fall, I welcomed my second child, a daughter. Hillary Ellen was born on October 28 and we became a family of four.

9

Giving the Community Control

The pressure to succeed in those early years was intense. I felt the need to be on top of every single thing that was happening in the organization. Barron (Buzz) Tenny, who played an important role at Restoration and then worked with me later at the Ford Foundation, recalled that as a demonstration project, we had "no margin for error." That's how he accounted for my insistence on signing every check, every lease, everything, "because if there was a scandal, the ball game was over." Our commitment to financial control, to quality control, to many different kinds of control, was serious. I didn't want to delegate something that could get away from me. There was too much riding on Restoration for that to happen. We were doing things that hadn't been done before and they had to be done right.

Buzz described many of our Restoration initiatives as "impossible," and he wasn't wrong. They were wide-ranging, usually completely uncharted, and the terrain we navigated always had unexpected bumps and turns.

The Restoration directorship was completely unexpected and unplanned, and yet there were times when it seemed like it was exactly where I was supposed to be and what I was supposed to be doing. Helping to establish the mortgage pool for Bedford-Stuyvesant was one of those times.

My earliest thinking about urban problems was formed in Bedford-Stuyvesant when I was a boy. It involved my mother's failed attempt to purchase a home, the bad real estate broker who took advantage of her, and the lawyer who didn't protect her during the botched deal. My first job after law school, at the Federal Housing and Home Finance Agency, fortuitously allowed me to learn a great deal about urban development. I was determining the eligibility of cities in the Northeast for federal assistance after reviewing their plans for development and the state of their zoning, building, and health codes. This experience—and my knowledge of Bedford-Stuyvesant—made me understand how vital it was to break the mortgage and finance logjam that was the source of so many issues.

Getting financing on reasonable terms was impossible in Bedford-Stuyvesant. The Federal Housing Administration (FHA) had redlined the area for insurance and banks had redlined it for lending. As a result, the typical situation most homeowners faced was a first mortgage from a mortgage broker, plus a second mortgage on top of it, with balloon payments at the end. Residents had heavy monthly payments and were usually confronted with refinancing within five to seven years because that was the typical duration of those mortgages. Also, a homeowner had to pay five or more points to secure that financing.

Homeowners had a heavy cash outflow to pay the mortgage plus utilities and other house and living expenses. To manage this, many of them rented out rooms in their homes, which made for over-occupied buildings that required more maintenance and upkeep. They didn't have money for that, and the result was rapidly deteriorating buildings. Our exterior renovation program was helping with this on the surface level, and in terms of community pride and ownership, but we needed better mortgage options and this required buy-in from banks, insurance companies, and the FHA.

We came up with a plan to get banks and mortgage companies to pool their money so the risk would spread among them. This meant we had to get the FHA to make its mortgage insurance feature available in Bedford-Stuyvesant. Finally, since we were proposing that banks and insurance companies work together to address a particular market, there were antitrust implications that needed consideration.

We had a group go down to the U.S. Justice Department to seek a waiver of the antitrust laws to allow us to proceed. We then turned our attention to the banks. We had a series of meetings at Citibank encouraged by George Moore, who was its chairman, and also a member of the D&S board, in which we described to banks and insurance companies in Manhattan how our mortgage pool idea would work.

Our staff would go to Manhattan for these meetings, which would go well, but then weeks would pass and nothing would happen. Frustrated, we finally decided we needed a new approach. "Perhaps we're meeting in the wrong locus," we concluded. "Let's get a bus and bring these people to Bedford-Stuyvesant to ride through the blocks we're talking about, meet the people, look at the houses, and then see what happens."

After much back-and-forth, they agreed, and we went to Bedford-Stuyvesant together and visited some of the blocks we'd been focusing on. The bankers met residents. They went into homes. And human nature took over. "I didn't know the neighborhoods were like this." "This looks nice." Coming face-to-face with real people and their homes made all the difference.

Within two months of our visit we had a $100 million mortgage pool commitment and all the clearance we needed in Washington. We quickly set up a mortgage processing unit in Brooklyn that would generate the paperwork to make claims against the money. From the beginning, we wanted our paper to look no different than the paper coming from any other originator that the banks and insurance companies were accustomed to dealing with, so instead of doing it ourselves, we went to the head of Chemical Bank, Bill Renschard, and a senior executive at Citibank, Bill Spencer, with a request: "Will you each give us an executive on loan from your mortgage unit who will come to Brooklyn at least three days a week and help us structure our unit to get all the systems and processes in place?" Renschard agreed immediately. "That's the first request someone's made of me in connection with this project that I can respond to positively," he said. The result was a senior mortgage person from Citi and one from Chemical spending six months with us training Jim McClendon, a local lawyer we recruited to run the pool, and several of his staff. After the system got going, we ultimately spun it off into a separate mortgage company owned by Restoration.

Eighty banks, insurance companies, and savings and loan associations had pledged financial support to encourage the development of the six-and-a-half-square-mile area of Bedford-Stuyvesant (that included five hundred blocks and some 450,000 residents). This made our mortgage pool the most significant commitment of its kind in the country. The money in the pool could be used to buy or rehabilitate one to four family homes, or consolidate existing debts on them. It was meant to help people already living in the area and encourage would-be homeowners to move in. Despite the barriers to borrowing, homeownership in Bedford-Stuyvesant ran at about 30 percent—the highest percentage by far of any inner-city area in the country. The mortgage pool was an important initiative for this particular community and one that showed that the community development corporation model could work. It required the full participation, expertise, and connections of Restoration (community), D&S (business), and the government entities whose involvement was necessary to make it a reality.

I introduced the mortgage pool publicly on April 1, 1968. Mayor Lindsay, who was present for the launch, said the program would "give us the kind of pilot guidance we need in other areas of the city." Senator Kennedy was there too, and stated that those "who preach dismay, despair . . . and violence are wrong. The fact is we can work together." Many people did work together to make the mortgage pool happen, and it also exemplified some of the most important principles of development as we defined them at Restoration.

As a community development corporation, we viewed our role as laying the foundation for the community to seize effective control of itself and to better understand how to make parts of the system work for it. From the beginning, we talked about development as an industry and how important it was that the industry be controlled by the people of the community.

We always believed that development was a process as much as it was a set of products. To help the community get into the habit of development, we knew we had to involve them in every step of that process. That's where the knowledge is generated and how it gets built upon. Most importantly, once that knowledge and capacity is there, no one can take it away. For example, once you have people within a community who have had firsthand meaningful experience in development—who know how to identify potential sites and find out who owns them, who successfully seek approval toward particular uses of a site, who organize and make presentations to secure the necessary financing, and who implement the plan and determine who designs and builds it, and so on—they will come to understand that this system, embedded in the process of development, is itself an industry.

I was getting into arguments all the time with people who would say, "Why do you want to create a construction company? Or a property management company? Why are you creating all these entities? You'll never be big enough to do everything the community needs." "Yes," I'd say, not disagreeing with their conclusion at all. But when they'd try to convince me that we should let big developers come in to build the facilities, I'd object. If they build it, the community's experience is limited to identifying a need, expressing it to someone, and then having someone else come in and deal with it. At the end of the process there is a housing unit or a widget. Everything in between remains a mystery. I think the better strategy is not to stop the developers from doing the work they want to do in Bedford-Stuyvesant. Let them do it. But at the same time, build development knowledge and capacity within the community on a parallel basis, because those other developers might change their minds, or their interests might change over time. If they do, local people and local institutions will still be here, because they have a long-term stake in the community. If you're really interested in development, then you've got to be interested in the process of development, and engaging local people in that process every step of the way.

There's a tenet we developed at Restoration I've lived by ever since. Its application is universal. It doesn't have to be physical development, it can be anything. If you want genuine knowledge building and real knowledge transfer to occur, you have to encourage the people closest to the problem to participate in the process.

The idea that you could do the development with and through the people themselves, who were the intended beneficiaries, was a rich and enormously powerful thought. It also came into play when I was hiring Restoration's first staff.

The inaugural staff at Restoration was a fairly young group, and we were all learning and growing every day. Jim Shipp, an early staff member, recollecting those early years once asked, "You had a bunch of young guys running around who didn't have much experience at all. We never doubted we could do it, we just didn't know how. What was your thinking to move in that direction, versus going after a bunch of very experienced people?"

When I selected staff back then, I knew they had to be comfortable in a fast-paced environment, in which you never knew exactly what was going to greet you when you walked in the door each day. Smarts, adaptability, honesty, and a healthy sense of adventure—these were qualities I knew I had to be able to count on. They also had to be hard-charging, ready to do things, and ready to figure out how, because much of what we would be doing would be new to all of us. I needed people ready to take that challenge and not be afraid of it because of their history, past experience, or background.

Ownership was also a very important concept for the Restoration staff. As Jim Shipp put it, "Once you were working on something, you owned it. It was yours and you had to make it happen."

One of my first hires was George Patterson. George and I had known each other from our days at Columbia where we were both student athletes—George played football and I was on the basketball team—and we'd remained close. We were both competitive by nature, and during college we'd always challenge one another to foot races. We laugh to this day about how George would sometimes start early to try to outrun me but I'd always outpace him by the end. "I cheated and I still couldn't win," George jokes whenever this subject comes up.

In 1967 George was teaching physics and coaching football at Poly Prep. He loved his job but I really wanted someone with his intelligence, loyalty, and fearlessness on staff, so I convinced him to come to Restoration. I told him he could always go back to teaching if he didn't find the job fulfilling, but I was confident we would be doing important work. Even before he officially came on board, he spent a great deal of time at community meetings taking the temperature of the various groups and leaders who were there, and developing a valuable understanding of the complex political context that Restoration now had to navigate. I was fortunate to have George there from the very beginning as we established our relationship with the Bedford-Stuyvesant community and as we launched our earliest programs.

On January 1, 1968, John Doar, who had been the head of the Civil Rights Division of the Justice Department, took over as the executive director of D&S (replacing Eli Jacobs, who had been doing the job temporarily). My feelings about the dual board structure were no secret to anyone, and when Doar was offered the job a meeting was held at Benno Schmidt's office, during which I questioned the D&S board, once again, about the arrangement. This led to a discussion in which the issues were penetrated much more deeply than before. "How do I explain John Doar to Bedford-Stuyvesant? What is his role?" I asked. Why did the board assume its interests and talents would be better transmitted to Doar and his staff than to me and mine? What did that mean? What was it based on? And if not on experience, education, commitment, or hard work, then what was it? Was it purely and simply race? We talked about it and everyone tried to formulate rational explanations. A legal point of view was offered about us being joint grantees with joint and separate responsibilities, and although that had some appeal to D&S board members, in fact, the responsibility did not have to be discharged through a separate staff and executive director.

The decision to maintain the structure and hire an executive director for D&S stood, but I was never convinced there was any good reason for it. Importantly, however, it did not affect my access to D&S. From the beginning, I had direct relationships with the D&S board, attended every one of its meetings, and provided input on all discussions and decisions.

I had no problem with Doar himself. He was committed, dedicated, hard-working, and sensitive in our initial meetings to taking steps that we thought were necessary to improve the working relationship between D&S and Restoration—for example, moving the D&S office staff to Brooklyn from Manhattan.

Senator Kennedy remained an important part of our efforts in those early days. Restoration was a priority for him, and he was always immediately responsive to any requests. He came to New York regularly, and whenever he did we would meet.

On March 16, 1968, just as we were getting the mortgage pool and some of our other first big initiatives off the ground, Robert Kennedy announced his candidacy for the presidency of the United States from the Caucus Room of the Old Senate Office Building in Washington, DC. This was the same location that John F. Kennedy had announced his candidacy eight years earlier. There was some talk on the part of his campaign team about whether I would go out and speak on his behalf or campaign for him in any way, but his position on this was clear. "The best thing you can do for me is stay here and make this Bedford-Stuyvesant project work," he said. And that is what I resolved to do.

10

1968

Bobby Kennedy would always say, "If you're only doing housing, you're not doing community development. If you're only doing small business lending, you're not doing community development. If you're only doing education, you're not doing community development. If you're only focusing on the cultural life of the community, you're not doing community development." For a development strategy to be worthy of the kind of effort we were all putting into this, it really had to, in Kennedy's words, "grasp the web whole." It had to simultaneously pursue work on housing, business development, job training, education, art, culture, and recreation, because all of these elements are necessary to a healthy community and a healthy society. From the beginning, Restoration believed strongly in this comprehensive view of community development, and once we had some momentum going we began to branch out in many directions, although the availability of resources always influenced the extent of the work.

In the spring of 1968, in an attempt to present the richness and depth of the community and counter the prevailing negative attitudes, we launched a television program on WNEW/ Channel 5 called *Inside Bedford-Stuyvesant*. The show focused on little- and well-known artists, writers, musicians, sports figures, and political and community leaders with ties to Bedford-Stuyvesant. It also included discussions about social, political, and economic issues of interest to the community, along with features about the work that Restoration was doing. It was a unique undertaking for a number of reasons. First, people of color were basically invisible on television at the time unless they were part of news footage about crime or riots. Second, there had never been a television show in the city that was written and produced by Black people, and this one was being aired on one of New York's leading independent commercial stations.

Although *Inside Bedford-Stuyvesant* was a local program, there was a powerful national dialogue at that time about race that punctuated the show's beginnings. Just a couple of months before the show launched, the Kerner Commission, which had been established by President Johnson to investigate the causes of the 1967 race riots, released its report on race relations. It stated that the U.S. was "moving toward two societies, one black, one white—separate and unequal." The report also offered sharp criticism of the media, condemning the coverage of racial issues and the use of scare headlines, and made recommendations for the future, one of which was that "the news media must publish newspapers and produce programs that recognize the existence and the activities of the Negro, both as a Negro and as part of the community." Our show was created in the midst of this complex race relations landscape. In fact, the official announcement of its launch took place the morning of April 4, 1968. That same evening, the devastating news of Martin Luther King Jr.'s assassination would send shockwaves throughout the nation. In New York City the next day, Mayor Lindsay visited Harlem and Bedford-Stuyvesant and, quoting Dr. King, urged residents to resist violence and maintain racial peace.

In spite of its undesirable time slot at 7 a.m., with a repeat at 1 a.m.—which was definitely not the best, but the best we could get at the time—the show became quite popular. Between 1968 and 1972, we aired fifty-two half-hour episodes that were written and produced by Charles Hobson, who'd previously been a producer at WBAI radio. The hosts were Jim Lowry, a staff member at Restoration, and Roxie Roker, who later starred on *The Jeffersons*. The show was primarily filmed outdoors in Bedford-Stuyvesant, giving it a casual, neighborhood feel, and guests included Harry Belafonte, Richie Havens, Broadway composers and musicians Eubie Blake and Noble Sissle, Cleon Jones of the New York Mets, jazz drummer Max Roach, and the Persuasions. Young people were an important part of the programming. In the episode that featured Max Roach, a group of young people surrounded him as he played outdoors on the campus of Pratt, and when Harry Belafonte was on the program several students from a local high school asked him questions. Neighborhood people were often interviewed as well, or just seen walking across the set—the set being the streets of Bedford-Stuyvesant.

The show presented a wide range of experiences and opinions in Bedford-Stuyvesant, some which were unusual for commercial television at the time. One of these moments was the performance of a poem by Leroi Jones (later known as Amiri Baraka) by a group of eight- to twelve-year-old youth called the Leroi Jones Young Spirit House Movers and Players. The poem is a strongly worded protest about race relations in America. The chorus includes the lines "America, America, why did you bring us here? Rape your mother, lynch your father. America, America, why did you bring us here?" Aware that the content would be controversial, the host, Roker, in her introduction stated, "You may not agree with what they are about to say, but you will agree that it needs to be said." Sonny Carson, who was a member of the Restoration board and known for expressing strong opinions, was also a guest on the show, as were members of the Brooklyn Black Panthers.

Many say *Inside Bedford-Stuyvesant* was the first in a national genre of Black public affairs television programming, and media scholars have studied and written about it over the years, commenting on its uniqueness in documenting a Black community. When Charles Hobson was asked about the program for a *New York Times* interview in 1998, after having put together a short film made up of excerpts from it, he said, "No other black community in America was documented the way Bed-Stuy was. . . . It was like truth, you know?"

The same month that we launched our television program, Restoration made another announcement. This one was the first to signal corporate investment in Bedford-Stuyvesant, and the corporate entity involved was one of the giants. On April 17, 1968, IBM announced plans to open a manufacturing facility in a leased building at Gates and Nostrand Avenues. Although the chairman and CEO of IBM, Tom Watson, was on the D&S board, and much of the official news attributed the IBM decision to that fact, in truth, we had to be very proactive and work hard to convince IBM to open its doors in Bed-Stuy. Initially, we heard from someone that IBM was considering the city of New York as a location for a manufacturing facility, and Harlem was being tossed around as a possibility. John Doar and I immediately went to Watson and asked for an opportunity to talk to the IBM people to ask them to consider Bedford-Stuyvesant. Watson's response was, "Fine. I'll see that you get to the right people, but you may not use my name and I will exert no influence in this regard. This is a call that's going to be made by them in their best judgment." He told us that if we understood and accepted those terms, he'd be glad to make the introduction.

A series of visits to the Armonk IBM offices ensued and we met with all the decision-makers. We asked them to be bold; we asked them to come look at potential sites in Bedford-Stuyvesant before they made any final decisions on location. By then we'd found an old abandoned warehouse on Gates and Nostrand and developed a preliminary plan on how it could be repurposed to suit IBM's needs. After a lengthy process, IBM decided to locate its facility in Bedford-Stuyvesant, but Restoration had to do all the legwork with the city and the property owners. We arranged the lease, and IBM used us to identify local contractors, so we were intimately involved with the renovation project.

The plant was projected to bring approximately three hundred jobs to the community, and salaries were expected to be a third higher than what equated at the time with a federal and state minimum wage for a forty-hour work week, making them consistent with salaries at other IBM locations. Mayor Lindsay called the move "pioneering and praiseworthy" and said it was sure to benefit both company and community.

The first manager of the plant, Ernest Friedli, said it would be a full manufacturing operation, including purchasing, receiving and inspection, warehousing, distribution, assembly, quality control, shipping, and cost accounting. However, when it officially opened in July, partially staffed and not yet operating at full capacity, the first product put into the facility was a power cable that was brought in by truck, unloaded, worked on in the building, and then shipped back out. Those of us close to the effort realized that IBM was essentially hedging its bets in those early days. My personal assessment was that if anything had gone awry at the plant, they would have easily been able to redirect those trucks, and those products, to another facility to get the work done. An interview Tom Watson did with Roberta Greene in 1970 seems to validate my perception. "Anybody who knows anything about Bedford-Stuyvesant is impressed with the effort, and is withholding judgment as to whether or not the ultimate goal will be able to be reached," Watson said. He continued, "I couldn't guarantee it will be reached either. There are an infinite number of problems in the ghetto that I thought Bob (Robert F. Kennedy) was pretty well aware of." Watson also noted that the people involved were inclined to get "starry-eyed" about the possibilities when it was "going to be difficult to make the Negro from a ghetto like Bedford-Stuyvesant, where the Negroes are generally poorly educated, a useful member of society. But I don't see any other choice but to try."

We knew, however, that having this plant in Bedford-Stuyvesant was our way to get our foot in the door, and perhaps attract other Fortune 500 companies, and we had confidence that in time IBM would become more confident in what we had to offer. And that's what happened. As time went on, it continued introducing products, one by one, until it had four products being made at the Brooklyn facility, one of which was only made at that particular plant, making it an actual manufacturing division of IBM.

After three years of operation, IBM was reporting positive results. The cost of the products made at the plant was below the established targets, the dollar volume was increasing annually, and the absenteeism rate was only 1.5 percent above IBM's other plants and far lower than that of other corporations in the area. There were 403 men and women employed there and 320 of them were members of the Bedford-Stuyvesant community, which meant they lived within a three-mile radius of the facility. Ninety percent of the employees were members of minority groups and 80 percent of the managers were Black or Puerto Rican. According to IBM, it had 5,500 applicants for these positions, and slightly more than half of those hired had been unemployed or working part-time before they came to IBM.

Most of the workers hired were unskilled, but they were very eager for steady work with decent pay. At IBM many were offered training, job security, and some fringe benefits. A number of them and the plant managers who worked at the facility went on to IBM assignments in other locations. The general manager in 1971, Halvan Lieteau, who was Black, made it clear that there was nothing mysterious or unusual about the productivity and satisfaction of the Bedford-Stuyvesant IBM employees. In an interview with *Black Enterprise* magazine he said, "It makes a big difference to a person if he's got a job versus no job, or a good job versus just a job, or a super job versus a good job. It's a fact, but sometimes it'll surprise you how a person will change. You give a man a good job, security, dignity, responsibility, and he won't need outside help anymore, he'll solve most of his own problems. It even changes his lifestyle."

We seized on the success that IBM was having and asked for two things. First, we asked if we could use IBM's experience as a testimonial when we talked with other corporations that we were trying to bring to Bedford-Stuyvesant. The second thing we proposed was that they consider building a new, modern plant in Bedford-Stuyvesant. The current building and its vertically stacked physical layout had always presented challenges for modern manufacturing systems, and with things going so well, we hoped IBM would consider investing in a new building with a more desirable design.

They agreed to a new facility and asked us to find them a suitable site for a new manufacturing plant, but they were not willing to let us use their experience as a testimonial to attract others. Their argument was that their experience in Bedford-Stuyvesant could be unique to them or perhaps they were still in a honeymoon period and not in a position to be used as a reference. It was disappointing, but we forged ahead looking for a site on which they could build a new manufacturing facility. IBM wanted us to be wholly responsible for the local process, but we had to do it all without using their name.

They rejected the first several sites we showed them, including the Brooklyn Navy Yard, which would have been the easiest in many ways. The site we found that they did choose, on Nostrand and DeKalb Avenues, had been earmarked for two public purposes, an intermediate school and a senior citizens' housing unit. Petitioning the city to change the designation of this site was far from simple, not the least because to the public at large, it just looked like we were trying to displace schoolchildren and the elderly. We knew we had a persuasive argument in that the plant would be a net addition to the community's resources, and not a displacement of them. We also knew there were alternative sites for the school and the senior citizens' home, but that the optimal and best use of this site would be for manufacturing. Jim Shipp, our point person on this project, went to many community meetings to persuade people that putting a manufacturing facility on the site would be the most beneficial use of it, but he had to do all of this without saying that the owner of the plant would be IBM, a fact that might very well have made his argument more convincing.

The site was re-designated, construction began, and in 1979, IBM's four hundred or so employees left the converted warehouse on Gates and Nostrand Avenues and moved into the new 168,000-square-foot manufacturing facility at Nostrand and DeKalb. The plant would operate for the next fifteen years as an integral part of IBM's manufacturing operations and as a source of good jobs and training for Bedford-Stuyvesant residents. In 1993, IBM sold the plant to its management and employees, making it an independent, minority-owned business that carried the name Advanced Technology Solutions Inc. ATSI was given a multiyear supply contract with IBM and did additional work for non-IBM customers.

IBM was a resource for Bedford-Stuyvesant for nearly thirty years, but we were never successful getting another top Fortune 500 company to come in. We had conversations with a number of them, but it seemed to be a period when, to the extent the corporations were interested in that kind of location, they wanted their own turf. They already associated IBM with Bedford-Stuyvesant. No one ever said that directly, but I always had the feeling that they were thinking, "Well, this isn't *ours*." I also sensed that the underlying development agenda we proposed wasn't something they saw as central to their future. IBM, on the other hand, did seem to have an interest in that agenda, as long as they were also protecting their bottom line. An article in a 1974 issue of *Black Enterprise* even called the company "an industry leader in social concerns as much as in sales and profits."

As Restoration welcomed IBM to Bedford-Stuyvesant in the spring of 1968, the world around us was anything but calm. Not only had our nation witnessed the assassination of Martin Luther King Jr. in early April, but the now infamous student uprisings at Columbia University only increased the level of tension in New York City.

I was actually called to Columbia during the demonstrations— protests against U.S. involvement in the Vietnam War and the university's plans to build a gymnasium in Morningside Park that would discriminate against local Harlem residents. I had no authoritative role there other than as an alumnus of the school, so I was able to talk to the student leadership non-confrontationally and we listened to one another. For reasons I don't pretend to understand, I found it relatively easy to communicate with the students about their concerns and then talk to the university leadership about what it might take to reach some accommodation. Talking and listening to people of different attitudes and beliefs has never been a problem for me. I had no other agenda at Columbia and I think that came through to the protesters. They were talking with someone who was genuinely interested in their position and was willing to serve as an intermediary with officials who were having a harder time understanding what the protests were about and addressing them. It seemed a very natural thing for me to go up and offer help in that way. It was a messy situation, which lasted a week, involved more than a thousand police officers, and ended with seven hundred arrests and more than a hundred injuries. It did, however, result in changes. The gymnasium wasn't built, and going forward the student body had more of a voice and there were improvements for Black students.

Bobby Kennedy had been on the campaign trail during that time, and in early May, fresh from winning the Indiana primary, he announced that he would soon be returning to New York. The New York presidential primary was scheduled for June 18 and he planned to campaign intensively in the state for the two weeks leading up to it.

11

The Loss of Robert Kennedy

Change was happening in Bedford-Stuyvesant, although not always as fast as some wanted. However, we were set on implementing a development model that empowered the community and provided tools for future success, and that can take twice as long.

Imagine you wanted to produce X number of housing units for low- and moderate-income people in a geographic area. There are a number of ways you can proceed. One is to put appropriate pressure on the city or the state, or a federal agency, or some combination of those, to get them to respond to that need. If you're successful, they will either renovate or construct housing for people at that income level. However, another way of looking at that same objective is to say we want X number of housing units, but we want to achieve that by finding and acquiring the land, figuring out how to finance the development of the project, and establishing training programs to ensure that as many community residents as possible are involved in the process. You will also want to develop the expertise within the community to lease and manage the units once they are built. If you opt for this approach you'll need to know how the banking system works (both private and quasi-governmental), how the land assembly process operates and how sites are designated, how to negotiate the acquisition of land and handle the possible relocation of people, and how to put financing packages together. This is a process of development that you will have established on behalf of your community. The knowledge they gained will never be lost. All the creative ways of adapting and modifying this process, which will be necessary as conditions evolve in the larger society, will essentially be in the hands of the people who have a long-term commitment to your community. That is what we were doing in Bedford-Stuyvesant. And that route can be a long one because you are basically creating an industry from scratch.

The financing and mortgage arrangements aren't coming from outside the community and then leaving as soon as the project is complete. The contractors aren't coming from outside, and you are having constant battles, sometimes with unions, over how you can get semiskilled people job and training opportunities and still not fundamentally violate what the unions have struggled to build over the years on behalf of their membership. You are involved in negotiations in every direction. But you develop a knowledge base that no one can ever take from you.

A perfect example is our renovation of the Sheffield Farms milk bottling plant into a modern office building that housed our corporate offices as well as commercial space, a community center, and the Billie Holiday Theatre. It was located at 1368 Fulton Street, and I viewed it as the beginning of a downtown core for the Bedford-Stuyvesant community. It would eventually be known as Restoration Plaza, and a shopping center would be added to the development. In the early days, though, that first phase was very slow-going. We created the Sheffield Management Corporation as a profit-making subsidiary of Restoration, and D&S, to oversee the project. Sheffield Management was the general contractor and it utilized local residents and businesses for the construction work and subcontracting. There were bumps and delays owing to our lack of expertise, but we stayed true to our vision of development.

Some of the challenges we encountered during those years brought us into contact with some intimidating figures. In fact, I'd often get intelligence from the police department about various things since not long before that, I'd been a member of the department myself. I appreciated their watch but always felt safe navigating the territory. There were times, though, when I later realized we were walking into situations that could have turned bad.

George Patterson likes to remind me of an instance, in the early days of the Sheffield construction, when one of the workers was successful in inciting a group of co-workers about pay scales, generally indicating that they were receiving unfair wages. The situation got heated and we arranged a meeting with this guy and a group of the unhappy workers who were threatening to strike. The meeting was to take place at the Sheffield site in a large room, down a set of narrow stairs. The area was not well lit, and George says he observed that as we descended the stairs, someone should walk in front of me while he walked behind, because the situation was tense and the physical layout could have made me an easy target. My mind was focused on calming the guys down and making them understand that the wages they were being paid were standard, comparable across the board, and that there was no favoritism going on.

At the time our offices were located downtown at the Granada Hotel, and the leader of this group seemed to be implying that something untoward was taking place downtown while the workers exiled in Central Brooklyn were being treated unfairly. I wanted to address that concern directly, so I invited him to come to work there every day to see exactly what went on. My goal was for him to observe the daily work of the office, get to know us, and see that there was no dishonesty. He took me up on the offer and before long became a supporter of our efforts. He stayed with Restoration through his training period, and we then placed him in a job with a construction company and gave him his own set of tools.

We had other labor issues while developing the Sheffield building and Restoration Plaza, and those emanated from the organized labor movement. As a rule, the unions were generally fine with us using our own people when we were doing exterior work on buildings on residential blocks as we had been doing until that point. However, when it looked as though something bigger was coming, prevailing wage issues emerged as they applied to construction work. Prevailing wages would have made several projects unfeasible for us, and we went to the unions and to the government with our dilemma. Ultimately, a modified waiver of the prevailing wage requirements was negotiated, and we were able to execute the Sheffield project using as much local labor as possible.

We weren't too far into the work, however, when we were challenged by a group of dissident unionists over a particular issue. They said they would shut down work on the Sheffield building unless we agreed to their demands. When reason failed to satisfy them, we decided to get bricklayers from outside the immediate area to augment the local bricklayers who wanted the work to continue. We found a group of Black bricklayers who came to do the work. We put up huge tarps on the back of the building so the work could continue without interference. Eventually there was a big confrontation with the dissidents in the courtyard of what became Restoration Plaza.

They realized we weren't going to stop working. We had too much invested in the work and in the community. The question became whether we could reach a workable accommodation with them, and ultimately, we managed to come up with something. It wasn't as much a Black-white issue as it was a union–non-union issue, played out against the backdrop of a depressed urban community with very high unemployment levels and a program that was attempting to address some of those issues.

It wasn't until 1971 that we were finally able to move into the Sheffield building, but when we did, we viewed the structure as a success not just in development and commercial terms but also because it was a sign of hope. We took a piece of real estate in the heart of the community, which had been a symbol of commercial failure and deterioration, and with assistance from local people, we turned it into good and positive change.

At the very beginning we were the only tenants, but before long it was a bustling community center with a bank, a Con Edison office, and many other businesses. The complex was financed through a $4 million loan from Chemical and First National City Banks, with a guarantee of $3.4 million from the Ford Foundation and a $2 million grant from the Office of Economic Opportunity. In addition, close to $700,000 was provided by the Astor Foundation for landscaping and an outdoor skating rink—an ice skating rink in the heart of Brooklyn, which was well loved by the community and a special location for our holiday party every year.

We were fortunate to have developed a partnership with Mitch Sviridoff, who was then vice president for national affairs at Ford, and he and they believed in what we were doing. That was important at the time since, as we were developing the site and then moving ahead with plans for the retail portion of the project, we had a kind of chicken-and-egg problem in Bedford-Stuyvesant. The prospective tenants, at least the major ones, didn't want to commit until they saw something that demonstrated to them that this project was real. And we really couldn't deliver anything until we had their commitments. So we went to Ford and told them we had to take a risk and begin building the center before we had a commitment from big retail anchor stores. We ended up borrowing the money to fund the project with help from the Ford Foundation—actually getting a loan guarantee from Ford—and proceeded to build the center before we had commitments from major tenants. Luckily the tenants came.

We knew that we didn't simply want to be landlords, either. That is, if, as a community development corporation, we were just a landlord and builder, and had booming successes among the tenants, then how would the community be benefiting beyond being consumers of the goods and services and employees of the business? That's why the deal we structured with one of our big anchor stores—the supermarket Pathmark—named Restoration as a partner in the business, sharing a percentage of the ownership. That was the first time Pathmark had ever made a deal like that, certainly in the inner city. The supermarket was a big success for both Pathmark and Restoration, although we did make the mistake of making it too small and had to quickly expand it into an adjacent building.

The retail stores came—slowly, but they did come—and Restoration Plaza was eventually the bustling one-stop service center for residents of the area that we hoped it would be, with a strong arts component that included the Billie Holiday Theatre and the Skylight Art Gallery. It eventually housed both national chain stores and local businesses, public utility offices, and the offices of Congress members Shirley Chisholm and Fred Richmond. We were able to look back on it as a success, but in the early days it was a challenging process, albeit one that we were committed to, and proud of.

We were eager for Bobby Kennedy to see some of our work closer up when he returned to New York. After Indiana, he had campaigned in Nebraska, Oregon, and South Dakota, winning two out of three primaries, and then declared a crucial victory in the California primary on June 4. But in the early morning hours of June 5, shortly after addressing the crowd at the Ambassador Hotel in Los Angeles and promising to heal the many divisions within our nation, Senator Robert F. Kennedy was mortally wounded in a crowded passageway as he left the ballroom through a service area, by a .22 caliber revolver wielded by twenty-four-year-old Sirhan Sirhan. He would die on the morning of June 6.

The news stunned an already shaken nation, and it knocked the wind out of those of us working to implement Kennedy's vision at Restoration. I knew the organization, its goals, and those working to achieve them were bigger than just one man, and I knew it was important to lead with a resolve that would illustrate to the staff and the community that the vital work we had undertaken would continue and our commitment would not waiver. It was challenging. We were all emotionally drained for a period, there was a kind of numbness that set in, and, of course, there was speculation about whether there would be ongoing support for the project, and for Bedford-Stuyvesant, from the people and entities who had made promises to Kennedy.

I did fear that some of the businessmen who'd committed themselves to the project and the D&S board might lose some of their enthusiasm, and perhaps we'd lose some of the foundation heroes. I believed they were committed to the ideas behind the Bedford-Stuyvesant effort, but they were also committed to Kennedy, the man. The prospect that he might become president of the United States increased the willingness of some to support the effort. That kind of practical concern was definitely in the air after Kennedy's assassination.

Kennedy had been critical in recruiting the prominent businessmen on the D&S side of our operation, and when there were low points, in the beginning particularly, when fundraising wasn't going as he'd hoped, he would step in and let them know. I remember one particular meeting held in the board room at CBS when he really gave them hell. It was incredible to believe they would even sit still for that. He was pointing right at them and saying that if this group couldn't come to grips with the problems Restoration was trying to solve and do the things asked of them, then what the hell was going to happen to the country? They were the best that the business world could produce. This worked, and I'm sure he did it one-on-one as well. These were not his personal friends either. They were people he had solicited to help with his community development vision and he expected the most of them.

Shortly after his death his family made plans for a living memorial to be designed by I.M. Pei, and there was also a foundation in the making to honor Kennedy's life and work. I didn't have any objections to this, obviously, but it seemed static and, at the time, unlike him. Yet, here was the Bedford Stuyvesant Restoration Corporation that he created. He had gone through all the turmoil and the battles. He recruited all the principal actors, and we now might be facing a challenge regarding whether we could keep our support going, and if we could, whether we could use that support to effectively bring about the kind of results we all wanted. It was the kind of risk that I think Robert Kennedy's life was built on.

With all of this in the air, the concept of the foundation was difficult to grasp. I realized that some of the people making decisions didn't know much about Restoration; they hadn't been here or met the people. And it certainly was less manageable than a foundation or a memorial.

In spite of all of this, the Restoration board, at our first meeting following the senator's tragic death, officially reaffirmed our commitment to the goals and purposes of the corporation and drafted a statement of our intent. By the end of June we'd also held a special board meeting with both the Restoration and D&S boards, and the businessmen on the D&S side pledged to remain supportive as well. There was a collective effort to recommit ourselves, perhaps even with an added push to make things work. We took the opportunity to review the first fifteen months of the corporation's work both for ourselves and for the public, and the list of accomplishments illustrated how much had been done but how much more was still necessary. A little later, Senator Kennedy's wife Ethel joined the board, which was important because symbolically it said that the Kennedy family would remain right there with us.

As always at the Bedford Stuyvesant Restoration Corporation, our actions were the most important evidence of our commitment, and we needed to get on with things, so we pressed ahead and we did so with a renewed energy, even during that dark time.

12

Dueling Boards

Vernon Butler was the first African American to receive an Aamco Automotive franchise in the United States. When he opened his shop at the intersection of Atlantic and Vanderbilt Avenues in Brooklyn in the summer of 1968, Butler, who had previously been employed as an accountant, said that he had a "burning desire to have something of his own." Shep Roberts had a similar story. He was about to launch Shep's Household Products at 964 Dean Street with four employees. The former Golden Gloves boxer/ex–social worker/inventor had been trying to open his own business for years. He had three patents already issued and one more pending, but he had been unsuccessful in procuring funding, until now.

Both men were beneficiaries of Restoration's Economic Development Program, which had made a commitment to invest in minority-owned small businesses that in turn would employ and train community members who needed work. We launched the program with great enthusiasm, and the earliest businesses were announced at a reception at our then headquarters at the Granada Hotel the month after Senator Kennedy's death. Mayor Lindsay, one of the guest speakers, spoke highly of the program, an initiative that was influenced and supported by Kennedy. Lindsay also made a point of mentioning how pleased he was that Ethel Kennedy had agreed to serve on the board of directors of our community development corporation in place of her husband. The Economic Development Program was an important one for us, although not always our most successful.

Hundreds of businesses were started or significantly expanded under the auspices of the program, but at times we may have done them a disservice by being too ambitious with our initial goals. When I look back and try to categorize them, the toughest businesses we tried to launch were in manufacturing. I remember backing a person who had experience working in plastic bag manufacturing. The equipment needed to produce plastic bags is very sophisticated. With our help and the help of consultants, he secured a contract with Kentucky Fried Chicken or a similar high-volume user. He had to renovate an abandoned facility to house the manufacturing operation. We had a preference for labor-intensive businesses mainly because of the number of jobs that would be created, and we also had a preference for businesses that employed people who otherwise might not have been employed. That meant there was often a skills deficit in the workforce, and a work-experience deficit, and some of the time, an education deficit as well. The businesses were often overloaded with these important social objectives at their inception. Perhaps they could have addressed all of this after being established for ten years, if they were successful, but trying to manage it all successfully at the start was too much. We were often guilty of unrealistic expectations. The more we could say the business was going to accomplish, the better we felt. It was an important lesson learned.

The businesses developed under the umbrella of Restoration were quite wide-ranging. Some were successful, garnered a great deal of attention, and also served as interesting models. One of these ventures, Design Works of Bedford Stuyvesant, directly involved a Kennedy family member, Jacqueline Kennedy Onassis. Onassis encouraged the prominent husband

and wife design team of D.D. and Leslie Tillett to serve as consultants to set up a business that would design and produce fabrics and textiles, and some jewelry and related items, based on African art and artifacts. The Tilletts had promoted the development of textile businesses in underdeveloped countries, and Mrs. Onassis asked if they'd consider doing the same in Central Brooklyn. They agreed, came up with a detailed proposal, and proceeded to recruit and train several talented young artists to design a line of fabrics that *Ebony* magazine called "the most original, colorful, exciting and thought-provoking in the country." When the studio had its opening, both Jackie Onassis and Diana Vreeland of *Vogue* were in attendance, and *New York Magazine* called the work "the most exciting collection of decorator fabrics we have seen." The work coming out of the company had a big impact at the time. There was considerable press coverage and celebrity interest, and *Ebony*'s feature praised Design Works for creating fabrics that were "not only making money but were offering a beginning lesson in African cultural history" as well.

Design Works also had its own print production plant and shipping facility. What started as a small business producing boutique items eventually became a company working with decorator supply firms that regularly had its designs licensed for various products including linens, towels, and carpeting. The company was financed by Restoration and commercial financial sources. Mrs. Onassis herself made a personal contribution based on what she described as a "deep and long-standing interest in the Bedford-Stuyvesant project generally," and because she thought the early designs created by Design Works employees had "great artistic merit." She felt strongly about the product coming out of the studio and was one of its great champions. Once, during an event to celebrate Design Works at the Metropolitan Museum of Art, she found herself standing to the left of me while the owner of a business who was licensing some of the company's art was standing to my right. Jackie leaned in and quietly asked me how much they were paying and if it was enough. She then asked the woman business owner why they weren't paying more. I had to laugh to myself, but I'm certain we increased our percentage on the basis of that interaction. It was just one example of her availability and persistence on behalf of Restoration.

As we were actively funding new business start-ups we were also considering longer-term revenue streams for Restoration, and cable television had been on my mind for a while as a potential resource. While I was thinking about what it would take to secure a cable television franchise for Central Brooklyn, Benno Schmidt brought Jock Whitney out to Bedford-Stuyvesant to see the work we were doing in the community. Benno was the managing partner at J.H. Whitney & Co., Whitney's venture capital firm. Jock was intrigued and a few days later he invited me to his office to meet. "What are the major obstacles you're confronting?" he asked. "And what do you see as the greatest opportunity?" I told him that the highest potential opportunity I saw was the possibility of getting a cable franchise for Restoration. It would be an ambitious and unprecedented undertaking but one that could be well worth the effort. He asked what it would take to secure the franchise and I told him that we'd need to be able to demonstrate to the city that we had the knowledge and the wherewithal to create and serve a cable system for the area, and we couldn't do that without an extensive engineering and market feasibility study. Through his foundation Whitney put up the money for the study, which allowed us to be a part of the competitive process. In the end we were awarded a portion of the coveted franchise. That was a big development for us. We knew a community-owned and -operated cable enterprise would be a significant economic asset to

Bedford-Stuyvesant, and it would also provide much-needed access to local communications and services. I saw it as a lifeline for Restoration in perpetuity, and as an enormous benefit to the community. It was a real opportunity. It was also the beginning of a long relationship with Jock Whitney, who would become very significant in my life in ways I didn't even imagine at that time. Years later, after my tenure, the leadership at Restoration decided to sell the cable franchise at a time when it needed access to funds. Although I understood the decision, it was hard to hear that news since I'd envisioned the franchise as a source of security for the corporation for many years to come.

The work we did at Restoration was 24-7. Many of the community functions we needed to attend took place in the evenings and on weekends. Both from the standpoint of strategy and as a matter of personal style, I consciously tried to be sure that I was not identified and established as the embodiment of the corporation. I didn't go to the political clubs. I didn't go to dances and social functions and the rest. The real strength of Restoration was in all the people who worked there, who got out and did what needed to be done. That is not about one individual. We were building an institution, and we wanted to create something that would survive. It was gratifying to see after a few years that Restoration was getting recognized, and at times even being held up as a model. I was beginning to get called on to serve new roles as well, many of which benefited Restoration's initiatives.

In 1969 I was appointed as a trustee of the board of Columbia University. Among the four new board seats that September, two of us—Dr. M. Moran Weston and me—were the first African Americans to serve as trustees in Columbia's history. Another institution of higher education recognized me in 1970, when I was thirty-six years old. Yale conferred an honorary Doctor of Laws degree upon me, citing the work of Restoration in its remarks: "The intractable racial and economic tribulations of the inner city have yielded to your energy and drive. Bedford-Stuyvesant has not only redeveloped physically but has also vastly improved health care and local enterprise. Your deep concern for humanity is bringing into being a working public and private urban partnership which is an important model to our whole nation." It was an honor, of course, but most importantly, the Bedford Stuyvesant Restoration Corporation was being noticed, and that would only help as we continued to realize our vision.

My family was growing in those years as well. My daughter Kerrie was born in March of 1969 and Kyle was born in July of 1970, making me a father of four. My life was just about as full as it could possibly be.

The more that we found our footing at Restoration, the more the dual board structure and the separate staffs became a point of contention throughout the organization. At some point it became apparent that the staff of Restoration was equal to or of better quality than the D&S staff, calling into question the need for two staffs, and echoing my original objection about all of us having counterparts. Ostensibly the purpose of the separate staffs was to bring guidance to the natives. Well, the natives didn't need it. On the Restoration side, Alvin Puryear was smarter and better trained than his counterpart on D&S, Owen Hague was smarter and better trained than his counterpart, the same went for Lew Douglass, and the list goes on. The D&S folks were still looking for a role.

From the beginning, John Doar's role was never clear to me. But he also wasn't in my way. I had a direct line to the D&S board and felt supported by them. In many ways I was closer to them than he was. It's also not unfair to say that he had limited, if any, experience in a situation where a large part of the control was in the hands of African Americans.

We got along well and he supported the work we were doing, but I don't think I welcomed him. What he brought to our efforts could never be explained adequately. I empathized because he was doing what was asked of him, but simultaneously I wondered about his contribution. The situation was tough on both of us.

In our daily roles we played out a kind of reverse tradition, in this case with a white guy having to give something up to a Black guy, not as a gift, but because the Black guy knows more about it than the white guy. We both seemed to be able to understand the situation without being angry and resentful, and we acted with appropriate respect. It was awkward at times, and in at least one meeting with some of the D&S board members there was a big blowup, but none of it was debilitating. It was a measure of where we'd come from, not a measure of where we were then. And we both knew we needed to deal with the current situation and figure out how to move ahead.

In truth, I wasn't prepared to kick over the apple cart. The principle wasn't worth destroying our whole effort, especially because it couldn't be divorced enough from me as an individual. I felt inhibited because with any change in the structure the direct beneficiary would appear to be me, and I didn't want it to seem that the battle was about that. However, I did know that I couldn't saddle the next person who came in to run Restoration with this dual structure, so I was sure something needed to change before I left.

John had a very distinguished career as a civil rights attorney. He also had deep loyalty, respect, and admiration toward Bobby Kennedy. He was human too, however, with the same drives we all have, to spend part of the time we have on earth doing something important and meaningful. So it was a difficult situation for him to accept, to be committed to an organization that was essentially saying, "We won't blow the whistle on the fact that you're not needed, but you ought to know that's how we feel." And our evidence wasn't based on emotion. It was based on fact. It was a hell of a role to be in.

John stayed for six years, eventually spending increasing amounts of time away from the organization. He always supported our work and our vision, and when he officially resigned in December of 1973, he said in his statement to the press, "You just reach a time when you don't think you're making the most of your time and energies."

When John Doar left, his position was not filled and the staff of D&S merged with the staff of Restoration, making the day-to-day operation of the Bedford Stuyvesant Restoration Corporation much more streamlined.

It was around the same time that we were being reviewed for another round of federal funding. We'd initially received $7 million under the Kennedy-Javits Amendment to the 1964 Economic Opportunity Act, an amendment passed in 1966 that provided financial support to public-private partnerships to invest in developing areas like Bedford-Stuyvesant. We had a great deal of momentum going, increasing acceptance from the community, and respect from Washington. We might have felt confident about renewed funding except for the fact that after his re-election in 1972, President Nixon, or at least some of his advisers, were determined to end the community development program. However, since Restoration had both Republican and Democratic support, they had to have a semblance of a process before they cut us off. Senator Jacob Javits had been a part of Restoration from the beginning and he still sat on, and was an active member of, the D&S board.

The feds organized a team of consultants to come see us, and ostensibly bring back a report that would justify the termination of federal support. When we realized we couldn't stop their process, we insisted that the team spend a reasonable block of time with us, and not simply drop in for two days and leave. They agreed, and the first visit of the five- or six-member team lasted about ten days. They came back again, at which time we reported on our work, gave them tours, and introduced them to the people involved. About halfway through the process, it became clear that the team's cohesion was starting to fragment. They couldn't quite hold together their negative premise in the face of everything we were demonstrating, living, and doing.

Unfortunately, the process did reveal a major crack in our organization, and one which could have cost us our funding. In the end, it also led to the resignation of the chairman of our board of directors, Judge Thomas Jones.

Judge Jones had raised certain issues during his interview with the team about potential problems and ethical violations. The allegations were baseless and the feds were not inclined to believe them. However, they reported the information to us in what seemed to be a warning. Why would our chairman be potentially sabotaging us? We wondered about the impropriety of him going to the funding source before coming to the board of directors, even if he believed such allegations to be true. The incident surfaced issues of trust that were not likely to be overcome. Judge Jones was part of Restoration from the beginning, and he was an articulate visionary who espoused great dreams and hopes for Black people, but there was no doubt that his resignation in January of 1973 was the appropriate course of action. Although it was true that Restoration's beginnings were part of a political scene in Central Brooklyn with complicated power dynamics, there wasn't room for any of that in the running of our organization.

Perhaps nine months after the start of the review process, I went to Washington to meet with the team. I learned they were going to turn in their report, which they shared with me, and I gave them my reactions. I also learned from some of the evaluators that the experience of actually being exposed to the work and what was happening had so divided the team that they couldn't reach a consensus on what they ought to do, despite the mandate they'd been given. That was a major achievement, though we were basically fighting a rearguard action in that instance. I didn't hear another word from them or the government, but when the report was released I knew there was disgruntlement because it didn't come out the way some in the administration had hoped.

The next communication I had from the feds was a U.S. Treasury check for $3 million with no cover letter. And I got another one for a like amount. We were more than a little surprised, and so pleased we took pictures of the checks. It was as though they just threw in the towel but couldn't bear to formally acknowledge to us the good they had found in what we were doing.

My mother, Viola Atherley Thomas

As a boy in Bedford-Stuyvesant

Columbia University, 1954

Columbia University basketball game, 1954

United States Air Force, 1958

Being sworn in by Robert Morgenthau, 1964

With Mayor John Lindsay and Senator Robert F. Kennedy at a press event
for the Bedford Stuyvesant Restoration Corporation, 1967

Talking to residents of Bedford-Stuyvesant, 1968

Surveying the streets of Bedford-Stuyvesant, c. 1969

Viewing construction on Fulton Street, Brooklyn, c. 1969

Reviewing plans at the Bedford Stuyvesant Restoration Corporation, c. 1969

With Jackie Kennedy Onassis at the Bedford Stuyvesant Restoration
Corporation, c. 1970

Yale honorary degree, 1970

Superblock dedication, 1975

President of the Ford Foundation, 1992

The Whitney Thomas family, 1994

With Vernon Jordan, 1994

With Kate and Nelson Mandela, 2007

With Penny Andrews and Steve Ellmann at the Twenty Years of South African Constitutionalism Conference hosted by New York Law School at the Ford Foundation, 2014 (Teresa M. Delcorso)

At the Twenty Years of South African Constitutionalism Conference hosted by New York Law School at the Ford Foundation, 2014 (Teresa M. Delcorso)

13

The World of Corporate Boards

At Restoration my activities and commitments expanded to touch other aspects of life in New York City and beyond. These experiences complemented my hands-on work in Bedford-Stuyvesant and paved the way for the next phases of my journey. At times, however, they drew me back to previous parts of my past in unexpected ways.

On April 25, 1970, a front-page *New York Times* story appeared that featured the account of a disillusioned New York City police officer by the name of Frank Serpico who had witnessed widespread corruption on the police force. He and a colleague, David Durk, had been unable to get anyone in the police department or the mayor's office to listen to their allegations of bribery and wrongdoing. Frustrated and disillusioned, they took their story to the *New York Times* and reporter David Burnham wrote a series of articles, noting that the city's leaders had failed to respond.

Within a month Mayor Lindsay had appointed a commission to investigate corruption in the New York City Police Department. It was to be headed by Whitman Knapp, who, among other things, was formerly head of the indictment and frauds division of the district attorney's office. Called the Knapp Commission, its mission, according to Lindsay's executive order, was to "not only investigate corruption in the Police Department, but to inquire into and evaluate existing procedures for investigating specific allegations and present practices to prevent corruption." The commission would also hire an investigative staff and hold hearings.

In addition to Knapp, the commission had four other members, and in May of 1970, I was appointed to, and accepted, one of the positions. Also appointed to the commission were former secretary of defense Cyrus Vance, who served under President Lyndon Johnson; Joseph Monserrat, president of the New York City Board of Education; and Arnold Bauman, a former assistant Manhattan district attorney and chief of the criminal division of the U.S. attorney's office of the Southern District of New York. Of the five of us, I was the only one who had previous experience with the police department.

Over the course of two and a half years we led an extensive investigation with a chief counsel, six associate and assistant counsels, and thirteen investigators. From the outset, I knew the work before us would be difficult. We were investigating a tight-knit brotherhood of police officers, and even though we had more than enough in the way of citizen complaints, we needed evidence from inside the department. We were fortunate that both David Durk and Frank Serpico agreed to testify, even though Serpico had been seriously wounded during a drug raid before the hearings.

Both Durk and Serpico provided headline-grabbing public testimony, as did former police commissioner Howard Leary (Leary resigned in September of 1970, soon after the Knapp investigations began) and many others. The report we finally issued in December 1972 turned out to be 283 pages long, and as the first line of its summary plainly asserted, "We found corruption to be widespread." And it was more pervasive and insidious than I'd expected.

We identified two categories of corrupt police officers: "meat-eaters" and "grass-eaters." Meat-eaters aggressively misused their power for personal gain and sought out situations that could be exploited for large sums of money. Grass-eaters accepted payoffs and gratuities from contractors, gamblers, restaurant owners, and so on, but did not aggressively pursue corruption payments. Grass-eaters were actually the heart of the problem. They existed in great numbers and they enforced a code of silence that branded a traitor anyone who exposed them. We believed that the overwhelming majority of those who took payoffs were grass-eaters.

We also determined that organized crime was the single biggest source of police corruption, through its control of gambling, narcotics, and illegal sex-related activities. The second largest source of corruption was related to businesses seeking to ease their way through the maze of city ordinances and regulations.

As a commission, we made many major recommendations for addressing the corruption in a systemic manner including appointing a special prosecutor to investigate police corruption, reorganizing the NYPD's Internal Affairs Division, and holding commanders accountable for their subordinates' actions. We also felt confident that the new police commissioner, Patrick V. Murphy, was serious about reform. He had announced his intention to make sweeping changes in procedures to deal with corruption, and it was important to us to make the patterns and depth of the corruption clear to New York City residents so they would encourage and fortify the new commissioner in his efforts.

While the Knapp Commission drew on my connections to law enforcement and my work with the police department, I was simultaneously entering a world outside of my work at Restoration that was new to me. Running Restoration put me in close contact with the D&S board people, all of whom were prominent business leaders. In order to be sure our work at Restoration was being supported and executed in the most effective way, and also because the dual board structure was never satisfactory to me, I made myself a steady and persistent presence on the D&S side of things. This is likely what brought me to the attention of Walter Wriston, who'd been the president of Citibank since 1967, and in 1970 became chairman (taking over from George Moore when he retired). Moore was a member of the D&S board, and Citi had supported our early efforts with the mortgage pool program.

When Wriston took over as chair, he took full advantage of changing the composition of Citi's board as existing members retired. I was one of his earliest recruits in 1970 (the same year that I was appointed to the Knapp Commission). When I was invited to lunch by Wriston, I went well equipped with arguments because I wanted the bank to make a larger contribution to Restoration. As it turned out, the purpose of the luncheon was to invite me to be considered for election to the bank's board of directors. I was surprised and flattered. I was thirty-six years old, with no experience on corporate boards, and I was Black, making me an atypical member of that particular group. (It was only six years earlier, in 1964, that the first two Black people were elected to a corporate board.) It was said of Wriston that he wanted the board to reflect his vision of the modern world, and also that he wanted people he could talk to about a broad range of topics, not just those having to do with Citibank. He wanted me on the board even though I had worked so closely with Bobby Kennedy, with whom he was not aligned politically.

At first I was a little uncertain of my response for a number of reasons. I'd been working for the past several years to get more capital into Bedford-Stuyvesant and areas like it around the city. I'd worked closely with banks in all of those efforts, and especially with the particular bank that was my host at that lunch. But my affinity was clearly with the community—

with the people and groups who had the need and not with the institutions providing the help. I wondered if that affinity would be put in jeopardy by board membership. If so, would the benefits that membership might bring to the community be worth the jeopardy?

In trying to answer those questions, I had to assess what I could effectively do on such a board. Could I really expect to be instrumental in promoting and encouraging positive change within the bank? If I felt I could, would those changes influence other institutions in a positive way? And—I guess because no matter how far you go in your life, you take some of your insecurities with you—I also wondered how I could avoid being merely a "token."

I had come to understand that in many businesses there was an increasing awareness of image, and one critical component of image was the opportunities for advancement that a business gave to minorities. Added to that was a second realization that good business, as defined, included more than the annual bottom line. It also required a climate of some order and predictability, and the assurance that such a climate would exist into the future. Those two evolving considerations fused into the idea that the corporation had a responsibility to help improve life in the community in which it operates.

With these thoughts in mind, I decided that board membership could present a unique opportunity to work for, and render service to, the broader community, while simultaneously aiding the bank in its goals. It's important to say, too, that the invitation itself seemed to indicate a raised consciousness on the part of the leadership of the bank; it was evidence that its corporate leadership had a desire to increase the number of ingredients going into everyday deliberations, and to begin facing some of the challenges that the newly emerging definition of good business was presenting.

As a director, I felt the first order of priority was to look honestly at the corporation itself, its employment practices, opportunities for advancement, and so on. If those facts didn't square with corporate philosophy, then it would be necessary to tailor a program to correct those deficiencies. And I knew it would be important for any internal changes that were made to benefit from the same talent that went into the profit areas. The best corporate minds should deal with questions like these. Can the purchase of goods and services from outside the corporation be accomplished in ways that confer benefits on the minority community and on its development and self-sufficiency efforts? In the course of regular business activities, are there ways to correct imbalances? For example, if a corporation is having a new building constructed or renovated, can a minority firm be used? If not, can it insist that the architects, engineers, and general contractors use minority talent? Can insurance be secured through minority brokers, or through the regular channels that have been encouraged to increase opportunities for minority people?

I knew that in a very real way the attention and emphasis a corporation gave to these areas would encourage multiple responses. First, there would be a response from the people who wanted to provide the service or goods. Then, when the organization or people trying to provide the service realized there weren't enough people to meet the demands, there would be a response from schools and universities, who would be compelled to change their long-standing practice of discouraging certain groups of people from entering certain professions. The list of consequences was only limited by one's imagination and willingness to think through what areas of opportunity existed.

I also believed that the presence of Black directors in the boardroom would have the effect of reminding management—

senior and middle management and first-line supervisors—that the speech the president or chairman made at some fancy dinner was more than just a speech. It reflected a genuine policy at the very top of the organization. If that message was clear, then those throughout the corporation, at all levels, would understand that their performance would be evaluated on criteria that included their ability to advance opportunities for minorities. It was my judgment that the corporate machine could optimally provide in both ways—on the money end and the social responsibility end.

I discovered that the role involved more than was traditionally assumed. The doors of the club had opened, and the inside wasn't as dark or secretive as might have been suspected. But in 1971, I knew my circumstance, by being invited through that door, was a unique one. I understood the responsibilities and burdens that all board members take on. At the same time, however, I knew that I couldn't avoid being a representative for masses of disenfranchised and powerless peoples. In that dual capacity, I would be attempting to hold corporations, government, and the institutions of our society more responsive to the needs of all.

I took to the work quickly, and the boardroom became an environment in which I found myself at home. The following year, I was asked by Bill Paley, who had been recruited to the D&S board by Bobby Kennedy, to join the board at CBS, where he was chair. Paley had built CBS into a communications empire, and he and I had gotten to know each other pretty well through our work together at Restoration. He was not only a great leader but a powerhouse in the world of media and entertainment. At the time corporate boards were often dominated by their founders, and at CBS, Paley, who was a larger-than-life character, had assembled a board of his closest advisers and consultants. For whatever reason, he decided he wanted to expand the reach of his board beyond people who were so closely connected, and beholden, to him. As part of that plan, I was appointed to the CBS board in 1971 at the age of thirty-seven. Henry Schacht, who was then president of Cummins Engine Company, was appointed at the same time. Henry was thirty-six. He had come to the attention of Paley through Irwin Miller, the founder and chairman of Cummins, who was a great statesman and very prominent business leader. Henry and I were much younger than the typical board appointee at the time. We became fast, close, and lifelong friends. We also spent some time puzzling over our new roles, especially the fact that we so frequently found ourselves having an audience with Paley, who'd seemed to have taken a special interest in us. We spent a great deal of time with him, seemingly more so than other board members, whether we were acting as sounding boards or giving counsel that he may not have wanted to hear. The relationship that I had begun with Paley at Restoration grew and transformed at CBS.

Within two years, I was invited by Irwin Miller to the Cummins board. I'd been working closely with Schacht on the CBS board already and the Cummins appointment would bring me more directly into his world. And Miller was someone for whom I had much respect. I accepted. I was still deeply immersed in my work at Restoration, but I found the corporate work satisfying and challenging in all the right ways.

"Unplanned" is a word I use not infrequently to describe things that have happened in my life, some more impactful than others. Finding a seat at the table in corporate America falls into that category. It is not something I sought, planned, or expected, but it would become a central part of my professional life for many years to come. When I first found myself in the boardroom it was not a space that had been open to Black Americans. In 1971, according to the *New York Times*, there were only sixteen corporations that had Black people on their boards. I was asked to join three in three years, and my tenure on each of those boards would last for decades. I'd go on to be appointed to many others too, including Alcoa, PepsiCo, Alcatel-Lucent USA, and Conoco. In more cases than not, I'd be made lead director of those boards as well, the first time a Black person would have the position.

I developed a reputation for being able to handle challenging situations, and I was trusted during times of crisis. It wasn't because I had a background in corporate governance or a degree in business. What I took to the boardroom and the corporation was very direct experience in the trenches. I believe part of what I did was to translate the needs that existed in areas like Bedford-Stuyvesant into forms that were recognizable by the usual sources of capital.

My counsel and leadership were based on my ability to think about situations in what some have called a holistic manner, but was just a way of managing that came naturally to me. I listen, I question, and I reflect, not just on the immediate outcome, but on how things will play out further into the future, both for those closest to the matter and for those in the broader society. I have always been able to see things, whether they be problems or opportunities, from multiple perspectives, and I've had success getting institutions and individuals to be open to collaboration. I'm a strong defender of equity and fairness, and time and again—whether it was during student protests, a corporate upheaval, heated political battles in Central Brooklyn, or, later, the institutionalized racist struggles surrounding South African apartheid—people, on all sides of an issue, were willing to talk and engage with me, maybe because they knew I was listening.

I was in an interesting position during those years, a Black man from Bedford-Stuyvesant being welcomed into some of the most prominent boardrooms in corporate America. Many people didn't know what to make of that. Fortunately for me, a friendship was forged at that time that proved enormously beneficial.

Mitch Sviridoff, who was then at the Ford Foundation, told me there was someone he thought I should meet. That someone turned out to be Vernon Jordan, who became one of my closest lifelong friends.

We first met over a long dinner at the Palm Restaurant. We knew of each other before (Vernon was the head of the United Negro College Fund at the time and would soon take over the Urban League), but that evening, over steak, wine, and whiskey, it was what we like to call "friendship at first sight." We had many things in common. We were both working for organizations that were serving Black people and Black communities; we had close professional ties to both activists and establishment figures; and we were both new recruits to the corporate world. The idea that we could be comfortable in both the Black community and at the highest levels of corporate power—which were exclusively white—made some people suspicious. We were working and living in Black *and* white America, and there were people in both of those worlds who didn't know what to think about that. It was tremendously helpful to have one another as we navigated our way through.

It was during those same years, the very early 1970s, when my marriage floundered and eventually ended, a sad and challenging time, and one spent worrying about how it would affect my four children, as all parents will understand.

Vernon and I would meet for dinner weekly and talk about everything. Our lives became intertwined professionally and personally in ways that we both came to rely on. We'd share many meaningful experiences, including our first trip to South

Africa in 1976, a fact-finding visit, he on behalf of Xerox, and I representing Citibank.

People often mistook us for one another. Our similarities were significant, physically and otherwise—but when once asked if we could be described as two sides of the same coin, Vernon characterized our differences in a nutshell, "Frank is quiet, I'm not so quiet, Frank is cool, I'm not so cool. . . . My emotions are more visible . . . and I talk too much, and Frank doesn't talk enough."

14

When Two Years Becomes Ten

When I became the executive director of the Bedford Stuyvesant Restoration Corporation in 1967, I agreed to do the job for two years. I thought that would be long enough to build a solid foundation from which the community development corporation could grow and thrive. I soon realized it wasn't possible to do justice to the scope, depth, and detail of the work in that amount of time. As the first program of its kind—a groundbreaking collaboration between a community, private business, and the government—the work was arduous owing to its pioneering nature. However, each month and year that passed brought tangible results, gains for the people of Bedford-Stuyvesant, and of course, important lessons through the bumps and failures we encountered along the way. I wanted to stay until I felt confident about the organization's stability and future.

Almost a decade had passed before I felt that sense of security. It was then that I was able to survey our work in the three major areas we designated—physical development; economic and business development; and cultural and social community-based programming—and see significant progress in all of them.

Physical development was a cornerstone of our strategy, and it focused not only on housing but also on community and recreational facilities; and retail, commercial, and industrial spaces. Importantly, in our ten years of operation we had stayed true to our vision that the community should play an active role in all phases of any development and construction that took place. This meant that architects, laborers, craftspeople, suppliers, and contractors were, as much as possible, drawn from the community. Overall, we put close to 7,500 people to work. We'd formed two wholly owned subsidiaries with this in mind: RDC of Bedford-Stuyvesant, Inc., a development company for all commercial and residential construction and rehabilitation projects; and the Bedford-Stuyvesant Restoration Construction Corporation, a fully owned general contracting company. Together these two entities created more than eight hundred new and rehabilitated units, and close to eight hundred more were in the development phase. We also formed our own Property Management Department, which was responsible for managing and maintaining all of Restoration's units. The Property Management Department also secured a contract with the Federal Housing Authority to maintain a thousand FHA buildings in Central Brooklyn. On the commercial front, the $6 million shopping center we built was the first ever developed for a minority low-income community in New York City. It was a civic, commercial, and recreational center and a testament to our vision of improving the quality of life in Bedford-Stuyvesant while simultaneously bringing economic and physical development to the area. It included 115,000 square feet of retail space and 60,000 square feet of office space, as well as a 30,000-square-foot open plaza and an 8,500-square-foot ice skating rink—a true community center in the heart of Central Brooklyn. Additionally, more than a thousand loans had been closed in the mortgage pool we started, representing an investment of $21 million.

In terms of business and economic development, we helped well over one hundred local people start businesses, and they ran the gamut from small shoe repair shops to major manufacturing companies. Restoration also owned a Nathan's and a

Baskin-Robbins franchise. One of our other objectives was to encourage existing companies to move their operations to Bedford-Stuyvesant to provide meaningful job opportunities for local residents, and, of course, we had great success in that area with IBM locating a plant in the community and then constructing a new $10.2 million plant a few blocks away. IBM provided more than four hundred jobs in Bedford-Stuyvesant, and 90 percent of those people lived within one mile of the plant.

Finally, we had robust offerings in the areas of community-based cultural and social programming. From our inception we were committed to all aspects of the community's life, and not simply economic rehabilitation. This was always important to Senator Kennedy's initial vision. There was a spirit that had to go along with the development work we were doing, and that spirit was anchored in the culture of its people. With this as a guiding principle, we devoted significant efforts to the encouragement of the creative arts, the recognition of talent, the projection of that talent, and also nurturing in youth from an early age both a sense of personal identity and a sense of identity with the community. This resulted in resources being devoted to the creation of the Billie Holiday Theatre and its children's component (the Theater for Little Folk), both of which offered a wide range of entertainment and educational programming. We also had a bustling Center for Arts & Culture that provided an outlet for artists to exhibit and sell their work, and was the site of class offerings in photography, dance, and painting. The space was even recognized by the Metropolitan Museum of Art as a worthy location for an exhibition of a Black art collection it put on loan to Restoration.

We'd also gotten ourselves into the business of education. We had an active committee working on education for years, and Medgar Evers College, which was officially established in 1970, was in part an outgrowth of a study we did in 1967 on post–high school opportunities for young people in and around Central Brooklyn.

Our neighborhood centers were another crucial part of our social and community programming. Four of them were established during my tenure at Restoration and were set up to deal with the human needs of the Bedford-Stuyvesant population, many of them urgent and precipitated by the lack of public services available to residents. The staff at our centers were equipped to help with health care, tutoring, housing concerns, and a host of other legal and social issues. The centers quickly took their place as important neighborhood institutions.

Throughout my time at Restoration, about two-thirds of our operating budget came from federal funding, namely through the Special Impact Program, and surprisingly, it remained fairly steady even through the Nixon and Ford administrations, when the federal government was not always generous in its support of organizations such as ours. We did have some difficulty at times, but the numbers were, for the most part, constant, and ironically the funding even increased during the Nixon years. The other one-third of our operating budget came from foundations and private giving. We often used this as seed money to leverage money from banks, insurance companies, and the traditional sources of capital to fund our development projects. Generally, this would allow us to secure leverage at a ratio of better than two- or three-to-one in terms of private to public dollars.

Our goal was to get capital circulating in the area in a way that it hadn't been for the last several decades, and to keep it circulating so the spill-off benefits could be felt by the people who lived in Bedford-Stuyvesant. We were seeing results of that happening. Most importantly, we had, as we'd intended, approached redevelopment as an industry that should be tapped for the people who lived in the community. The product was only one part of the benefit to be derived from the development activity. If, for example, we were engaged in a housing project, we sought out local ways to acquire land, to develop sites, to build the buildings, to do the financing, and to buy the supplies and materials. We also employed local people and then hired local people to manage the buildings. Our way often took longer, because we were not only building the physical structures, but establishing the process from the ground up as well as encouraging a capacity and a turn of mind that allowed the community to feel a sense of ownership in the outcome.

There was another major accomplishment that couldn't be measured in numbers, but it was one I didn't lightly dismiss. It was the reconciliation that took place in the community that allowed the development process to move forward in the first place. When our efforts began in the late 1960s, the Black Power Movement and the pressure to separate and exclude were at their peak. We were consciously, openly, and aggressively asserting that the future for development and for a healthy community and society was a future that involved Black and white people working together. We were prepared not just to articulate that but to demonstrate it through the activities of the organization. We endured the slings and arrows along the way because we believed our approach would lead to a healthy future, not separate societies.

Another accomplishment, of course, was establishing the very notion of community development through a public-private partnership, which was pioneered by Restoration and then spread across the nation. We created this model and were able to make great strides as we blazed new trails in the world of urban development. The road was certainly rocky at times, and there was a learning curve organizationally and operationally during that first decade, but the public-private collaboration was beginning to show real results in Central Brooklyn.

It was late in 1976 when I decided to leave Restoration. Not only was the organization healthy then, but it clearly would be for a long time to come. The staff were excellent and dedicated, the board members on both the business and community sides continued to work hard for the organization, and the Kennedy family was still very supportive of our efforts. In December, I wrote a memo to the staff announcing that I would leave in May, and would work with Judge Joseph Williams (chair of the Restoration board) and Benno Schmidt (chair of the D&S board) to ensure a smooth transition.

In that memo I told the staff that it had been my privilege to work with them on behalf of Bedford-Stuyvesant for the past ten years. Those years were, in a real sense, a continuation of the nurturing that the Bedford-Stuyvesant community had given me as a youngster in its streets playing punchball, in its playgrounds playing basketball, and in its neighborhood schools. They were years of growth in my understanding of how to make things happen and how to identify and preserve what is healthy in a community.

I also wanted them to know that beyond the specific measurable achievements that were well known to all of us, I was most proud of the attitude we came to take for granted around Restoration—namely, not "Can we do it?," but rather "When will we do it?"

My plan when I left Restoration was to resume my law practice and take some time to sort out what I'd been doing. I'd received an offer from then president-elect Jimmy Carter to serve as his secretary of housing and urban development but I turned it down, telling him that the only federal job I was interested in was the one he was about to occupy. Honestly, I just didn't feel that the cabinet post was what the last ten years at Restoration had positioned me to do. Two things went through my mind. First, did I think I could make a unique difference? I didn't see that I could. And, as I envisioned how my time would be spent, it seemed to me I would be spending half of it or more testifying before committees of Congress about existing programs, a lot of which I had questions about.

South Africa was also on my mind. The same year I announced my resignation from Restoration I traveled to South Africa for the first time. My trip took place shortly after the student-led Soweto protests in June 1976. The Soweto uprising began on the morning of June 16, when twenty thousand schoolchildren in the Black township of Soweto marched to protest a government policy that required the mandatory use of Afrikaans (the language of the Afrikaner whites, who are descended from the original Dutch settlers) in their schools. The police response to the march resulted in the fatal shooting of a thirteen-year-old student, Hector Pieterson, which triggered further protests, much more violence, and the killing of many more students.

Part of what took me to South Africa after the Soweto uprising was a growing personal interest and deep concern that the anachronism of white minority rule on the southern tip of Black Africa defied the moral and ethical efforts of the majority of people inside the country to change it, as well as defying the trends toward majority rule in the rest of Africa. There was mounting evidence around the world of colonialism ending and representative government coming into place, and at least the beginning of a conversation about what kind of economic systems would best serve the new nations. Yet here sat the South African government going in the opposite direction.

The race-based human suffering in South Africa was something I could not ignore. There was also the fact that, increasingly, American corporations were being asked to demonstrate their respect for human rights by the actions they did or did not take in their global operations. Regarding South Africa, this involved their employment and operating practices as well as their attitude toward making new investments, or possibly withdrawing from South Africa altogether. I wanted to go and see the situation for myself.

At the time I was a director of Citibank and Vernon Jordan was a director of Xerox. Both companies had operations in South Africa. The reports we were getting from the management were that the companies saw themselves as positive forces in South Africa: they defied government prohibitions against Black workers in higher-level jobs, they were making education available for Black employees and their families, and they were making supportive payments with respect to housing. I talked to the people at Citibank and told them I didn't know how I could be helpful, but that I was uncomfortable with the growing sense that South Africa was heading in a direction that was opposite its long-term best interest, and the interests of the United States. However, I didn't know enough and I wanted to go there and learn.

Vernon was in a similar position, and the two of us decided to visit South Africa together, along with two senior executives from Citi and Xerox. The four of us visited the plants and facilities of the two companies. Vernon and I went on our own to look at some of the homeland areas. At that point the South African government was beginning to argue that the majority of the Black people in the country were actually citizens of neighboring independent states, or "homelands," and that the urban Blacks in South Africa proper were there not as South African citizens, but rather as visitors simply selling their labor. The government was also saying that the world community ought to look in the "homelands" for evidence of representative government, not in South Africa as they defined it—a clever but obviously flawed argument.

During our trip, Vernon and I met with a wide cross section of South Africans from the Black, Coloured, Asian, and white communities. We concluded relatively quickly that the scheme being articulated by the South African government was a contrivance and did not reflect reality: homelands represented only 13 percent of the land of South Africa, while 87 percent of the country was reserved for whites; the Black people who lived in the urban centers and townships were never given a choice about their citizenship; some who had no contact with the homelands for generations were deemed by government fiat to be citizens of those areas. We began a series of discussions with white South Africans about the arbitrary way in which these homeland areas were created and the arbitrary assignment of citizenship of South African urban-based Blacks to these areas. How was that consistent with the nation's history or the wishes of the majority of the people? We had similar discussions with some of the homeland leaders.

In the plants and in the banking facilities we met with Black employees, many of whom told us that the jobs they had were the best jobs available to Blacks in South Africa; they saw themselves as being advantaged vis-à-vis other Black South Africans. Many of them noted they were learning things that would be useful to them forever, not just on the job, and also that more opportunities were being created by some of the multinational companies than by the South African government or private sector, including some positions where Blacks supervised white employees, a practice which was against the law and prevailing policy at that time. So, there was confusion—a series of both benefits conferred and wrongs committed simultaneously that could not be neatly aligned or easily evaluated.

We met with many students and listened to them describe the horrors of apartheid and the horrors of the education system that had given rise to the 1976 rebellion. The young people expressed growing impatience with their own parents, who, they felt, were too conditioned to the old system and were not challenging it sufficiently. At that point Black South Africans were just beginning to express their resentment toward the United States for its inaction. There was still faith that the U.S. could make a meaningful impact on the South African government and help change existing conditions in the country. What was needed in the United States was more knowledge about the reality of conditions in South Africa.

We also met Mangosuthu Gatsha Buthelezi on this trip. Buthelezi was chief minister of KwaZulu, the Zulu homeland, and a major figure in South African politics. He came across as a leader who was committed to the liberation struggle, with his own view of how best to accomplish it. He seemed to understand the Afrikaner mentality without sacrificing the Zulu pride, and felt there were windows of opportunity through which fundamental change might occur in South Africa. At the same time, he insisted that the grand apartheid scheme of independent homelands was a farce to which he would never submit, and that he would not negotiate with the central government on a regional or national solution as long as Nelson Mandela was in jail and the African National Congress (ANC) was not free to operate within South Africa.

Vernon and I came back to the U.S. and were invited on the *Today Show* to share our findings with Tom Brokaw and others. We said that the United States should be paying more attention to South Africa, and that U.S. corporations had to become more proactive in expanding opportunities for Black South Africans if they were going to do business there. We argued that it wasn't clear which course of action was better for U.S. corporations: to pull out completely or stay and break as

many of the unconscionable South African government restrictions as possible. Obviously, this stirred up a lot of reactions
here because there were people who had been following South
Africa closely, including expatriates who had a well-developed
set of beliefs—principally, that the only thing to do was to completely isolate South Africa, and U.S. corporations should get
the hell out.

The trip left me intrigued, puzzled about the situation there,
and enormously impressed by the people—Black and white.
They all talked so openly about the issues, and some with a
degree of earnestness that was moving. Some of the Afrikaners, for example, would painfully make the case that they had
fought their own war of liberation at the turn of the twentieth
century. They had struggled, and their National Party had
just come to power after World War II, and while they had political authority, they had very limited economic authority—
the English-speaking white South Africans really controlled
all of that. The English, at least on the surface, were more
sympathetic to the Black liberation struggle, some even outspoken in their support of it. Now, looking back, I think they
saw it as a modest trade-off: a way to trade political power-
sharing with the Black majority in exchange for preservation
of a market-oriented economic system. I think they were pushing the Afrikaners to think along those lines of possible compromise. They all feared the unknown of the ANC, however,
many having persuaded themselves that the ANC was in
large measure a puppet of Soviet-style communist ideology. As
a result, many of the arguments made by the Afrikaners and
English-speaking white South Africans were about their fear
of being dominated by a Soviet-style system. They saw the ANC
and other liberation groups as a Trojan horse for this unwanted
system to come in and take over.

I returned to the U.S. thinking, my God, what an incredible place, but I could see it heading toward its own tragedy, and the U.S. stumbling along, not quite knowing what it should or shouldn't do.

All of this was still very much on my mind when I left Restoration and set up shop on Fifty-Third Street in Manhattan.

15

An Unexpected Presidency

The year I left Restoration turned out to be a busy one. In addition to setting up my practice, I accepted an invitation to become a trustee of the Ford Foundation. I knew several of the trustees and some of the senior staff from other civic and business activities, and also from the close partnerships I'd had with Ford during my tenure at Restoration beginning as far back as 1967. I also was asked, and agreed, to become interim head of the John Hay Whitney Foundation for nine months while Archibald Gillies, its permanent director, unsuccessfully ran for a seat on the New York City Council. I'd become quite close to Jock Whitney during my time at Restoration and had been a member of the Whitney Foundation board for several years.

I had a personal relationship with the Whitney family by this time as well. While I was on the Whitney board, Whitney's two daughters, Kate and Sara, were also asked to join. I knew Jock and his wife, Betsey Cushing Roosevelt Whitney, but it wasn't until Kate and Sara joined the board that I spent any time with them. Kate will tell you that she was a very quiet person in those days, so she didn't reveal a great deal of herself during those meetings, but one evening, after she'd been on the board a couple of years, we both had to leave a meeting early and found ourselves in the elevator together. Kate uncharacteristically talked my ear off on the short trip down, and according to her when we reached the street I said, "Kate, I'm sorry, but I don't think I understood a word you said." We knew, though, that we wanted to continue the conversation after that, and we did. Both divorced, with seven children between us, we began to see more and more of each other, and our friendship developed into what would become a lifelong relationship.

Dr. John Knowles, the president of the Rockefeller Foundation, approached me with a compelling proposal as I was settling into my post-Restoration life. He indicated that some members of their board were thinking about the feasibility of forming a study commission on U.S. policy toward southern Africa, particularly South Africa. They were concerned that the level of misunderstanding that existed about South Africa, owing to both the general lack of information and the amount of misinformation, hampered the ability to have thoughtful policy debates or to fashion nonpartisan national policy about the region. This was very much aligned with my current thinking. After my trip the year before, I'd already decided that I wanted to contribute in some way to bringing about positive change in South Africa. When they invited me to lead the effort, I accepted.

I spent several months doing research and gathering information to determine the feasibility of a study commission focused on southern Africa. There was a great deal to consider, including whether a commission was the best way to proceed, the pros and cons, the risks and potential, and whether we could guarantee the objectivity of commission members. In the end, however, I was persuaded that there was a hunger and a need for fact-based information about the region that also considered ways in which public and private U.S. actions could have an impact on changing the apartheid system. This hunger extended to the public, parts of the business community, and to many people in the world of policy. My report identified the fundamental difference—and the central policy problem—

between U.S. policy toward southern Africa and toward the rest of Africa as the result of institutionalized racial discrimination in South Africa and its dependencies. It also identified the capacity of institutional racism to contaminate all of the surrounding states and even to potentially spread beyond their borders. My findings supported the feasibility of a commission wholly independent of, even if financially sustained by, the Rockefeller Foundation. My report also offered suggestions on the commission's composition, terms of reference, processes, timetable, and probable costs.

Soon after I turned in the report, I was invited to a Rockefeller Foundation retreat in Williamsburg, Virginia, where the report and its recommendations were discussed. The outcome of that two-day meeting in September of 1978 was the foundation's decision to move ahead and create a commission on U.S. policy toward southern Africa. Rockefeller was prepared to fund the commission in its entirety and to draw members from the categories recommended in the report, if I would agree to take the lead as chair.

After some deliberation I agreed. The foundation had committed to provide all funds in advance, which was one of the terms I thought important to avoid any interference with the direction or pace of the commission's work. I knew the work of the commission could come under criticism since the subject of South Africa was a challenging one and it was necessary to know that if criticism was leveled from outside sources during the study, the commission would always be in full control of its process. I estimated it would take about two years to complete the assignment, after which we would need some time to disseminate it to audiences in the United States, Europe, South Africa, and other parts of Africa. I began to rearrange other things in my life, with the idea that I would give the commission one-third to one-half of my time.

In the midst of all of this, the Ford Foundation was searching for a new president. McGeorge Bundy, who had been at the helm of the organization since 1966, had announced several years earlier that he wanted to retire when he reached the age of sixty, which would happen in 1979, and the board had begun a search for his successor. Prior to serving in the Ford administration, Bundy had been national security adviser in the Kennedy and Johnson administrations; before that he was dean of the Faculty of Arts and Sciences at Harvard University, and a member of the school's Department of Government.

At the time, Ford was experiencing what some, including the *New York Times*, categorized as a mid-life crisis. Now in its forty-first year of existence, Ford had recently experienced a concerning financial downturn, and it was clear that the status quo could not be maintained going forward. The foundation had made a number of illiquid investments and then got caught when the market collapsed. As a result, there was one twelve-month period when the foundation's assets dropped from $4 billion to $1.7 billion and its cash flow was significantly reduced. Henry Ford II had surprised the board in late 1976 by resigning, stating that while Ford had a "magnificent record of achievement," it was not sufficiently respectful of the economic system through which the money had been generated. He also criticized the foundation for still trying to address as many different problem areas as it did fifteen years ago, with half of the income, and as a result, "tackling some of these rather thinly and thus not too effectively." Bundy had already reduced the staff by about 50 percent, but the blueprint and mission for taking Ford into the next decade would be created by its next leader.

As a trustee, I was fully aware of the president search, although not a part of the seven-member search committee. The committee considered hundreds of candidates, and those of us on the board were updated regularly on this matter. The rest of the world was watching too. With total assets of around $2.8 billion, Ford was still the biggest and wealthiest foundation in the country, and its future direction, structure, and programs would have an impact not only on American philanthropy, but on social development in the U.S. and in the rest of the world.

I'd been on the board for almost two years, and had signed on to chair the Rockefeller Study Commission on U.S. Policy Toward Southern Africa just a few months earlier, when the Ford search took an unexpected turn, at least as far as I was concerned. Ford asked me if I would consider being interviewed for the presidency.

I was just getting settled into my life after Restoration and the commitment I'd made to Rockefeller was a significant one. As a trustee, however, I was equally committed to the future of Ford. I had recently traveled to India and Bangladesh to see the work the foundation was supporting, and I was intrigued by the possibility of helping Ford through the current crisis. Interviewing for the position was certainly unplanned, but I was starting to think that some of the most interesting opportunities I'd encountered were those that had found me, not necessarily the other way around. I agreed to the interview.

I was very forthright during the interview process, which took place on a weekend. I remember thinking that they might not like or agree with my answers to the questions they posed, but I was going to be as open, honest, and direct as possible. I'd been on the board long enough to have clear opinions, and my goal was to move Ford in the right direction, not to land the job. The job hadn't even been on my radar. If they still thought I was a good candidate after hearing my frank responses, then it would be a position I would consider seriously. It was a robust exchange.

Afterward, I went to Manhasset, where I was staying with Kate and her family. The Ford people called and asked me to come back into Manhattan on Sunday to meet with them again. That's when they offered me the job.

I'd been candid with them about what I thought was necessary to ensure the future health of the foundation. When the trustees asked me to accept the presidency, it was with the understanding that the organization was still bleeding, and that it hadn't yet rethought its programs and the consequences of that rethinking for staffing and the organization as a whole. In fact, Alexander Heard, the president of the board of trustees and of the search committee, made clear to the press at the time that the forward commitments of the foundation had been kept to a minimum so the new president would have as much leeway as possible in shaping its future. I knew the challenges involved in assuming the presidency would be enormous. I'd also just made a big commitment to the Rockefeller Foundation and was just beginning to adjust to the structure of my new professional life. Yet, I kept thinking that everything I cared about—conditions of life in this country and abroad—was on Ford's agenda. I also thought I could be effective in the role, and importantly, I was confident that I would be able to count on the support of the board to get the work done. All the vibrations felt right to me. It seemed like an opportunity to build on the crazy, unpredictable combination of experiences I had to that point, in an institution that was flexible in its resources. Ford could be a powerful force and also open to taking risks and initiating meaningful action.

I decided to take the job but was serious about my commitment to the South Africa Commission and the Rockefeller Foundation, and I shared that with Ford. They said they were equally as interested in South Africa and suggested that I restructure the work of the commission so that I could take on both tasks. Rockefeller agreed to this approach. I formally accepted Ford's offer in January of 1979 with the understanding that I wouldn't officially start until the following June. That would give me some time to launch the study commission and close down my existing office.

The official announcement of my appointment as the seventh president of the Ford Foundation was made on January 30 and it was major news. The front-page *New York Times* piece that appeared that day reported that the other finalist for the job was Dr. Richard Lyman, the president of Stanford University. The same piece quoted Alexander Heard, president of the Ford board and chancellor of Vanderbilt University, who said, "Mr. Thomas's training, experience, knowledge of the foundation and wide-ranging understanding of problems facing America and the world equip him admirably to propose and chart a course for the foundation in the years immediately ahead." Heard was also quoted in another outlet saying that what impressed my fellow trustees about me the most was my ability to analyze difficult problems and come up with well-reasoned judgments. "You get a feeling with him that he is able to focus calmly and rationally on whatever the subject, with a sense of self-confidence and a ready willingness to point out his limitations," he said. The announcement also said the appointment was likely to affect the course of other foundations, since they look to Ford as a leader, and that it elevated me into a role as one of the "most influential black leaders in the United States."

I didn't define myself as a leader. No one had voted for me. No one had asked me to speak on their behalf. Of course, I was proud to be identified that way but was sometimes suspicious about what that was based on. I felt a responsibility to the issues, and that was a happy coincidence for the Ford job. However, although one is always sensitized by their background and interests, you can't transfer your role as an advocate into your role as the head of an enterprise whose role is broader than advocacy. In discharging your responsibilities, you should always be informed by your natural instincts and experiences, but not limited by them.

Much was made about the fact that Ford had appointed a Black president. My good friend Vernon Jordan was president of the National Urban League at the time and he was quoted in the media saying that my appointment "was the most significant black appointment of his time." "Frank Thomas is the right man," he said. "But he wasn't simply competing with a black person; he was competing against the world." Vernon said it was the first real example of a case where white people turned over meaningful power to a Black person. McGeorge Bundy said it was the first time a Black man had been appointed to a job of that magnitude that "didn't have black marked on it."

Many of the newspaper headlines that appeared throughout the country also made a point of mentioning race. From the *New York Daily News* ("Black Named to Head Ford Foundation") to the *Chicago Tribune* ("Black Lawyer Heads Ford Foundation") to the *Detroit Free Press* ("Ford Foundation: A Black at the Top"), the headlines suggested that my race was a significant part of the story. The Ford Foundation, however, made the decision never to mention my race in the biographical note released with the announcement of my appointment, nor in the remarks given by Alexander Heard. The focus was exclusively on the strong experience and characteristics I possessed that made me eminently qualified to lead the foundation. Ford was even criticized afterward for failing to mention race at all. A *New York Times* op-ed said Ford had exhibited "an excess of delicacy," and criticized the foundation for not finding the words to "celebrate the fact that, among other things, Thomas is black." Another critical opinion piece said that although the time might be coming when it will no longer be relevant to point out that "this or that exceptional achiever is black, that time is not yet at hand."

From where I stood at the time, I understood that a barrier had been broken with my appointment and I realized the impact that was having. I also knew it would become a platform from which other achievements could be made. It would touch the outer reaches of what was possible for those who identified with me by opening up an avenue that was traditionally marked "private." It said we had tangible evidence that the limits of what's possible is not really known or predetermined.

I also knew, however, that if the only consequence of my being at the Ford Foundation was that the organization had a Black president, then that would not have been a very significant step forward. What I needed to do was to bring my particular experience and exposure to the institution in a way that would tap resources that had gone unnoticed and untapped in the past.

It was certainly true, though, that I may not have been a traditional choice for the job. I was Black. I was a first-generation college graduate, born in the Bedford-Stuyvesant section of Brooklyn and still living there in a home I refurbished on Lafayette Avenue while running the Bedford Stuyvesant Restoration Corporation.

After the interview one of the board members said something to me that I thought was revealing in this regard. One of the things that struck him during the process, he said, was that the broadest visions of how the foundation could deal with pressing issues throughout the world came from someone from the streets of New York, someone whose background, on the surface, was Bed-Stuy, and among the most narrow.

Most of the reactions to my appointment were positive, although my friend Bill Paley, whom I'd worked with on the D&S board during my time at Restoration and also as a member of his board at CBS, was quite upset. "Frank, why did you take a job with Ford? Why didn't you come and work with me?" he wanted to know. I assured Bill that I thought this would be much better for our ongoing relationship.

I didn't think much about the reactions, which I knew would be subject to change. I knew I'd accepted a challenging job, and everyone would be watching. The substance of the work had to be my focus. The questions were immediate. "Will you reduce the number of areas in which Ford works?" "Will there be a change in international programming?" "Will you cut budgets? Staff?" I didn't have a developed agenda or blueprint at that early stage and responded that I imagined a shift in emphasis, rather than a wholesale shift out of any area and into others. I also said I fully expected Ford's international programming to continue. And I mentioned my interest in developing domestic and international programming that would utilize local people and groups working on their own issues and problems and create ways to tie them into broader policy efforts.

I knew I liked to build programs from the bottom up, and to those questioning my approach, I reminded them about my experience at the Bedford Stuyvesant Restoration Corporation, where I always tried to involve the people of the neighborhood, rather than imposing a master plan upon them.

Beyond that, my first order of business was to figure out a way to organize my life so that I could simultaneously begin my work on the South Africa Commission and move into an office at the Ford Foundation to start my detailed evaluations of the organization and its programs in order to make assessments about the future.

16

A South Africa Study Commission

The period between 1979 and 1981 was one of the most intense I've ever experienced. It required me to go all out, all of the time—and there was rarely anything left at the end of the day. There were stretches during that two-year period when I could only laugh to keep my balance. I would wake up and the papers were still spread around me on the bed. I worked from the moment I woke up until my eyes couldn't stay open any longer. Between the South Africa Commission and the Ford presidency, every ounce of my energy was fully engaged at all times on problems of concern to many people.

The Study Commission on U.S. Policy Toward Southern Africa began taking shape in the spring of 1979, shortly after my appointment at Ford. An independent, tax-exempt nonprofit corporation, the Foreign Policy Study Foundation, Inc. was established to receive and administer the Rockefeller grant, with the commissioners serving as its board of directors. The first order of business was to hire a staff and map out a research program. Marc Fasteau was appointed staff director and general counsel, and Milfred Fierce was named research director. Marc was in private practice at the time and had previously served on the staffs of several congressional committees. Milfred and I grew up a few blocks from one another in Bedford-Stuyvesant. We attended different high schools but we met as teenagers on the local basketball courts. When I asked Milfred to join the effort he was a history professor at Hunter College. He had a sabbatical planned for the year, but after some convincing, he agreed to put aside the book project he intended to work on during that time and join the staff of the commission. He was reluctant initially, not feeling himself expert enough about the region, but I assured him that I wanted the group to gather information and learn together. I was looking for people without preconceived notions. Milfred's engagement would go far beyond what even he imagined when he accepted the research director position. In fact, he wouldn't return to his sabbatical book project for another fourteen years. Milfred brought valuable historical context to the work we did on South Africa, and while he empathized with the liberation struggle and fervently hoped for its success, he was also able to see beyond it to other concerns, such as the need for mass education, economic development, and the fundamental improvement of the quality of life for the oppressed.

I then identified people I thought would be ideal commissioners and invited them to join the effort. I explained that the commission's charge was to determine how the United States could best respond to the problems posed by South Africa and its dismaying system of racial separation and discrimination. And I outlined our mission as meeting the pressing need for a carefully researched, thoughtful appraisal of the policy options available to the U.S. for dealing with the difficult political, economic, and moral issues posed by developments in the region.

Eleven highly capable people accepted my invitation. They came from diverse backgrounds including business, philanthropy, government service, labor, and academia. All of them were serving in their individual capacities and not as representatives of the organizations with which they were affiliated. From the outset, the commission members made no claim to a dispassionate attitude toward South Africa. They all shared the firm conviction that apartheid was wrong and they were eager to see a transition to a more just society. However, they pledged to give a full and fair hearing to all points of view. The commission members included Robert C. Good (president of Denison University), Charles V. Hamilton (professor of political science at Columbia University), Ruth Simms Hamilton (professor of sociology and racial and ethnic studies at the University of Michigan), Alexander Heard (chancellor of Vanderbilt University and also on the board of the Ford Foundation), Aileen C. Hernandez (an urban consultant), Constance B. Hilliard (international director of the Booker T. Washington Foundation), C. Peter McColough (chairman of Xerox Corporation), J. Irwin Miller (chairman of the Cummins Engine Company's Executive and Finance Committee), Alan Pifer (president of the Carnegie Corporation), and Howard Samuel (president of the Industrial Department of the AFL-CIO).

We decided to spend one year gathering information and to refrain from tackling policy questions until we felt confident of the facts. This extensive fact-finding procedure had the merit of draining some of the emotion out of the issues and allowing us to focus more clearly on the complex realities. One of the commission members with extensive experience on other commissions also gave us some advice that we took on board: "It usually takes a year to reach a point of maximum disagreement within a commission, and at least another year to put things together again. The danger is that if the second phase is rushed because of arbitrary deadlines, the quality of the analysis will suffer in pursuit of a quick consensus." There were a few times over the course of our information gathering when I had to remind the commission not to get ahead of itself. Commission members were taking in a great deal of information, and some of them already had some previous knowledge of, and experience in, the region and were eager to get to the second part of our task. I was careful not to rush to the second part, however, and we gave ourselves a full year for information gathering.

A steady stream of background reading began flowing to the commission members in the summer of 1979, and in the fall we began more formal exploration of the issues before us through a series of meetings in New York. A wide range of knowledgeable people were called in to offer information, and we examined topics including South African history, Black and white politics, the law and practice of apartheid, the South African economy, the internal forces for change in South Africa, and the South African military and internal security. We also considered South Africa's relations with the rest of Africa and with the international community in general, American interests in South Africa, past and present foreign policy toward South Africa, and the Soviet and Cuban roles in southern Africa. This was followed by a two-and-a-half-week trip to South Africa in early 1980—and we traveled widely. Commission members visited Johannesburg, Cape Town, Durban, Port Elizabeth, Pretoria, Ulundi, and Transkei, and during those visits talked with cabinet members, government administrators, leaders of the white parliamentary opposition, businesspeople, farmers, union leaders, journalists, and scholars. We visited urban African "townships" and rural resettlement communities occupied by Africans newly evicted from "white" areas. We listened to the views of African leaders and angry young residents of Soweto, the large township outside Johannesburg, and we met with representatives of the Indian and Coloured communities. Some of our commissioners met one-on-one with banned dissidents who were forbidden to see more than one person at a time. We asked to go to Robben Island, off Cape Town, where Nelson Mandela had been imprisoned since 1964, but we never got an answer from the government. We also asked to see Prime Minister P.W. Botha, but received the same non-response.

We did get to meet with Foreign Minister Roelof "Pik" Botha, who spent several minutes telling us that he didn't really want to meet with us and didn't care what we ultimately said because he knew in advance what that would be.

I do think the fact that we were an integrated group, traveling and working together, had some impact on the Afrikaners we met. Our physical appearance was a demonstration of principles that were being lived out in the U.S., which pointed out to them, of course, the core of their own problem. We came away with a clear sense that despite all the rhetoric to the contrary, all sides in South Africa were concerned about the impression the U.S. had of them. Moreover, it was eye-opening to many of us to discover that the Africans and the Afrikaners regarded each other as legitimate residents of the region. Both groups indicated that their problem was figuring out how to live together and share power.

It was during our first trip that the undertaking became very high-stakes for all involved. Theory came alive as we met with people throughout South Africa and could see, hear, and experience all we had been reading about. Listening to people's stories while crouching down, unable to stand up straight, ten thousand feet underground in a gold mine, gave our work an immediacy. In addition, it caused us to universally recognize and accept the need for merciless schedules and a virtual double-time pace in order to meet our two-year deadline.

The commission sometimes split into smaller groups to cover more ground. We did the same in subsequent travels elsewhere in Africa, in Namibia, Botswana, Lesotho, Mozambique, Malawi, Zambia, Tanzania, Kenya, and Nigeria. Staff members accompanied the commission and made additional trips of their own to South Africa and Zimbabwe.

As our research continued, in the spring of 1980 we held meetings in New York, Washington, DC, and San Francisco, at which representatives from a wide spectrum of U.S. groups and institutions presented their views on policy toward South Africa. Their recommendations ranged from support for immediate, all-out armed struggle against the South African government to what amounted to acceptance of the status quo. Civil rights, anti-apartheid, religious, congressional, and student groups were represented, as were university administrators, corporations, research and public policy institutes, and state and local governments. In the late spring and early summer of that year, commission members, operating in groups, also held meetings in England, France, and West Germany with government officials, business leaders, and others who were engaged with issues related to South Africa.

We spent time after these meetings sorting through what we'd learned and assessing the current course of events in South Africa, the prospects for change, and the range of American policy options. Then, in November, we returned to South Africa and renewed the discussions we'd had with South Africans on our first trip. We elicited other views and sought reactions to emerging ideas as we tried to gauge the impact of proposals under consideration.

Through the remainder of 1980 and into 1981, the commission held a final series of meetings to draft our policy recommendations and to review and edit the background chapters of the report. We also consulted with our advisers and their staffs: G.A. Costanzo, vice chairman of the board of Citibank, and William Sneath, chairman of the board of Union Carbide Corporation, as well as three former senior government officials—Henry Kissinger, Donald F. McHenry, and Cyrus Vance. We spent a total of seventy-five days in meetings and fact-finding trips and many days doing individual work.

Though the members of the commission had moments of profound disagreement and debate, in the end we achieved a

genuine consensus on all the major issues and presented a unan-
imous report that outlined possible courses of action that
could be taken to pressure South Africa to abandon its apartheid system and join the rest of the democratizing world.

Our report was published by the University of California
Press as a five-hundred-page book titled *South Africa: Time
Running Out*. As it made its way into the world, I was aware
that it would be addressing a hugely diverse audience. I was also
aware that, when dealing with a subject as emotional and complex as South Africa, there is a tendency for all of us to only grab
a piece of the elephant. The difficult thing is to see that there is
indeed a very large and complex object confronting us. It was
my hope that readers would not only read the section of the
report that interested them most, but that they would read the
others as well, and that they would consider our research and
recommendations in their totality.

The report was released just as the Reagan administration was
settling into office in Washington, and there was certainly talk
of a shifting emphasis in foreign policy, of less stress on human
rights and more on strategic and economic "realities." While
those realities were both present and important in our policy
toward South Africa, the issues of political freedom and civil
liberties in that country also had a tangible impact on the United
States at the time. It was the hope of the commission that policymakers would carefully weigh all aspects of the South Africa
question, as we tried to do, before they decided on a course.

The report presented a vast amount of our research for all to
consider. Some reviewers of the report even commented about
the level of detail included. Anthony Sampson, writing in
the *New York Times*, stated, "The study approaches the highly
charged problems of South Africa in a laborious manner, as if a
team of lawyers had been asked to look through all the official
statutes, documents, and reports. Whole sections are written in

the style of an encyclopedia, going through the country's history date by date." However, Sampson was also quite taken with the breadth and scope of the voices involved. "But between these grave assessments are sandwiched a series of snappy and outspoken interviews with South Africans of all races," he says, and he goes on to quote some of the passages that stuck with him. "'Afrikaners are a nasty bloody race,' says an English-speaking sculptor, 'absolutely humorless. They should never have been let loose here.' 'The blacks have exactly the same complaints today as the Afrikaners had under the British,' says an Afrikaner investment banker. 'It is only a matter of time before we get organized,' says a Black clerk in Soweto, 'we talk about it together every day.'" Sampson suggested that the interview sections might explain more about the tensions of South Africa than all the statistics, facts, and analyses that were included. He also said that the effect the interviews had on the report was as if "a board meeting were suddenly interrupted by a noisy group of protesters. After they leave, the discussion seems all the more solemn and impersonal."

In reality, these elements could not be separated. The voices of the people, the facts, the statistics, the research, and our analyses were all vital to do the delicate work we'd set out to do. We knew a revolution was in the making in South Africa, and we also knew there were no easy solutions. One of the realities we made clear in our report was that the choice was not between slow and peaceful change and quick and violent change, but between a slow, uneven, sporadically violent evolutionary process and a slow but much more violent descent into civil war. We explained that it must be viewed as a process of undermining and eventually overcoming white power, rather than as a single eruption or cataclysmic event.

In short, we concluded that the United States had five major interests in South Africa and the surrounding region:

(1) protecting U.S. military and strategic interests and minimizing Soviet influence in southern Africa; (2) ensuring adequate supplies of key minerals imported from South Africa; (3) advancing political freedom and civil liberties for all South Africans; (4) maintaining satisfactory diplomatic and commercial relations with other African countries; and (5) maintaining commercial relations with South Africa. We also presented a comprehensive list of realities and trends that reflected our findings, all of which helped us to recommend a policy based on the simultaneous pursuit of five objectives. The objectives were intended to serve as an integrated framework for action by the U.S. government and by private organizations. The five objectives were as follows:

1. To make clear the fundamental and continuing opposition of the U.S. government and people to the system of apartheid, with particular emphasis on the exclusion of blacks from an effective share in political power.
2. To promote genuine political power-sharing in South Africa with a minimum of violence by systematically exerting influence on the South African government.
3. To support organizations inside South Africa working for change, assist the development of black leadership, and promote black welfare.
4. To assist the economic development of the other states in southern Africa, including reduction of the imbalance in their economic relations with South Africa.
5. To reduce the impact of stoppages of imports of key minerals from South Africa.

We also recommended actions for each of these objectives to be taken by the U.S. government and U.S. corporations. For example, for the first objective, we recommended that the government broaden the arms embargo to cover foreign subsidiaries of U.S. companies, broaden the nuclear embargo, and offer no recognition of or economic aid to "independent homelands." And to U.S. corporations, we recommended no expansion and no new entry; that they commit resources to what we called the "social development expenditure standard" to improve the lives of Black South Africans; that they subscribe to and implement the Sullivan Principles (a code of conduct that called for companies to eliminate segregation, unequal pay, and discriminatory promotion, and to train Blacks for advancement); and that they implement and follow guidelines for U.S. shareholders.

Importantly, we didn't see our work ending with the report's publication. We spent a couple of years disseminating the information we'd gathered, even returning to each of the countries from which we had drawn knowledge or examples. We gave it as much visibility as we could, understanding the urgency of the situation and believing in the value of what we had produced. We sent copies to the White House, to every member of Congress, to every ambassador to the United States and to the United Nations, and to most businesspeople with South African connections. We also sent copies to many other people engaged with South African issues.

Time Running Out received a great deal of attention at a time when South Africa was being debated with intensity, and it did seem to reach the audience we'd hoped. One day, shortly after it was released, I even saw the book on a best-seller shelf at a Doubleday bookstore in Manhattan.

Those who were interested in a total quarantine of South Africa or complete disinvestment were not pleased with the commission's recommendations. However, it was our strong opinion that there had never been a causal connection between a total economic boycott and political change. We recommended that an official U.S. anti-apartheid policy be paired with U.S. business policies that furthered the interests of Black South Africans. In addition to urging more companies to subscribe to the Sullivan Principles, we urged stockholders in those companies to use their leverage to demand such policies. We also, however, did call for a freeze on further expansion of U.S. firms and no entry by new investors. And we urged firms with enlightened employment practices to expand and compete against companies that were discriminating against Blacks.

Businesses with a razor focus on next quarter's bottom line also weren't fond of our recommendations, but many nonetheless viewed *Time Running Out* as valuable. An op-ed in the *Chicago Tribune* in June of 1981 called it "an unusually thoughtful study that should be given a careful read by President Reagan and his policymakers. It may provide the basis for a policy that can serve both the ideal of racial justice and the reality of South Africa's strategic importance."

The South Africa Commission was, for me, a labor that taxed my endurance and gave me enormous satisfaction. As I was leading the commission, I'm not sure I knew that the work I was doing in South Africa was just getting started. The other thing just getting started during that time was my presidency at the Ford Foundation. I was deeply immersed in figuring out a way forward for the organization, and that required careful analysis and tremendous focus while being under close and critical scrutiny by those who did not welcome the inevitable change.

17

Reimagining the Ford Foundation

When I became president of the Ford Foundation, I was given a striking gift—a shield from New Guinea—that became part of my office decor. Perhaps it was meant as protection from the daggers that would fly once I began to make changes. There was significant change, and there were daggers—many of them— but from the beginning I was simply doing the job I was hired to do.

One of my mandates when I arrived at Ford was to address the concern of the trustees, and much of the staff, that the foundation had not adequately dealt with the question of over-extension, even though the program budget had been cut by 50 percent over the preceding five years. There was a sense that Ford was trying to do too many things in too many areas and, consequently, was losing its impact. Additionally, there was discussion that the cost of the foundation's management in relation to total grant dollars awarded was rising at too rapid a rate. The structure of the organization was also a cause for concern at that time. It did not encourage natural interaction among the staff because it had grown up in such a segmented fashion. Breaking down the barriers between the divisions seemed like an initiative worth exploring.

In sum, I knew the institution needed to be changed fundamentally, not just at the margins. With this in mind, I began an exhaustive review of operations that lasted eighteen months and included every program and person who worked for the foundation. Understandably, this wasn't exactly welcomed in all quarters of the organization. The current staff were accustomed to the status quo, and change is never easy. Now they were facing the unknown at the hand of someone many of them viewed as an outsider.

During the process, much was made of my style, managerial and otherwise. There were grumblings when I installed venetian blinds in my hallway-facing office windows, criticisms that I didn't mingle enough with staff, and gossip about whether I traded in former president Bundy's car for a different model. I thought the attention paid to what kinds of plants I had in the office or the car I drove was a little silly, but not all that unusual. I figured it just came with the turf. I knew Ford-watching was a common pastime among members of the foundation community and the media, and rumors, factual and otherwise, were par for the course. At least one newspaper reported that it was universally agreed that Bundy ran the foundation like a college campus, while my style was more that of a corporate executive. The press was eager to capitalize on any hint of anxiety or discontent among the staffers. Ford was, after all, the biggest and most powerful foundation in the nation, and it had the means to affect the course of social development both in the U.S. and abroad.

Not surprisingly, when the trustees approved my restructuring program in the spring of 1981, and we took the first steps to implement the plan, the controversy that was sparked was intense.

The reorganization was nothing less than a full-court press, but I was asked to lead Ford out of a period of drift and indecision, and small changes would not have solved our problems. I'd also assumed leadership during a period when philanthropy was painfully adapting to the challenging circumstances and shrinking resources of the 1980s, with the government reducing its own activities and calling on foundations to increase theirs.

Along with the restructured program agenda I suggested, there was a proposed staffing cut (from about 800 to 550). While most staff saw the wisdom of the programmatic changes and accepted the need to further reduce staffing, some, having survived the 50 percent cut by Bundy, were deeply upset. Senior program officers were among those who lost their jobs. It was dubbed the "May Day Massacre" or the "Mother's Day Massacre" because it happened in May. Although generous financial settlements were given, four of those officers filed charges of age discrimination.

The public attention paid to all of this was somewhat unusual because in the past, a deep sense of institutional loyalty and an active old-boy network helped ensure the inner workings of Ford were cloaked in an aura of secrecy. After the restructuring, however, departing employees were talking to the press and airing their gripes in public.

From my vantage point, I was alarmed by the top-heavy bureaucratic structure and the paternalism toward grantees. I wanted to know why we had so many ex-staffers working as consultants for one hundred or two hundred days a year. I also noted that there were people at Ford who behaved as though the purpose of the institution was primarily to preserve the jobs of the people who worked there. Additionally, the institution's resources had changed enormously, and the style of operation was no longer appropriate.

It was my President's Review of 1980 that laid out the new program agenda and the rationale for our decisions. It emphasized the need for further retrenchment in light of the foundation's reduced assets and increased management costs resulting from inflation; closer cooperation among programs and staff in the U.S. and between the U.S. and overseas, so we could become one foundation rather than a number of independently functioning units; and greater collaboration with other funders—public and private, at home and abroad.

The major programmatic changes included the reorganization of the foundation's programs into a single division, with grant-making organized around themes that united our activities in the U.S. and overseas. We would continue to spend 30 to 40 percent of our program budget on international activities, but in fewer overseas locations. We would retain nine overseas offices in the three continents in which the majority of our work was located: in Bangladesh, India, and Indonesia for programs in Asia and the Pacific; in Egypt, Kenya, and Nigeria (with a sub-office in Khartoum, Sudan) for Africa and the Middle East; and in Brazil, Mexico, and Peru for Latin America and the Caribbean.

Finally, we announced that in the years ahead the foundation's program work, both in the U.S. and abroad, would be focused around six major themes:

- Urban Poverty and the Disadvantaged
- Rural Poverty and Resources
- Human Rights and Social Justice
- Education
- International Political and Economic Issues
- Government and Public Policy

Cutting across the themes were approaches we had emphasized in recent years and special concern for several groups, including low-income women, disadvantaged racial and ethnic minorities, and refugees and immigrants. Attention to women's legal rights, for example, came under the theme of Human Rights and Social Justice; non-farm rural employment in developing countries or supported work programs for mothers on welfare in the U.S. would be addressed under either the Rural Poverty or Urban Poverty theme. Within several of the themes, coordinating partnerships with, and support for, community and neighborhood organizations was one of our most important approaches to problems, along with maintaining a focus on promising developments in communications technology.

Throughout my time at Restoration, while on the board at Ford, and then as president, women's initiatives were important to me. During my first summer at the foundation, the women at Ford developed a program paper, the first big program paper I took to the board as president. It called for doubling the size of Ford's women's programs. Susan Berresford was put in charge of helping with the expansion, which among other things included directives asserting that the role of women and minorities must be considered in all of Ford's activities. This presented itself in a number of ways, one being ensuring that women were part of the programs themselves. For example, were women in developing countries sharing in programs to help small rural farmers or to secure credit? Another was asking organizations who applied for money from Ford if women and minorities were represented on their boards (an inquiry that surprised many).

We "practiced what we preached": by 1982, 51 percent of Ford's professional positions were held by women, the first woman head of an overseas office had been appointed (Bangladesh), and Susan Berresford had been named the foundation's first woman vice president. (She would go on to be the first woman president of the Ford Foundation in 1996.) Also, Alvin Puryear, an African American man, was named vice president of administration in 1980, making him the first senior-level African American (besides me) within the foundation.

We did have to scale back in some places; there was less money going to universities for research and fewer grants for scholar-exchange programs. There were also a number of areas in which we had strongly engaged that now were not designated as major themes, most notably arts and culture, resources and the environment, and population.

We did anticipate some continued support of the arts, however, particularly within our six thematic areas. For example, grants were made to encourage minority groups in the performing arts and to offer inducements for performing arts groups to improve their financial management.

Recommendations emerging from a review of needs and opportunities in resources and the environment set the highest priority on intensifying efforts in local conservation and management of land and water resources. The bulk of our activity in this field would be conducted within the theme of Rural Poverty and Resources.

We decided to phase out a discrete program in population research after some two decades of extensive support in this once neglected field. The decision came at a time when governments and other major funders had picked up responsibility for many large-scale projects. To help ensure the stability of two of the country's principal centers of population work, we made a substantial tie-off grant to the Population Council, which concentrated on the population problems of the developing world, and a smaller grant to the Alan Guttmacher Institute, the leading source of policy research on reproductive health issues in the United States. We intended to retain the capacity to follow through on a limited number of targeted research grants, and to shift the focus of our support to women's reproductive health.

Finally, as my 1981 review noted, concurrent with the realignment of the foundation's programs, there had been a shift in program leadership. The vice presidents of the three major divisions through which the foundation had operated for ten years had retired. Harold Howe II retired as vice president of the Education and Public Policy Division and went to the Harvard Graduate School of Education. David Bell, vice president of the International Division, would be leaving the foundation later in the year. And Mitch Sviridoff, vice president of the National Affairs Division, was appointed to direct the Local Initiatives Support Corporation, an initiative of the foundation. To manage the single new program division, two vice presidents had been appointed: Susan Berresford, in charge of U.S. programs, and William D. Carmichael, in charge of Developing Country Programs.

I recognized and rewarded talent when I saw it, and I didn't abide by the unspoken tenure system that had previously existed at Ford. I also made appointments based on a person's capabilities and promise, regardless of whether the right credentials were attached. I believed in fresh perspectives and ideas, and I wanted to ensure that I made the institution I inherited stronger than it already was.

In my first few years, I affirmed that the foundation would continue to recognize the impressive capacity of local institutions and individuals to undertake and sustain initiatives aimed at improving the quality of life. Our work in the U.S. and abroad had helped to develop this capacity, which focused on the areas between a city's central business district and the suburban ring, the neighborhoods where immigrants and rural migrants had traditionally settled, and which called for a holistic approach toward a broad range of urban problems—schools, jobs, housing, health, welfare, and other social services. Later in the decade we supported community development corporations (CDCs), among them the Bedford Stuyvesant Restoration Corporation, which, of course, I headed for ten years; the Watts Labor Community Action Committee in Los Angeles; the

Woodlawn Organization in Chicago; Chicanos Por La Causa in Phoenix; and Mississippi Action for Community Education in the Delta.

The community development movement had proved to be an effective means for bringing life back to stranded neighborhoods and disadvantaged people. Innumerable local organizations had become skilled at leveraging private and public capital to carry out local tasks more effectively than government agencies usually could. Community development also yielded by-products that could not be quantified: for example, the restored confidence of local residents, a new sense of hope, and the easing of racial and ethnic tensions.

In recent years, Ford had worked to increase the impact and reach of its program activities through the formation of partnerships with other organizations, public and private, national and local. One of its strategies was to enhance the capacity of existing national organizations or to create new ones to address particular societal needs. Such national organizations brought together financial and other resources from all sectors and provided technical and financial support to community organizations. We encouraged the establishment of networks of local institutions engaged in similar activities to facilitate the exchange of useful knowledge and experience. Connecting a national organization to a network of local entities was an especially effective way to operate a nationwide activity. The national institution served as a clearinghouse of ideas and a disseminator of cross-project learning. The community groups adapted the collective learning to fit local needs and act as the local "eyes and ears" of the national body.

The Local Initiatives Support Corporation (LISC) illustrates the benefits of this approach. Launched in 1980 with nearly $10 million from the Ford Foundation and several major U.S. corporations, it was an outgrowth of the foundation's experience supporting CDCs in low-income communities in the late 1960s and 1970s. LISC provided technical assistance, loans, and grants to community organizations and helped them attract new sources of public and private capital for business and residential development. LISC was a testament to the large and growing number of successful local organizations that were ready to expand and diversify their community development programs. The effort built on the solid record of achievement by men and women who were directly affected by adverse conditions in all kinds of communities: residents who had for several years displayed energy, imagination, and leadership in arresting decline and making their environments substantially more livable.

By the end of 1982, LISC had already assisted close to two hundred projects nationwide and attracted almost $40 million in commitments and contributions from corporations and foundations around the country (including $16 million from Ford). Its capital had in turn been leveraged for high returns: loans of $4.9 million generated residential construction projects valued at $128.3 million; loans of $3.7 million for business and industrial development resulted in projects valued at $29.6 million. By the end of the decade, LISC had raised more than $300 million for community-based development projects and had attracted an additional $1.3 billion from public and private sources.

LISC's experience illustrated the important role that local funders could play in the community development process. That the business community had been actively involved in the LISC effort at both the national and local level underscored the fact that parts of the private sector were ready—indeed eager—to lend resources and talents to social investment projects with a favorable ratio of public gain to business risk.

We were trying to accomplish a great deal while living with the reality of ever-shrinking funds. Although we could decry the changes that were brought about in some areas on the federal level, and encourage thinking about alternatives to those policies, there was also a great need to take advantage of the opportunities that remained, and of some that were created by those changes. That is why I was increasingly leading Ford into partnerships with big business, tapping its funds and expertise when possible. My experience on the ground in Bedford-Stuyvesant also led me to work through community and grass-roots organizations.

While we were grappling with the economic challenges of the early 1980s, I put forth a new philanthropic vision in my first annual report for the Ford Foundation that embraced my belief that the nation would be better if the private sector assumed a fuller role in the redress of social problems. I called on philanthropic institutions, especially foundations, to create closer partnerships with business. I also suggested that Ford and other foundations would see a more concrete return on their investments if they assumed more of the characteristics, techniques, and priorities of corporations and private businesses. I called this approach "balance sheet philanthropy," and I stated that professionally staffed foundations were uniquely qualified to facilitate this approach and act as a powerful mediating institution between corporations and nonprofits and the people they serve. Although the phrase "balance sheet philanthropy" (the idea of using capital, rather than income, to achieve a charitable purpose) isn't one that stuck around, the concept has been embraced and built upon over the many years since then.

However, it was also never acceptable to me, as a social development strategy, that the federal government, which ought to be the means through which all our collective interests are served and mediated, should withdraw its concern from basic human welfare. Housing, food, health care, and education are national needs, because a nation doesn't thrive unless the great bulk of the people have the capacity to meet these basic needs. So it's not simply doing *for others*—though some of us would argue that may be justification enough—it is also doing for the *collective us*.

As shifts in policies took place under Reagan, the obvious question was, "If not the government, then who?" The quick answer tended to be the private sector would do it all. But none of us believed the private sector was capable of doing it all. And some of us questioned whether the private sector *should* do it all.

If you looked at the numbers themselves, in gross terms, in 1982, annual federal support for social programs was reduced by most estimates by about $35 billion. The entire foundation community had about $2.5 billion available for grants. Private corporations had about $3.5 billion available, so you were still looking at only $6 billion available to mitigate the impact of a $35 billion decrease. There was a fairly big cloud on the horizon that needed to be addressed: the government was renouncing its role to ensure that the basic needs of citizens were met. My view was that the government's role was large and pervasive, and it could be executed in a variety of forms. Some of those might have been wholly oriented to the private sector, such as providing funds or incentives. Others might have been through public-private partnerships, while others would be executed wholly by the government alone. For me, the appropriate mix within the spectrum of possibilities is what the debate needed to center on, not whether it was an appropriate objective of government to see to human welfare.

Another idea that was important to me was giving more money to people who would administer programs on their own to develop self-reliance and not dependency. I felt strongly, too, that the institution should be supporting the people closest to the problems, and that those people should have more control over the consultants that were hired to advise them. That was a change from the way things were done in the past when the Ford Foundation hired the consultant and loaned them to the grantee. When I was at Restoration and we were grantees, I remember the system working in this way and the consultants not being very useful to us. I knew giving the grantee the power to hire the consultant would make the process more productive.

I was mostly indifferent to the frequent criticism aimed in my direction throughout that period of change, but it did irritate me that the critiques were overshadowing the achievements that Ford was making. It was disappointing that it took so long for wise, principled observers of the foundation to recognize the powerful, important initiatives that were underway and that they were spending time looking backward instead of forward.

It took some time for the press to settle down as well. After a few years of skeptical questions and pointed critiques, when Ford started showing positive results, I was called into an editorial meeting at one of the major New York City newspapers and asked how things were going. The same people who had not shown much confidence in me were now patting me on the back and telling me that my efforts were exactly what was called for. "It was obvious that things really needed to change," I was told. To which I could only reply, "So now that I've survived you, what I did was obvious?"

18

A Changing Landscape
in South Africa

After *South Africa: Time Running Out* was published in 1981, and the South Africa Commission spent a couple of years disseminating the information we'd gathered, the group subsequently disbanded. There was, however, a pressing need to keep together the growing network of people interested in, and knowledgeable about, South Africa. An entity named the Study Group was established inside the Ford Foundation to continue this work.

The situation in South Africa was becoming more urgent as each year passed. By the middle of the decade it was clear that the question wasn't *whether* change would come—it would, but whether it would come after descent into civil war with all its violence and attendant bloodshed and bitterness, or whether it would result from a less violent political process of the kind that can only begin at a negotiating table.

Through periodic meetings and travel, the Study Group kept informed of developments, trends, and evolving U.S. policy regarding South Africa. Periodically, we scheduled trips to South Africa with Cyrus Vance, who was secretary of state in the Carter administration, and Robert McNamara, who was secretary of defense in the Johnson administration, and others—mainly people who expressed interest in becoming better informed about South Africa but weren't able to devote the necessary time to it. We basically did the homework and took them with us on the trips.

In May 1984, we sponsored an all-day conference at the Ford Foundation with approximately forty attendees, including several from South Africa. The agenda consisted of a report on the findings of the South Africa Commission, an update on developments in South Africa and the region since 1981, and a review of current issues. Five additional conferences were held over the next three years, each with thirty to sixty participants from diverse backgrounds, including Ford Foundation staff, academics, journalists, business leaders, foundation executives, representatives of anti-apartheid groups, members of Congress, present and former government officials and staff, delegations from South Africa, and representatives of South African resistance groups in exile.

Some of the South Africans who attended, arriving from South Africa and from countries of exile, came to the meetings at great personal risk, in several cases coming out of hiding to be there. The topics discussed ranged widely over issues relating to the future of South Africa and its people—labor, the economy, education, health care, housing, regional and international relations—and U.S. and international policy toward the country.

The Study Group also sponsored two new publications during this time based on *South Africa: Time Running Out* that were intended primarily for secondary school students and teachers.

On March 1, 1985, the Study Group met at the Overseas Development Council in Washington, DC. Ted Koppel and members of the staff of ABC's *Nightline* were present at the meeting. Koppel was preparing for a broadcast from Johannesburg, the show's first ever from outside the United States. He knew of the Study Group meeting from earlier conversations with me and others, and asked if he and his staff could attend.

That same day, Vernon Jordan and I and several other members of the group met with Reverend Leon Sullivan at the Embassy Row Hotel. Rev. Sullivan, a prominent African American Baptist minister and a member of the board of General Motors, was the author of the Sullivan Principles, a code of conduct drawn up in the late 1970s to guide U.S. firms operating in South Africa under apartheid. The Sullivan Principles called for desegregation of the workplace, equal pay for equal work, training programs for Black workers, promotion of Blacks to management positions, and recognition of Black trade unions. By the early 1980s, 137 companies had signed on to these guidelines, most of the major companies doing business in South Africa. But adherence to the principles was voluntary and compliance difficult to monitor; this in part was why the principles were controversial, especially among anti-apartheid activists, many of whom dismissed them as ineffective and argued instead for disinvestment. Disinvestment was commonly defined as the withdrawal of capital from investment in South Africa, or specifically the sale of stock in a company that had direct investments in South Africa.

We discussed a number of issues at the March 1st meeting, including the current situation in South Africa, disinvestment, the extent to which the Sullivan Principles were being adopted by U.S. companies, and the need to influence British, French, German, and Japanese firms. Rev. Sullivan commented that the disinvestment movement had been helpful in pushing companies to embrace the principles, especially South African companies that had nowhere else to go. English-speaking South Africans could move to Australia, the UK, or the U.S., but Afrikaners had few outside options. But the Sullivan Principles were getting pushback from companies, and criticism from many Blacks, and an independent advisory group was needed to monitor compliance.

People say, and I would agree, that when you are dealing with a complex, difficult situation like apartheid, you get to a point where you recognize that each position has consequences for everyone involved. This means you might find yourself in favor of aspects of each position. At such times, the one litmus test I always use is if the policy prescription you are offering ends up making you feel good without changing conditions on the ground, then you ought to be suspicious of it. We all should feel some pain and uncertainty as we try to be effective in these circumstances. In the case of South Africa, when talking to students and others, I would say, "If you decide you want to sell all your stock in a company that is doing business in South Africa, I would urge you to sell, but hold on to ten shares, hold on to something that gives you a legitimate voice in the affairs of that corporation and then go and press your point at the annual meeting, write letters, do all the things that are available to you as a shareholder. Don't sell it all and say to yourself that you are pure while the problem remains."

In working out the study commission's prescriptions for corporations, the approach was essentially the same, which is "No new investment, but do not completely divest." In other words, the corporation should retain its existing South African assets and become a model employer, defying the restrictions of apartheid—for example, by promoting people on the basis of merit without regard to color or gender, by creating educational programs for its workforce and their families, and by explicitly seeking out and trying to help those who have been disadvantaged by the apartheid system. At the same time, the corporation should feel some economic pain, since it is missing opportunities within the country by not making new investments, explicitly because of apartheid. Yet, the corporation shouldn't be pure and removed from that system. It should remain engaged, because if it did decide to sell out, in most cases its interest would be turned over to Afrikaners or others who would feel no significant pressure from their shareholders to be a force for change within the system.

The commission had constructed a policy schematic for the corporate community and for universities and individuals, and we tried in our report to be very explicit not only about what we were recommending, but why we were recommending it and what we thought its potential impact could be. I think it's one of the reasons the report had such a long shelf life. It was compelling to almost every thoughtful reader; even the Afrikaans language press in South Africa recognized its worth. According to those outlets, even though they disagreed with its recommendations, they felt everyone who had an interest in the health and future of South Africa should read the report. That put things into perspective for me in an interesting way.

The problem was how to explain the recommendations to groups of people whose concerns and attitude were simply encapsulated in the question "Are you for sanctions or against sanctions?" It wasn't a simple answer. We were for them. Those sanctions that were in place needed to remain in place, and there needed to be a prohibition on any new investment. But we were not in favor of pulling out all existing investment. If that happened, current investors remain tortured so long as apartheid remained entrenched. That was certainly the honest view that we had, and I'd say it was the most responsive to the realities of South Africa and of the United States.

The groups that wanted the green light that investment was good, that their presence was liberating, that infusing our values into that system was the most revolutionary thing we could do— that group was outraged at the no new investment recommendation. They said it was a recommendation to withdraw, because either you're growing or you're dying, and therefore it makes no sense to be there and not to be able to put in new money.

Then, in the early-to-mid 1980s, there emerged a growing core of young, impatient Black leaders in South Africa who felt that the self-avowed defenders of democracy in the West had failed to detach themselves from the apartheid regime. Many who had been on the side of limited engagement called for the United States to be clear to itself and, more importantly, to Black South Africans, that it was on the side of democracy, freedom, and choice. The more nuanced approach that we had recommended in 1981 was no longer seen as viable.

The South African government's behavior had gotten more outrageous, and most, if not all of us, felt comfortable altering our recommendations at that point. We had fought the great fight for five years. The fact was that long-term we were losing the hearts and minds of the majority of the people, and that was more detrimental to them and to our interest than taking a more aggressive stance on divestment policy. And so, with good conscience, we were able to make the shift, and explain it both to the South Africans and to others.

Sadly, Leon Sullivan didn't see disinvestment as a strategic necessity. I think he saw it as rejection and defeat of his Sullivan Principles, and he took it very personally. The Sullivan Principles had become the lightning rod for the attacks asserting that the presence of American corporations was not contributing to significant political change. This was a stinging blow for Leon, since he knew, as did we, that ultimately Sullivan-like principles would be necessary in a future South Africa free of apartheid.

In July 1985, a Study Group delegation visited South Africa. Several of us stopped in London on the way, where we met with journalists, academics, business leaders, current and former members of Parliament, including former prime minister Sir Edward Heath, members of anti-apartheid organizations, and others. The full delegation arrived in Johannesburg on

July 21, just as the government announced a new state of emergency. There were rumors that the delegation was some kind of "official" body representing the U.S. government, and members were bombarded with questions from the South African and foreign media about the purpose of our visit. Despite the tense political climate, the government did not interfere with the Study Group's meetings or its movements. There was, however, evidence of government surveillance of the leaders of the delegation.

Often dividing into smaller groups, we met with individuals representing all segments of South African society. There were meetings in Johannesburg with South African trade union leaders, including Cyril Ramaphosa, secretary-general of the National Union of Mineworkers, and with Harry Oppenheimer, chairman of the Anglo-American Corporation, and some of his colleagues; we met with Gatsha Buthelezi in Ulundi, capital of the KwaZulu homeland; we attended a seminar on international affairs in Durban. The delegation also met with a number of South African government ministers: F.W. de Klerk, who was then minister of national education and chairman of the Ministers' Council in the House of the Assembly; Barend du Plessis, minister of finance, who at that time appeared likely to succeed P.W. Botha as president; Roelof "Pik" Botha, foreign minister (unrelated to P.W. Botha); and Gerrit Viljoen, minister for cooperation and development. There were discussions with anti-apartheid organizations and leaders as well, particularly in the volatile Eastern Cape region. Several of these individuals were under banning orders and met with the delegation at great personal risk.

It was around this time—the mid-to-late 1980s—that we began to notice a transformation in the attitudes of many Black South Africans toward the United States. What had been a kind of implicit faith in the U.S. as a potential source of liberation was turning dramatically negative. Some of this was obviously related to politics here in the U.S. There were changes in government, and the pronouncements of the new assistant secretary of state for African affairs, Chet Crocker, about U.S. policy and "constructive engagement" with South Africa never quite landed despite being well intentioned. In the eyes of many, under the leadership of Ronald Reagan, who was reelected in 1984, it appeared that the U.S. was cozying up to the apartheid regime.

On our visits, we began to hear from Black South Africans about the alignment between an undemocratic apartheid regime and a U.S. government that openly promoted democracy. The Black activist community and even some Black religious leaders were asserting that the U.S. was more interested in preserving Afrikaner power and authority than in pursuing the values with which the U.S. was associated. It came as a huge shock that the U.S. was no longer widely seen as an ally in the liberation struggle but rather as a force for maintaining the status quo. For many of us, this brought about a dramatic shift in thinking about U.S. policy toward South Africa.

I recall Cy Vance and Bob McNamara, in particular, coming back and saying they were going to make the case with their contacts in Washington that something dramatic had to be done in order to get out of this box. They perceived, correctly, that the U.S. was losing the long-term strategic struggle. There was a growing alignment of apartheid, democracy, domination, and market systems in South Africa.

In December 1985, Secretary of State George Shultz asked the president to create a task force on South Africa. The Democratic-controlled Congress had begun an end run around the administration to create a sanctions environment, and the administration was struggling with what it should do. President Reagan had imposed limited sanctions against South Africa by executive order in 1985. The following year, Congress passed a strong set of economic sanctions over the president's veto. Shultz asked about a dozen people to serve on an advisory committee, including me. He communicated to us that he was open to different ideas, and that it would be a bipartisan effort. Frank Cary, former chairman of IBM, and William T. Coleman Jr., secretary of transportation in President Ford's administration, would be the co-chairs of the twelve-person committee. The committee's purpose was to recommend to Secretary Shultz "what U.S. policy toward South Africa would most effectively influence peaceful change and promote equal rights in that country."

After much agonizing, I agreed to participate in the advisory board, but doing so almost cost me my relationship with a number of Black South Africans, among them Mamphela Ramphele and Malusi Mpumlwana, both gifted and powerful leaders in the liberation struggle. Ramphele and Mpumlwana were, with Steve Biko, founding members of the Black Consciousness Movement. A medical doctor who also holds a PhD in social anthropology, Ramphele was elected vice-chancellor of the University of Cape Town in 1996 and in 2000 became a managing director of the World Bank. Mpumlwana was regional director of Africa Programs at the W.K. Kellogg Foundation (1996 to 2006) and after that became a senior policy adviser to Kellogg. He is also a bishop of the Ethiopian Episcopal Church.

Black South Africans had boycotted any kind of meeting with the Shultz advisory group. They simply refused to meet or talk with any of its members.

In one of the most painful sessions I think I've ever had about South Africa and apartheid, Ramphele and Mpumlwana told me they'd decided they wouldn't meet with me because I had joined the advisory group. They asked, "How could you do it?"

They weren't pleased with the administration's position on the sanctions, and also didn't believe its intentions were serious. They said that I was compromising myself by joining the advisory group. I responded that if the product of the advisory group turned out to be what they feared it would be, then they would be welcome to denounce not just the product, but me as well, and I would accept that. However, I explained that I thought there was a real chance that the advisory group could be much more than what they feared, and I couldn't in good conscience not try to make it happen. Eventually there was embracing and crying. It was incredible. We were all navigating through a very difficult period, and every time you ventured forth to strengthen or create a bridge, it became clear that you were treading on very, very fragile territory.

I did join the advisory group and worked pretty hard to ensure that our report would be a positive step in the liberation struggle, which it was. The group met regularly throughout 1986 and we submitted our findings in January 1987. It was a good report that advanced the aspirations of the majority of South Africans that apartheid must go. We were grateful to have stayed with the project despite all the threats that had been leveled at us.

In April 1986, a small Study Group delegation visited London and South Africa. The disappointment and frustration of Black South Africans was palpable, as was their hostility toward U.S. policy in South Africa and the region. Nonetheless, many people were eager to meet with us to voice their dissatisfaction with U.S. government policy. Black South Africans appeared unimpressed by South African government "reforms," such as the abolition of the pass laws and the anticipated end of the Group Areas Act. The pass laws restricted the movement of Black South Africans throughout the country by requiring them to carry passes at all times, and the Group Areas Act

(1950) created racially separated areas in towns and cities where Blacks, Coloureds, and whites could live and work.

Securing the release of Nelson Mandela was the priority now, as was unbanning the African National Congress (ANC) and beginning meaningful negotiations for a new political order in South Africa.

In May, John de St. Jorre, who had been a senior staff writer for the study commission, completed a short report for the Study Group on developments in South Africa since the publication of *Time Running Out* in 1981. The report indicated areas in which *Time Running Out* needed updating, and led to the decision to publish the "South Africa Update Series," which would consist of five or six titles produced over an eighteen-month period, and might also include research papers on related topics. De St. Jorre was subsequently appointed editor of the series.

Around the same time, the Study Group was conducting periodic meetings bringing together South Africans—Black and white—Americans, Europeans, and others. One of these meetings especially stands out in my memory. It took place on May 30–31, 1986, at the Harrison Conference Center in Glen Cove, Long Island, and I'm certain it left an indelible impression on all involved.

Among the participants were Thabo Mbeki, then based in Lusaka, Zambia, and head of the ANC's Department of Information and Publicity; Mac Maharaj, an Indian member of the ANC executive committee and leader of an underground revolutionary network inside South Africa; and a group of people from the ANC in exile, as well as South Africans living in the country. The white participants included Pieter de Lange, rector of the Rand Afrikaans University in Johannesburg, and chairman of the Broederbond, a secret Afrikaner organization with direct ties to the ruling National Party. The Broederbond

(Brotherhood) was founded by a small group of Afrikaners in 1918 to promote Afrikaner political, cultural, and economic interests. It was influential in building the National Party, and from 1948, when the party came to power, counted many government leaders among its members. There were a couple of others present as well, including Vance, McNamara, and our usual crowd, but no journalists. All those meetings were kept off the record, although occasionally a U.S. State Department person asked permission to come, and we would grant them entry, as long as they identified themselves. At this particular meeting, there were a couple of State Department people.

At some point after the meeting began, de Lange gave a presentation on higher education in South Africa. In the middle of the presentation, a fellow from the ANC in London named Jurabi couldn't restrain himself. He may have been reacting to something de Lange said in his presentation, or perhaps it was based on his knowledge of de Lange's leadership of the Broederbond. Whatever the catalyst, there was an incredible outburst. He stood up in his seat and started shouting, "I'll kill you, I'll kill you!" The whole room was stunned into silence—there were about thirty of us in this session, which I was chairing.

It was a time of great tension and anxiety in South Africa, with periods of violence and not infrequent states of emergency. The explosion set us all on edge. Relating this incident never gets any easier because it is still difficult to believe that it even happened, and also because there was so much at stake. Even the least emotional interactions between these groups were precarious and carried a tremendous amount of weight; an explosive situation like this one could be catastrophic.

I calmly turned to Jurabi and said, "Everyone understands the depth of your passion and your hurt, but that conduct is not appropriate. You need to get yourself under control, or you have to leave." I then called a ten-minute break, and the other ANC members corralled him. After the break, we resumed the meeting without incident.

The importance of that meeting was not so much the outbreak, but the critical fact that it was the first time that de Lange (a white leader close to the South African government) met Mbeki (an ANC man), and they spent several days talking. It was de Lange's first contact with the ANC in exile, and in a sense the first time that there was any real contact between the ANC and the National Party. Although de Lange was not an official of the National Party, the Broederbond was extremely close to the National Party at that point.

At the conclusion of the meeting, de Lange came by the Ford Foundation and saw Bill Carmichael and me. At the time Bill was vice president of our Developing Country Programs. De Lange thanked us for inviting him to the meeting and said it had changed his life. He told us that because of the experiences he had during our meetings, he now believed it was possible to negotiate with the ANC, that they were not the ogres that he and the overwhelming majority of Afrikaners believed them to be, and that he was going to change his mission in life and resign from the university to create a small think tank. He was going to go out among the Afrikaner people to try to persuade them of his discovery, and thus lessen their resistance to negotiating. It was incredible to witness the extraordinary reactions that some people had to that meeting and its aftermath.

In de Lange's case, he lived up to his word. One could speculate that de Lange was so successful in convincing the Afrikaner leadership that it was time to negotiate with the ANC, he set the stage for F.W. de Klerk's willingness to not only negotiate with the ANC, but to oppose apartheid and support the release of Nelson Mandela from prison without conditions, which he did after he became president, succeeding President P.W. Botha, in 1989.

19

Positive Results

As we did our work at Ford within the new structure, the financial health of the organization improved steadily. At the start of the decade, in 1980, the endowment stood at $2.3 billion; by 1989 it had risen to $5.6 billion (while the foundation simultaneously expended $2 billion on grants and operations).

The gains owed in part to two significant shifts in our budget practices. First, we concluded that budget levels should be about equal to the real rate of return we could expect to earn on our investments over the long term. We judged that rate, in the first ten years or so, to be about 5.8 percent. Second, to protect budgets from volatile changes based on short-term swings in the value of the endowment, we established a thirty-six-month rolling average of our asset values as a general guide to determining new budget levels. To reduce volatility further, we fixed our overall budget on a two-year cycle. Finally, we provided a 10 percent reserve in the program budgets, which allowed us to hold or release all or part of the reserve depending on the market performance during the two-year period.

By establishing biennial budgets using an annual spending rate of 5.8 percent of the average value of the investment portfolio and a thirty-six-month period over which to measure that average, we felt we would be able to budget on a predictable basis. (The federal government payout requirement for private foundations was 5 percent.) Further, we believed we would preserve the real value of the endowment over time by, in effect, spending only the real return. If our investment experience was better than the 5.8 annual rate of return, we would use those additional earnings to build up the endowment.

In retrospect, those decisions—to live within the real earning capacity of our assets and to budget in a way that would better take into account fluctuations in the value of the endowment—seem fairly simple. But they had a profoundly positive effect on the foundation's financial health, and the endowment continued to increase during my tenure.

In my final President's Review in 1995, I noted that the foundation's assets were valued at about $7.7 billion and our annual spending had grown from $119 million in 1979 to $420 million. During the period from 1979 to 1995, $4.2 billion was expended to further our mission.

Numbers don't tell the full story. There were some foundational changes in the ways we operated during my years at Ford as well. These became obvious to Ford watchers fairly quickly. Even by the mid-'80s the perception of the foundation was changing. An article in the *Chronicle of Higher Education* in 1986 said that after years of being criticized as a loner, Ford, in recent years had earned a reputation as a partner. The article spoke specifically about Ford's efforts in recruiting community foundations across the country to work collaboratively with the foundation on problems of teen pregnancy, and Ford's success in persuading big business to invest in the renewal of urban communities. Also mentioned was the establishment of a number of independent agencies to carry out work in fields ranging from refugee policy to local economic development, along with the enlistment of cosponsors for such organizations. Our work in the Third World had also become more explicitly involved in social justice than it had been in the past, making us more inclined to directly address the needs of poor people and assist them in improving their circumstances as opposed to pursuing more macro-economic development and growth initiatives.

Many said I brought a very different perspective to the presidency of Ford—that of a grantee. My goal was simply to maximize resources and put them in the hands of people who were close to, and solving, the issues and problems being tackled.

At the core of my philosophy was always identifying and reinforcing people's local initiatives; this is always the wisest investment of money—in people. When you focus on local initiatives and then connect them to higher reaches of government and policymaking, you can multiply impact. Making connections between initiator and policymaker was key.

It was heartening to see that after just a few years the early and loud criticism I had received, some that came from very responsible and reliable sources, disappeared. I just had to try to keep my vision strong, beyond the immediate criticism, or attack, or comment, and recognize that much of it was not centered on me, but on the uncertainty and anticipation of change, and the difference in style and personality that I brought to the organization. I might be overstating it a bit, but what was always interesting to me was that after some time passed, the changes that I instituted at the beginning became everyone's idea of exactly what had to be done! That actually became a real-life lesson for me, teaching me that leadership is not simply about taking a referendum at each stage of a process. Leadership is also about absorbing enormous amounts of criticism.

In 1982, *Ms.* magazine named me a Ms. Hero (awarded to "Men Who've Taken Chances and Made a Difference"). The paragraph that accompanied my photo credited me with "doubling grant-making to women's programs (from $4 to $9 million a year); for promoting and hiring women, including the first woman vice president, head of education and culture, and head of a field office abroad; for mandating an examination of all programs, domestic and international, for their effect on race and sex equality; and for bringing a spirit of practicality, democracy, and excellence to a foundation once seen as the heart of the Eastern Establishment." The work we were doing at Ford to promote equality was important to me. I was greatly influenced by the strong, smart women who raised me and knew that as women they faced even higher hurdles than I did. My sister Audrey was actually working at *Ms.*, a magazine founded by my lifelong friend Gloria Steinem. I first met Gloria when she came to visit the Bedford Stuyvesant Restoration Corporation as a reporter for *New York Magazine*, and we've been close ever since.

A year later, in 1983, it was an honor to be awarded the Alexander Hamilton Medal from the Columbia College Alumni Association. Awarded to members of the community for both distinguished service to the college and exceptional accomplishment in any field of endeavor, it was a meaningful acknowledgment since my connection to Columbia was one that was, and would be, important to me throughout my life. As I said the evening I was awarded the medal, if someone would have asked me to imagine the setting in which I would have been most pleased to receive an award and engage in a celebration, it would have involved Columbia, the school I love and respect, in a setting with classmates and friends, many of whom I'd known for more than thirty years, with at least some of my family present. That is exactly what was provided for me when I was awarded the Hamilton Medal.

Especially meaningful was that two men who were very important to me, Benno Schmidt and Vernon Jordan, spoke that evening. Benno and I met, of course, when he helped persuade me to lead the Bedford Stuyvesant Restoration Corporation.

We worked together very closely there, laboring in that extraordinary vineyard in our effort to blend self-reliance with the public and private sectors in order to produce the best that each was capable of. We remained close after I left. And Vernon and I shared triumph, tragedy, and everything in between since our first meeting.

For me, the evening allowed me to reflect back on my days at Columbia—the academics, the basketball, all of it. It was a time when you worked from the time you arose until you went to sleep. You simply reached out and partook of the enormous variety of information, insight, judgment, and talent that surrounded you. Much of the work I had done in my career built upon a foundation of knowledge, exposure, and sensitivity that I traced to Columbia College. All the issues we were working on at the Ford Foundation—whether it was peace and security, youth unemployment, human rights around the world, poverty (both urban and rural), higher education—all drew upon my Columbia background.

At Ford, we had the extraordinary job of directing resources toward the resolution of critical problems facing the world. It was a job where failure was defined as being too timid to try new approaches toward the resolution of old problems. All over the world people were struggling to achieve more opportunities for themselves and their children while simultaneously searching for enduring connections with something larger than themselves—some sense of community, some sense of value beyond their individual circumstance. Wanting more choices, more opportunities, and stronger ties and connections is a universal quest, common to people the world over. People are worried much less about their absolute economic condition than they are about the capacity to improve that condition and about the fairness of the system in which they live. They care little about the label the system carries if one tries to describe it.

Closer to home, my own sense at the time was that the recession that had gripped the country in the early 1980s had created a national mood of suffering. The sentiment seemed to be that we were all in this depressed condition together, across economic, geographic, racial, and ethnic lines. My guess was that the moment of greatest worry would come after we worked ourselves out of the recession and most people went back to work in industries across America, and the differential impact of deprivation was no longer masked by shared suffering. That's when we would need robust leadership at all levels, government and private—which historically we had a record of providing, although that record had appeared to be tainted over the previous few years.

In 1983, around the time I received the Hamilton Medal, the new structure at Ford was now well established, as were some of the early initiatives. The Local Initiatives Support Corporation (LISC) had raised more than $300 million for community-based development projects, and its successes illustrated the pivotal role that funders could play in the community development process. The active involvement of the business community in the LISC effort both nationally and locally illustrated how the private sector was ready to lend resources to social investment projects when the ratio of public gain to business risk was favorable.

In my President's Review for that year, which focused on the transnational aspect of the foundation's work, I mentioned the building of community development organizations as one of several areas of productive interchange between our programs in the U.S. and the developing world. The foundation's long experience with CDCs in the U.S. helped us better understand the problems faced by similar organizations in developing countries. Our efforts to assist these organizations overseas were still at an early stage, but our overseas offices were working with community development groups to some degree, with the most extensive activity taking place in India, Bangladesh, Egypt, and Mexico.

The fact that we had organized the foundation's program staff into a single division encouraged us to address issues from a transnational point of view, and also enabled us to take maximum advantage of the presence of Ford staff overseas as well as the natural links between our work in the U.S. and our work abroad.

Another area in which the transnational approach was significant during that time, and was also mentioned in my 1983 President's Review, was infant mortality. Although infant mortality had declined in all but the poorest countries in the thirty years prior, it was still unacceptably high in the developing world, with one child in four dying before reaching school age. And even though overall child mortality rates were lower in the U.S. than those in developing countries, in some depressed communities, death rates still were comparable. For example, a rural county in Tennessee in 1980 reported an infant mortality rate of 31.5 per 1,000 live births, while the infant mortality rate in Malaysia that year was 30.3 per 1,000. Another dimension of the problem in the U.S. was the disparity in the rates of infant death and illness between white and minority children, one example being that low birth weight (a key predictor of health problems in early life) was twice as common among Black infants.

Through its Child Survival/A Fair Start for Children program, Ford supported efforts to improve the rate of survival of disadvantaged infants and young children through inexpensive, yet effective, techniques to prevent and treat common childhood maladies, and also by training local practitioners and midwives in preventive and therapeutic techniques in areas where people were far removed from sophisticated and often prohibitively expensive medical care. Education was also provided to community leaders and young women about the nutritional advantages of breastfeeding and the use of readily available foods to combat intestinal and nutritional disorders. Those approaches were also used effectively in India, Bangladesh, Egypt, Indonesia, and Sudan.

In the U.S., the foundation was also running a home-visiting program to improve the health and mental development of Mexican American children in East Austin, Texas, that was based on knowledge gained in Latin America. There was also a foundation-funded preventive health program for Hispanic migrant workers in South Florida that used strategies developed in Central America.

Three of the foundation's programs—International Affairs, Human Rights and Social Justice, and Urban Poverty—were engaged in work, both national and transnational, that year to benefit refugees and migrants. At the time, it was estimated that the number of refugees, migrants, asylum seekers, and safe-haven seekers exceeded thirty million people (ten million of whom were refugees from political, social, or environmental upheavals in their home countries).

We were heading into a year when everyone was affected by the tragedy that was sweeping across much of Africa. Children and adults were dying of starvation in Ethiopia, Chad, and Sudan. The immediate cause of this crisis was a prolonged drought, but the more fundamental cause was the pressure of increasing population on economic resources and the food supply in the region. Food surplus aid was necessary of course, but equally urgent was the need to address underlying population, resource, and governance problems.

The Ford Foundation supported programs to increase agricultural production for many years in its overseas work to alleviate hunger, malnutrition, and exceptionally rapid population growth. We'd invested more than a half billion dollars since the early 1950s in these efforts. We also committed to new initiatives including agroforestry, farming systems research, and water management.

Complementing that work, we worked rigorously to reduce the pressure of growing populations on the resources available to provide them with an adequate standard of living. Our approach to population growth shifted over the years, particularly as large-scale funding for family planning programs in the developing world became available from governmental and intergovernmental assistance agencies and from the countries themselves. By the mid-1980s, our new course was influenced by the fact that improved contraceptives and access to them could not by themselves reduce excess rates of population growth. It had become clear that the success of population programs depended on millions of men and women making personal choices about sexual activity, contraception, and child-rearing. These choices would be profoundly influenced by how these adults made a living, how secure they felt in their futures, and especially by factors including women's education and parents' expectations for their children's life chances. With this knowledge, the foundation designated four priority areas to be addressed in our effort to influence population issues.

The first focused on women's incomes, education, and health (in both the U.S. and developing countries). The second, which was related, focused on high-risk mothers and children. The third area was the development of effective population policy, which we hoped to achieve by funding policy-related research. And the fourth centered on the migration of peoples throughout the world, which we believed represented a significant population problem. Our work in that area emphasized protecting the legal rights of refugees and migrants, analyzing the causes and consequences of refugee and immigration flows, and helping migrants and refugees settle in their new locations.

In 1984, there were 565 Ford Foundation people world-wide, compared with 1,500 in 1974 and 750 in 1979 (when I became president). I'd made a decision when I was hired to put available money in grants for people, rather than in the operation of an institution, and that is exactly what we were doing.

20

Mandela's Freedom

On February 11, 1990, Nelson Mandela was released uncondi-
tionally after twenty-seven years in prison. Mandela's freedom
had long been a demand of the ANC and others, and discussions with and about Mandela had been quietly underway for
some time. It was widely known, however, that Mandela was
firm in his demand for unconditional release. He would not tol-
erate restrictions on his liberty and autonomy. He had been
offered freedom with conditions many times, something he was
never willing to consider.

There was never much hope that P.W. Botha's Nationalist
government could or would reach agreement with Mandela, especially with the whole world tuned in. Mandela's release by
President F.W. de Klerk, when it happened, was thus a welcome surprise, unexpected even for veteran South Africa watchers, many of whom didn't believe they'd see Mandela freed in
their lifetimes. De Klerk first announced the lifting of the ban
on the ANC, the Pan Africanist Congress, and the South African Communist Party, as well as the removal of restrictions
on a number of domestic organizations including the United
Democratic Front and the Congress of South African Trade
Unions. Nine days later Nelson Mandela walked out the front
gate of the Victor Verster Prison in Cape Town. Photographs
of the historic moment show Mandela on that sunny afternoon,

arm in arm with his then-wife Winnie, each raising a fist in triumph.

I'd been cautiously optimistic for many months that change was coming. 1989 was a year of dramatic political shifts in many places. The Berlin Wall came down, the Soviet structure started to disintegrate, and the import of these events was instantly communicated, and their effects felt, around the world. More directly, in May of 1989 I traveled to South Africa and had a conversation with de Klerk that was not only memorable, but one of the most incredible conversations I've ever had with him or any other national leader. I left feeling that de Klerk had genuinely become persuaded by the growing unrest in South Africa and the winds of change in other parts of the world, and that bold action was imperative.

Milfred Fierce and Wayne Fredericks of the Study Group were with me on that trip. I'd met de Klerk on many occasions before, during the time he was a minister in the South African government. I often sought him out when I was visiting. He prides himself on being a lawyer and I'd had several arguments and discussions with him about group versus individual rights. I also knew that there were conflicting views within his own family. His brother became the co-founder of the democratic movement in South Africa, and I'd always been intrigued that the two could be so far apart politically.

De Klerk had replaced P.W. Botha as head of the National Party in February of that year, and as state president in September. We went to see him late on a Friday in May at his office in Cape Town. We did a lot of listening; he did most of the talking. He laid out his fears and apprehensions, and he spoke about the timing and implications of Mandela's release. He also talked about how he was going to deal with Mangosuthu Gatsha Buthelezi (president of the Inkatha Freedom Party, which was originally a Zulu cultural movement but then was transformed into a political movement under Buthelezi's leadership in the 1970s and renamed the Inkatha Freedom Party in 1990), and the fact that he didn't have full control over the South African military because its soldiers saw him as too soft.

He told us that he was not planning to immediately remove the state of emergency that was then in effect, even though there was enormous pressure coming from many sides to do that. He said if he removed it as one of his initial acts and the violence continued to spiral out of control, he would have to reimpose it, and then it would be *his* state of emergency. At the time, it wasn't considered his. His issue was *when* the time would be right to remove it. His move would be taking the state of emergency away, not introducing or reinstalling it.

De Klerk also talked about the changes he was considering in his search for an accommodation between all the people of South Africa. He felt there had been considerable improvement in the atmosphere for negotiations, especially among those who were not in the spotlight—ordinary people on the street, town councillors, urban Blacks, and others. He planned to consult with all groups—homeland leaders, urban Blacks, church and labor groups, among others—and seemed committed to working hard to build bridges of trust. He appealed for time and for operating room from the international community.

He identified his immediate challenge as bringing Blacks into the national body politic without one group dominating another. White domination had to end, but it could not be replaced by Black domination. South Africa had to find what he called "a balance of power," since there was concern, even in the Black community, about domination by one group over another.

De Klerk said that Mandela should and would be freed, and that Mandela must participate in negotiations if they were to be considered legitimate. He added that all legitimate interest groups must be equally represented in negotiations in order to break down mistrust.

He was fully aware much of this would be controversial and that there would be negative responses from all sides, but he believed that the National Party had to risk losing white support on the right in order to find an acceptable solution to South Africa's central racial and political problems. In his calculus, lost support on the right (seats in parliament) would be offset by gains on the left.

De Klerk ended our conversation that day by emphasizing the importance of not excluding Buthelezi and Inkatha from any talks, as there could be no permanent settlement without them. He added how important it was to find a formula for lasting peace in the region now that the Cubans were departing from Angola and Namibian independence was imminent.

I found myself starting to smile during our discussion with de Klerk on that Friday. The subject was familiar—we'd been talking about political liberalization in South Africa with him off and on for a couple of years—but his arguments and ideas were different than before. "I know what you're thinking," he said when he saw the look on my face. He said he still believed in group rights but suggested that maybe we could have a free association group. I said I'd buy that idea. I was struck by his combination of seriousness and focus as well as the degree of introspection that, paradoxically, allowed him to lighten a bit and connect back to things we had discussed much earlier.

I think it's fair to say that everything de Klerk indicated to us he was going to do, in substance he did. But at the time, as I talked to various groups of people in the weeks and months following the meeting, including some in the U.S. government, they were incredulous. "You guys have been working in this field for a long time, do you know this man?" they said. "You've got to be nuts to believe everything he says."

Even that summer, during a stay in Martha's Vineyard, I had spirited conversations, including one with my friend Bill Gray (then a congressman from Philadelphia, serving the Second District of Pennsylvania, who would later become president of the United Negro College Fund), who corralled me and asked, "What's this I hear you are going around saying?"

"Bill, look," I replied, "I understand your reaction, I really do, but my experience this spring tells me I'm right about this." I didn't tell him the full substance of my meeting, which I regarded as confidential, but I did say that I was convinced de Klerk was a leader who was in the process of changing.

Later, when Mandela's release was announced, my reaction was not surprise. However, it was as important an event as almost any other I can think of. It seemed that de Klerk, feeling increasingly pressured to take action, calculated that if a deal was going to be made that would lead to a peaceful future, the last best hope was to negotiate with Mandela. He was the only one who could make such a deal stick, if he decided it was the right course of action. I think that was the strategic assessment de Klerk made.

It was the right calculation. In addition to the humanitarian dimension, saving a lot of lives and bloodshed, it gave the country a genuine chance to sort through some of its very tough issues. All signs suggested that South Africa had fully accepted and was committed to a constitutional democracy, based on majority rule with protection of minority rights, as its national model.

Following Mandela's release, my periodic visits to South Africa and the region (Zambia, Zimbabwe, Mozambique, Namibia) continued, but now they included spending a lot of time with Mandela, in addition to others with whom I often acted as an intermediary, including de Klerk and Buthelezi, as they and some twenty other parties endeavored to reach agreement on an interim constitution for the new South African government.

Mandela and I had an immediate connection from our first meeting in South Africa not long after his release, and our bond remained strong until his death in 2013. There was an ease about our communication and a deep level of trust that allowed us to speak freely about a wide range of subjects. People have asked me many times over the years about the basis of this bond and it really was quite simple. We knew we could speak our minds to one another with confidence that our conversations would stay between us, unless we decided differently. Mandela had been imprisoned for twenty-seven years, and in many cases what he knew about various issues and events was what he'd been able to gather from behind the walls of a prison. He was eager to share his impressions of so many things and wanted to know mine as well. Understandably, there were many issues preoccupying him in those early years after his release. We talked about life, the role of government, and more generally about his frustrations and hopes.

Mandela's first visit to the U.S., which took place just four months after his release, was an eight-city tour that consisted of a grueling schedule for the then seventy-two-year-old who had recently undergone surgery to remove a benign cyst from his bladder. In addition to meeting President George H.W. Bush at the White House, Mandela addressed a joint session of Congress and the United Nations General Assembly. The objective of his visit was to keep pressure on the white South African government, economic and otherwise, so he also met with business leaders, some of whom still had financial ties to South Africa. There were stadium events and ticker-tape parades over the course of a packed twelve-day schedule, and he still could not come close to meeting the demand for his time and attention.

There were many noteworthy events in 1990, including the first formal talks between the South African government and the ANC that May (with Nelson Mandela serving as the ANC's deputy president) and the return of ANC president Oliver Tambo to South Africa that December after having spent thirty years in exile. That same month the ANC held its first Consultative Conference in South Africa after thirty years, which was attended by 1,600 delegates and concluded with a mandate to "serve notice on the regime that unless all obstacles are removed on or before 30 April 1991, the ANC shall consider the suspension of the whole negotiation process" with the government. The ANC also announced that 1991 would be a year of "mass action" and rejected a call to relax international sanctions against South Africa.

There were many things threatening to disrupt the negotiating process during the years following Mandela's release, including escalating violence involving segments of the ANC and Buthelezi's Inkatha Freedom Party, parties on the far right, and the "third force"—government military intelligence and police officers operating in secret.

However, of the numerous attempts to derail the negotiations, the assassination of Chris Hani in 1993 perhaps came closest to succeeding. Hani joined the South African Communist Party (SACP) in 1961 and was a member of the militant wing of the ANC. He'd gone into exile in 1963 to avoid imprisonment and returned in 1990 after the ANC and the SACP were unbanned by de Klerk. In 1991 he became secretary-general of the SACP. Hani, a charismatic and popular figure in the ANC, had a particularly strong following among young people. In his two years as leader of the SACP, he had made considerable progress in rebuilding the organization as a national political party and played a significant role in the negotiating process. On April 10, 1993, he was shot and killed outside his home by a member of the AWB (the Afrikaner Weerstand Beweging, or Afrikaner Resistance Movement), a far-right extra-parliamentary group. The assassin was a white immigrant from Poland who was subsequently arrested on the report of a white Afrikaner woman. Hani's assassination raised the threat of new violence, and of the collapse of the peace process.

Nelson Mandela took to national television to appeal for calm. "I appeal to all our people to remain calm and to honor the memory of Chris Hani by remaining a disciplined force for peace," he said. "I am reaching out to every single South African, black and white, from the very depths of my being. A white man, full of prejudice and hate, came to our country and committed a deed so foul that our whole nation now teeters on the brink of disaster. A white woman, of Afrikaner origin, risked her life so that we may know, and bring to justice this assassin. . . . Now is the time for all South Africans to stand together against those who, from any quarter, wish to destroy what Chris Hani gave his life for—the freedom of all of us."

As Mandela later observed, it was the ANC, and not the government, that sought to calm the nation in these precarious circumstances.

Less than a week after Chris Hani's assassination, Judge Richard Goldstone and I were meeting in my office at the Ford Foundation. Goldstone was a South African judge who had been working within the system for years to dismantle the laws of apartheid. In 1991 he was appointed by President de Klerk to chair the Commission of Inquiry Regarding the Prevention of Public Violence and Intimidation, subsequently known as the Goldstone Commission. He also served as a judge on the Constitutional Court of South Africa from 1994 until 2003. Our paths had crossed several times during the preceding ten years. The first was following a conference sponsored by the Aspen Institute, on the application of international human rights norms to domestic jurisprudence, that Ford had helped fund. After the conference Judge Goldstone wrote to me expressing his thanks and noting that he was going to apply what he had learned to his role as a judge in South Africa. Judge Goldstone was true to his word, and over the ensuing years earned broad respect among those who advocated freedom and justice in South Africa.

He'd only been in my office a short time that morning when he received calls from both de Klerk and Mandela. Both were requesting that the commission he chaired conduct a formal investigation into the Hani assassination. The importance and sensitivity of the issue to the processes underway in South Africa were quite clear, and I did what I could to help. Years later, Judge Goldstone, in his book *For Humanity: Reflections of a War Crimes Investigator*, described what happened in my office that day: "I shall never forget how warmly and spontaneously Franklin Thomas gave his office over to me and put his secretary, telephone, and fax machine at my disposal. From there the necessary instructions were issued for a preliminary public inquiry to be held in Johannesburg a few days later."

Although Ford had a long funding history in South Africa, as Judge Goldstone was leaving my office, I wondered what some future researcher, noting the Ford Foundation fax ID on the correspondence he sent that day, would make of my role and the role of the foundation in the instructions to investigate Chris Hani's assassination.

21

President Mandela

I have been privileged to know South Africa from several perspectives. It was as an interested visitor in 1976 that I first discovered South Africans' energy and zest for life, marveled at their country's natural beauty, and saw firsthand the ugliness of apartheid. I later chaired the Rockefeller Foundation–funded study of U.S. policy toward southern Africa, with a special focus on South Africa, that resulted in the published report *South Africa: Time Running Out*. As president of the Ford Foundation, that report formed the basis for my continuing close attention to South Africa, along with an annual multimillion-dollar program commitment to the country. And always, I have looked upon South Africa as a friend and admirer of its people, a people who needed so much and asked for so little, and who claimed a part of my life since my first visit.

The Ford Foundation's work in South Africa began many years before Nelson Mandela's release from prison in 1990, and it focused on support for human rights, legal assistance, education, and community development organizations in Namibia as well as in South Africa. The President's Review for 1986 reported on a $1.9 million special appropriation voted by Ford's trustees in 1985 to expand the foundation's programs in both South Africa and Namibia.

For the foundation, the challenge had been to find opportunities to help meet the human needs of oppressed Blacks in ways that also contributed to preparing them for the day when they would assume their rightful role—first as full partners in negotiation of their country's future, then as potential leaders of a democratic South African government. Our assistance had thus taken the form of expanding educational opportunities that would prepare Black South Africans for positions of present and future leadership, development of public interest law and legal services, and the strengthening of Black community-based self-help organizations.

Support for efforts to improve educational opportunities for Blacks had been a central focus of the foundation's program in southern Africa for a decade, and a large share of the special funding was committed to expansion of this program. Grants to the Institute of International Education allowed its South African Education Program to launch two new initiatives. One placed undergraduate Namibian students in American colleges and universities, the second supported graduate-level training in the United States for members of the South African and Namibian clergy, who had a special commitment to the social ministry. In part, this program recognized the unique leadership role being played in the apartheid crisis by South African priests and ministers such as Archbishop Desmond Tutu, Rev. Allan Boesak, and Rev. Beyers Naudé. These religious leaders had attributed their effectiveness in significant measure to opportunities to study and reflect outside of South Africa's restrictive atmosphere.

Since there was little the foundation could do to improve the inferior state-run Black primary and secondary schools, our strategy had been to facilitate remedial and enrichment programs offered by nongovernmental organizations. A new effort initiated by the South African Committee for Higher Education Trust, a foundation grantee, offered some eighty recent secondary school graduates a one-year "bridging" curriculum to help prepare them for studies at two of South Africa's strongest institutions of higher education, the Universities of Cape Town and the Witwatersrand.

Another focus of the foundation's work in South Africa had been an attempt to address violations of human rights and promote the rule of law. One thrust of this program had been our support since 1979 of public interest law centers in the country's urban areas, where attorneys helped Black South Africans cope with the burden of residency regulations and influx control restrictions on Black Africans' movement in urban areas, assisted Black industrial workers, and provided counsel and litigation services on a wide range of legal problems. Increased attention was now being paid to the legal needs of rural Blacks, spurred in large part by mass forced relocations. Thus, part of the special appropriation had been committed to expansion of the work of the Transvaal Rural Action Committee (TRAC) of the Black Sash, one of South Africa's most important rights and education advocacy groups. TRAC had become an effective supporter of rural communities that were threatened with or were already victims of forced removals, and a major force for strengthening community-based self-help organizations in remote areas.

Funds from the special appropriation also funded a number of projects at the Universities of Natal, Cape Town, and the Witwatersrand; an unusually effective community development organization that assisted small-scale businesses in a rural area of the Cape Province; and a Ford Foundation–based study group, which I chaired, to review and assess the evolving situation in southern Africa, with particular reference to its implications for U.S. foreign policy.

In 1993, with the political transition underway, the foundation decided that it could better manage its South Africa program with a field office based in the country. In April of that year, an office with a staff of five Americans and nine South Africans was opened in Johannesburg. It was officially inaugurated in January 1994.

Ford wanted to help all the people of the new South Africa build a peaceful and prosperous society. After opening our office, we began to focus on the public interest sector more broadly, going beyond our long-standing work in public interest law to include activities in rural development, women's issues, community development, and public policy research. We believed that a strong public interest sector that keeps elected officials accountable to the people they govern was vital to any democracy. And we were convinced that one of the foundation's best advantages in any country was our freedom to work with nongovernmental organizations (NGOs) devoted to public policy and advocacy. For example, the Legal Resources Centre, an NGO the foundation had supported for many years, was bringing before the new Constitutional Court cases that would be crucial to making South Africa's political and justice systems work. Another example was the National Association of Democratic Lawyers Trust, which received foundation support to provide legal training in rural areas.

The same year that we were opening the Ford office in Johannesburg, I was on the selection committee for the Philadelphia Liberty Medal. Established in 1988, the Liberty Medal is awarded annually to individuals or organizations "who strive to secure the blessings of liberty to people around the world." The award was initially administered by the Philadelphia Foundation until, in 2006, it was taken over by the National Constitution Center.

That year, we nominated de Klerk and Mandela to receive the award jointly, and I was asked to go to South Africa to help persuade them to accept it. On that visit, I spent time with both de Klerk and Mandela determining the various conditions each had for traveling to the U.S. and accepting the award together. I learned that de Klerk was prepared to go to Philadelphia to accept the award, but that he didn't feel he could go unless he was recognized as head of state and was assured of a meeting with President Clinton. He was also apprehensive about how he would be received by the public: he did not want to run the risk of being heckled by anti-apartheid protesters.

Mandela made clear to me that he saw the joint award as an opportunity to advance the negotiating process. There were several outstanding political issues that still needed to be resolved, like the timing of the elections and the establishment of a Transitional Executive Council that would, in effect, be the government until the elections were held. Mandela proposed that if those issues could be resolved, he would stand side by side with de Klerk at the ceremony, so if there were hecklers, they would both be heckled, and he also agreed to support de Klerk's request to meet with President Clinton.

The negotiations were successful and both men agreed to accept the award together in Philadelphia. On that visit I saw them both for the first time the night before the ceremony, which was to take place on July 4, at a reception being held in their honor. Mandela was smiling and happy when he arrived. He was meeting my wife Kate for the first time that evening, and as soon as he saw us in the receiving line, he leaned in for a very warm greeting and spoke directly to Kate. "Now I know why Franklin is so effective," he said. De Klerk, too, was in very good spirits. "Nelson persuaded me to accept," he said to me, "and I'm glad I did. Nelson and I are both lawyers and we reason from facts. That's why we were able to work out these issues."

The ceremony took place at Independence Hall in front of approximately two thousand invited guests and thousands more who crowded into the mall that houses the Liberty Bell. Mandela, de Klerk, and President Clinton all addressed the crowd, and while there were some protesters, they only caused a minor disruption. In Mandela's speech he cited Frederick Douglass, who marked the Fourth of July 141 years earlier, during the era of slavery, with the words "This Fourth of July is yours, not mine."

There were some anti-apartheid activists who had expressed concern that Mandela was being used by de Klerk, but their concern was misplaced. It was a win/win situation: de Klerk got to meet the U.S. president and Mandela secured the critical agreement on the Transitional Executive Council. Mandela would also get to meet President Clinton, but de Klerk's meeting would come first.

Throughout 1993, negotiations for a transitional government in South Africa moved forward while violence continued. The big struggle between the ANC and Inkatha Freedom Party (IFP) was intensifying; negotiations between the ANC and the National Party were beginning, and Gatsha Buthelezi was not at the table. Buthelezi and the IFP boycotted the multiparty forum that drafted the interim constitution and set the date for elections in April 1994. In alliance with the right-wing Conservative Party and several smaller groups, Buthelezi sought to derail the settlement and declared his intention to boycott the election. Mandela and de Klerk offered him concessions, which he rejected as inadequate. For Mandela and de Klerk, it was essential that the IFP, the third major party in South Africa, participate.

It was becoming increasingly apparent that the Gatsha/ANC split was serious and growing, and it no longer looked like posturing. In fact, there was serious concern that it could disrupt any chance of political cooperation.

I knew Gatsha well and I'd had many lengthy conversations with him over the years, which almost always followed a similar pattern. He would start off by berating me in some fashion for something the Ford Foundation had done or failed to do.

He would basically read a message to me. He would attack, then put away the speech, and then a substantive conversation would ensue.

I knew that he was very smart and strategic in his thinking. I knew further that in his mind, he had fought the good fight against the apartheid government. He had not accepted full independence for the KwaZulu homeland, holding out for the release of Mandela and the unbanning of the ANC. Given the violence between Inkatha and the ANC party, I think it is fair to say that we were perhaps more sympathetic to him at this point than was warranted. Nevertheless, I was sympathetic, and I think he knew that.

In January of 1994, I was preparing for the official dedication of the Ford office in Johannesburg, when I got a call from the U.S. State Department on behalf of the administration asking if I would agree to take a letter from President Clinton to Gatsha. I was clear in my response: "I will see Gatsha, and I am open to any briefings you want to give me on what is going on and the like. But I do not want to take an official letter. I am traveling as a private citizen, not as an emissary. If I become a carrier, I lose all the uniqueness that allows people to want to talk to me. I don't make any secret about the fact that I am willing to talk to policymakers, but taking an official letter would be a mistake." There was a great deal of back-and-forth with the State Department and Tony Lake, the national security adviser, trying to persuade me differently, but they ultimately accepted the fact that I would not be delivering a letter for them.

I knew they had many other channels through which to deliver the letter. They had our ambassador, they had administration people, and they had members of Congress going back and forth to South Africa. It didn't make sense for me to take the letter, and I felt it would taint my long-standing relationship with Gatsha.

While I was in South Africa I met with Princeton Lyman, who was then U.S. ambassador. I first met Princeton in 1979 when he was ambassador to Nigeria and the South Africa Commission was beginning its work. Since then we'd developed a friendship and I had much respect for him personally and professionally. He told me that the delegations from Congress, people from the administration, Secretary of Commerce Ron Brown, and others who'd been to South Africa had not been successful in one-on-one discussions with Gatsha, who arrived at every meeting with at least two people, which always tended to be more ritual than substance.

"Don't be surprised if you aren't able to get a one-on-one meeting, despite your relationship with him," Princeton and others warned me. Princeton offered to help arrange a meeting, but I declined, preferring to do it on my own. In fact, my colleague Milfred Fierce had gone down a week in advance and had already made contact with Gatsha's people. He delivered an invitation from me to Gatsha and the Inkatha leadership to the opening of the foundation's office in South Africa and Gatsha had accepted. If you can picture it, this is in the middle of the powerful division between the ANC and Inkatha, in the midst of bloodshed and general chaos. People were choosing sides, and yet there was also progress happening with the negotiations between the National Party and the ANC.

Gatsha showed up at the Ford reception, which was being held at one of the big hotels in Johannesburg. I greeted him and said I really wanted to talk, and if his time was short, I would break away from the reception and talk to him then. "No, this is an important event for the foundation," he said, "People are here to see you and be with you. My time is okay." He stayed until the end of the event, and then he and I went upstairs to speak, one-on-one, with Milfred and one of Gatsha's colleagues in the outer room.

"I am here to talk to you about your role in the upcoming elections," I said. "I want to try to understand how you could allow the elections to happen without your participation. It is so inconsistent with everything I know about you and all that you have fought for all of your life. I would like to try to both understand and be helpful."

"I understand you have a letter for me," he said.

"I don't," I replied. "I don't carry letters." Gatsha looked at me and just grinned.

A moment like that takes your breath away! One gets accustomed to the fact that there is rarely total secrecy in the system, but the fact that he knew about the letter amazed me.

We then sat and began our talk. Gatsha recited for me the ins and outs of the relationship that he and Mandela had since Mandela's release from prison. He recounted all of the slights that Mandela had visited upon him and the efforts to which he had gone to overlook those slights. He talked for more than an hour. When he was done, I asked him how much of the conversation I could share with Mandela, whom I would be seeing the next day. "All of it," he said. I told him I would do my best to be helpful.

The next day Mandela came to the Carlton Hotel, where I was staying. He came up to my room, we had lunch, and we talked. I started describing to him just the beginnings of my conversation with Gatsha. He stopped me and took the next forty-five minutes to tell me all of the slights that Gatsha had visited upon him and the extraordinary efforts to which he had already gone to try to bridge this gap. He also talked about the tension within the ANC that was based on the feeling that he had gone too far in trying to accommodate Gatsha.

We talked very candidly about all of it. About where things were in the political process, how this was a historic moment for the country, and that we couldn't let it slip away because two people who ought to be allies were at each other's throats, and by their example were allowing, if not encouraging, the violence that was escalating between their followers. That was just not acceptable; it *couldn't* be acceptable. We reached a point in the conversation when he looked up and said, "Tell me what you think I should do."

I gulped, took a deep breath, got myself together, and told him what I thought. My view was that he had to reach out personally to Gatsha. "You have the greater power in this situation," I explained, "and taking the first step is not a diminution of power, it's an affirmation." Gatsha was suffering from, among other things, a perceived loss of face. He had envisaged a three-party process that included Mandela, de Klerk, and himself. It had become a two-party process, with Gatsha never being in the circle. Having fought the good fight, he was hurt and deeply resentful, and feared for his and Inkatha's future role in the governance of South Africa.

Because Gatsha previously had a pretty good working relationship with the National Party, I told Mandela that Gatsha had to believe that his absence from the negotiations was Mandela's doing. It was also important to remember that the National Party had been prepared to make a deal with Gatsha, but he had refused to accept the deal while Mandela remained in jail and the ANC was banned. Mandela and I went back and forth, and he finally said, "I'll do it, but I have to do some serious work with my own people first," he said. "You have to know how difficult this is. My people are furious with him."

"I don't pretend to know all of that," I responded, "but I do know that if you don't do it, things will be worse."

I spoke with Princeton before I left Johannesburg and indicated that I was cautiously optimistic that Mandela and Gatsha would make a final effort to have full participation in the upcoming elections. I said I believed that Gatsha would not let

this election take place without his participation, or at a minimum he would not prevent his constituents from participating,
even if he held back himself. With many fits and starts, that is
essentially what happened.

Only five months elapsed between approval of the interim
constitution in November 1993 and the election, set for
April 1994. As the transitional government worked to prepare
for the country's first-ever democratic election, violence continued, threatening disruption of the elections and civil war.
(The agreement approving the interim constitution called for
the establishment of a multiparty Transitional Executive Council to govern the country until the election of a new parliament and an Independent Electoral Commission to organize
the elections.) Until the eve of the election, it was by no means
certain that the polling would go forward peacefully, or indeed
go forward at all. Gatsha Buthelezi's IFP, joined with a coalition of right-wing groups in the "Freedom Alliance," led the opposition to the transition process. The February deadline to
register for participation in the election passed, with none of
these groups signed on.

The principal Conservative Party did register—as the Freedom Front—in time for the extended deadline in early March,
splitting the conservative coalition and marking the end of
a serious threat from extremists on the right. This left Buthelezi
standing alone.

Fighting continued in KwaZulu-Natal and other homeland
areas, and in Johannesburg, where the IFP twice organized
mass rallies to protest the settlement. The second of these, at
the end of March, ended in a confrontation at ANC headquarters, which left some fifty people dead. Mandela and de Klerk
renewed their efforts to bring Buthelezi into the process, to
avoid further bloodshed and to ensure that the election would
take place without further disruption. They offered to extend

the deadline for registration to accommodate the IFP but refused to postpone the election, which was one of Buthelezi's demands. In mid-April, just days before the election, Buthelezi signed on.

During these months, I worked to generate support for the South Africa Free Election (SAFE) Fund, an organization established by a group of Americans to raise funds in the United States to support nonpartisan voter education, registration, and monitoring for the April election. In partnership with the Ecumenical Assistance Trust (EAT) of South Africa, SAFE made grants to projects identified and recommended by EAT, which distributed the funds to South African NGOs. Projects included voter education workshops and materials; train-the-trainer programs; media projects (radio, television, and print); and initiatives aimed at particular groups such as rural voters, women, or regions of the country where there had been violence or resistance to the elections. The Ford Foundation was an early contributor to SAFE, as was the Charles Stewart Mott Foundation, which ultimately became one of SAFE's largest donors.

In April, South Africans went to the polls to vote for the legislature that was to enact a final constitution two years later. It was the first national, nonracial, and democratic election ever held in South Africa. Some twenty million people voted, many of them illiterate, most of them for the first time. More than nine thousand polling places had been set up, and the voting took place over three days in anticipation of a large turnout. People stood in long lines, often for many hours, waiting to cast their ballots. In his book *Long Walk to Freedom*, Mandela spoke of "great lines of patient people snaking through the dirt roads and streets of towns and cities; old women waiting to cast their first vote saying that they felt like human beings for the first time in their lives; white men and women saying they were proud to live in a free country at last."

It was later estimated that 86 percent of the electorate had voted. When the votes were counted, the ANC had won an overwhelming victory, polling more than 60 percent of the vote, against the National Party's 20 percent. Buthelezi's party, the IFP, won more than 10 percent. This would translate into a cabinet consisting of eighteen members of the ANC, six members of the National Party, and three members of the IFP. There had, inevitably, been irregularities in the voting process, given the complexities of organizing the first election in which the entire population had the vote. But no one doubted the ANC's triumph.

The interim constitution provided for a system of shared governance for a period of five years after the election. The majority party would elect the president; a party that won 20 percent of the vote could name a deputy president; and parties that won more than 5 percent of the vote would be entitled to seats in the cabinet proportional to their share of the vote. Accordingly, Nelson Mandela was elected president and named Thabo Mbeki first deputy president; de Klerk became second deputy president and Buthelezi minister of home affairs, one of three IFP members of the cabinet. This was the Government of National Unity.

22

An Inauguration

1994 was an extraordinary year. On a crisp, sun-swept May day in Pretoria, the world witnessed one of the most remarkable transitions ever when Nelson Mandela was inaugurated president following the first free and popular election in South Africa's three-hundred-year history.

The occasion was made all the more powerful because of Mandela's personal history. Imprisoned for twenty-seven years for refusing to accept the racial discrimination imposed by the apartheid system and for insisting that all people deserved political rights, Mandela had become the conscience of his nation and the world. His election was also the result of his extraordinary ability to communicate to all people his clear understanding of right from wrong and to practice forgiveness on a scale rarely seen.

Several days after the election took place, on May 5, President Clinton had given an inspiring speech at an event held in Washington, DC, about the transition that was underway in South Africa. He noted its historic importance to the future of South Africans and the rest of the world, especially the United States.

The president's language was characteristically beautiful, and the substance resonated strongly with me. I found that some of the language and structure mirrored that of the report we

published in 1981, *South Africa: Time Running Out*, which made
me very proud. In part, President Clinton said:

> South Africa is free today because of the choices its leaders and
> people made. Their actions have been an inspiration. We can also
> be proud of America's role in this great drama. . . . Now we must
> not turn our backs. South Africa faces a task of building a toler-
> ant democracy and a successful market economy. . . . To show
> that reconciliation and democracy can bring tangible benefits,
> others will have to help. . . . America must be a new and full
> partner with that new government so that it can deliver on its
> promise as quickly as possible. . . . I'm writing the leaders of the
> other G-7 countries and asking them to join us in expanding as-
> sistance to South Africa. And we urge the international financial
> institutions, such as the World Bank, to do the same.
>
> We are taking these actions because we have important inter-
> ests at stake in the success of South Africa's journey. We have
> an economic interest in a thriving South Africa that will seek
> out exports and generate greater prosperity throughout the re-
> gion. We have a security interest in a stable, democratic South
> Africa working with its neighbors to restore and secure peace.
> We have a moral interest. We have had our own difficult strug-
> gles over racial division, and still we grapple with the challenge
> of drawing strength from our own diversity. That is why the
> powerful images of South Africa's elections resonated so deeply
> in the souls of all Americans. Whether in South Africa or Amer-
> ica, we know that there is no finish line to democracy's work.
> Developing habits of tolerance and respect, creating opportunity
> for all our citizens, these efforts are never completely done.

On May 9 the new multiracial parliament convened, and pro-
claimed Mandela president. Writing in the *New York Times*,

Bill Keller reported that Mandela's arrival in the parliamentary chamber was "announced by a bare-chested tribal imbongi, or praise-singer, shouting tributes to this most famous prisoner of apartheid." Mandela entered the chamber side by side with de Klerk, who moved across the aisle to take his seat as leader of the opposition; Mandela embraced Buthelezi and shook hands with his former opponents. Keller noted that the parliament was "roughly a mirror of the public, which is about 75 percent black, 15 percent white, and 10 percent Indian and mixed-race," and that the new speaker, "for centuries a white man in a black morning coat, was an Indian woman in a sari, Frene Ginwala, an eloquent lawyer and women's rights campaigner who found cause for celebration in the more than 70 women elected among the 400 lawmakers."

Later, Mandela addressed a jubilant Cape Town crowd: "We place our vision of a new constitutional order for South Africa on the table not as conquerors, prescribing to the conquered. We speak as fellow citizens to heal the wounds of the past with the intent of constructing a new order based on justice for all."

On May 10, 1994, when Mandela was sworn in as president, I was fortunate enough to attend the inauguration ceremonies. I was a member of the 46-person U.S. delegation, which was headed by Vice President Al Gore and First Lady Hillary Rodham Clinton. Mrs. Gore, Secretary of Commerce Ron Brown, Secretary of Agriculture Mike Espy, Senators Paul Simon and Carol Moseley Braun, Representatives John Conyers, Ronald Dellums, Charles Rangel, Benjamin Gilman, Harold Ford, John Lewis, Kweisi Mfume, Maxine Waters, and Elizabeth Furse, former NYC mayor David Dinkins, Rev. Jesse Jackson, Maya Angelou, Coretta Scott King, Colin Powell, and National Basketball Association commissioner David Stern were some of the others in the delegation.

Invitations to this milestone event were widely sought after, and attendees came from across the world. I was invited to attend by the ANC and by the United States government as part of its delegation. It was more convenient for me to fly to South Africa commercially than by U.S. government aircraft, but once in Johannesburg, I connected with the U.S. delegation and traveled with them during their stay, and particularly on Inauguration Day.

There was a memorable celebration the evening before the inauguration at the Market Theatre, with speeches and entertainment reflecting the joy and sense of human accomplishment all attendees were feeling. The Market Theatre, which was founded in 1976, had gained international recognition as South Africa's "Theatre of Struggle" during the years of apartheid. As a theater of opposition, it challenged the regime through its productions, which included the plays of Athol Fugard, and by opening its doors to people of all races in defiance of the government's segregation laws.

The evening's festivities were also a moment of pause before what everyone knew would be a sustained and challenging struggle to translate the political victory of electoral democracy into attainable opportunity for all citizens, particularly the great Black majority who had been systematically excluded from adequate education, health, housing, work, and social advancement. It was almost a moment to refresh and regroup before the next phase of the struggle began.

The next day, we assembled outside the Carlton Hotel for our early morning bus ride to Pretoria. Excitement was everywhere. Even the most sophisticated and experienced among us were filled with anticipation, and perhaps some tension. We would be witnesses to history. Our mood was lightened by a delay in our departure—despite a very tight schedule—so that Dave Dinkins could return to his room to collect a particular outfit he planned to wear later in the day. The delegates groaned at Dave, but he was determined—and so we waited.

The trip was uneventful. As we approached Pretoria, we passed several landmarks, including the Voortrekker Monument, preeminent symbol of Afrikaner nationalism, which commemorates the "Great Trek" north from Cape Town of thousands of Dutch-speaking white settlers seeking independence from British rule.

My own emotions that day were complex. There was overwhelming joy at the imminent transition of power to a popularly elected ANC government and its leader Nelson Mandela, with all that would mean to the people of South Africa—Black and white—and to people across the world. There was also apprehension and worry that some diehards would try to derail the process, even at this last minute. So, as our bus wove its way to our destination, I found myself looking with special care each time our vehicle stopped, or we crossed an intersection, or a cluster of uniformed armed soldiers or police appeared along our route. I don't know if others on our bus had similar feelings, but I suspect some of them did.

Our first stop was the LC de Villiers stadium at Pretoria University, which was our assembly point and where private cars and buses were required to park. From there, passengers were transported to the stately and impressive Union Buildings, where the inauguration would take place. The Union Buildings were actually one building with two wings. Designed by Sir Herbert Baker to symbolize the coming together of the British colonies and the Boer states in the Union of South Africa (1910), the two wings were intended to represent the equal partnership of English and Afrikaner peoples. Completed in 1913, the building was the residence of the president and the seat of government.

We arrived at the grounds several hours early. Coffee and light refreshments were available, and we talked among our-

selves, greeted others in attendance, and kept track of the arrival of dignitaries from across the world.

The arrival of each new contingent of eminent persons helped
build the mood of excitement and anticipation. Nervous laugh-
ter seemed to come from every corner of the stands as we waited
for the ceremonies to begin. My seatmate was NBA commissioner David Stern.

The formal proceedings that day were a healthy mixture of
solemnity and lightness of spirit. Two praise singers preceded
Mandela's entrance, and he danced a few steps to the pulsing
music of the African Jazz Pioneers. All knew the significance
of this formal occasion and all that lay ahead.

President Mandela's speech, which was delivered before a
crowd of world leaders, reflected his appreciation of South Africa's history and the aspirations of its people:

> Today, all of us do, by our presence here, and by our celebration
> in other parts of our country and the world, confer glory and
> hope to newborn liberty. Out of the experience of an extraordi-
> nary human disaster that lasted too long, must be born a society
> of which all humanity will be proud. Our daily deeds as ordi-
> nary South Africans must produce an actual South African
> reality that will reinforce humanity's belief in justice, strengthen
> its confidence in the nobility of the human soul and sustain all
> our hopes for a glorious life for all. All this we owe both to our-
> selves and to the peoples of the world who are so well repre-
> sented here today.

He also offered words of gratitude and healing:

> We deeply appreciate the role that the masses of our people
> and their . . . leaders have played to bring about this conclu-
> sion. Not least among them is my Second Deputy President,

the Honourable F.W. de Klerk. We would also like to pay tribute to our security forces, in all their ranks, for the distinguished
role they have played in securing our first democratic election
and the transition to democracy, from blood-thirsty forces
which still refuse to see the light.

The time for the healing of wounds has come. The moment
to bridge the chasms that divide us has come. The time to build is
upon us. We have at last achieved our political emancipation.
We pledge ourselves to liberate all our people from the continuing bondage of poverty, deprivation, suffering, gender and
other discrimination. We succeeded to take our last steps to
freedom in conditions of relative peace. We commit ourselves to
the construction of a complete, just and lasting peace.

At one point in the ceremony, Mandela praised former president F.W. de Klerk as "a true son of the soil of Africa." Later,
he clasped hands with de Klerk and Thabo Mbeki, then deputy
presidents. As he raised their joined hands high, he called on
all the people of the country and the world to support the Government of National Unity. At that moment, there was a palpable sense that the people of South Africa, weighed down by
generations of violent repression, had an enormous burden lifted
from their souls and that a brighter future was possible for
them, their children, and their grandchildren. For freedom-
loving people everywhere it was the culmination of support for
democratic forces in South Africa that spanned several decades.
For me personally, it was the most moving and inspiring moment imaginable.

As I observed the delegations from 130 nations and particularly those from Africa and the Middle East, I hoped that
South Africa's demonstration of what was possible through
outstanding leadership, trust, and compromise would send a
powerful message of peaceful change to their nations.

Several African nations held free elections in 1994, a peace process had begun in parts of the Middle East, Haiti's freely elected president was returned to office, several nations in Eastern Europe and the former Soviet Union continued their progress toward democracy, and political and economic reform continued in Vietnam and China. Global economic growth and the expansion of world trade supported the political change of that year. Increasingly, nations understood that to compete successfully for foreign capital, access to markets, and domestic savings, they had to commit to international norms of political stability, freedom of expression, and openness. Modern communication also made it harder and harder to hide repression, and the pressure toward compliance with recognized standards of behavior was great. In short, the conditions for greater freedom and prosperity seemed to be in place in most parts of the world.

However, that provided little basis for complacency. There was (and is) still widespread poverty, injustice, and conflict in the world. At the time, the war in Bosnia, massacres in Rwanda, and suppression in Chechnya were some events that reminded us that freedom was fragile and the world was still a dangerous place.

A few minutes after President Mandela finished speaking that day, the South African Air Force—helicopters, transports, fighters—flew over in a stunning salute, culminating with the jets' contrails, in the colors of the new flag, blending in the sky overhead, symbolically and literally joining all of the colors of this amazing country into an amalgam never before seen. That magnificent spectacle reinforced the message Mandela had just delivered to South Africa and the world.

The luncheon that followed the ceremony on the lawn at the Union Buildings featured food offerings that reflected a wide diversity of tastes—roughly similar to the diversity of the

attendees. No palate needed to go unsatisfied. The seating order at the luncheon was random, with many people spending
time with long-standing friends and first-time acquaintances in
equal measure. Symbolic, I thought, of the occasion, and what
was to come for the new nation and its Government of National
Unity.

When the luncheon ended and the crowd began to dis-
perse, there were long delays as people searched for the buses
to which they were assigned. This turned out to be a special
challenge as few knew exactly where to go. Some were offered
rides in cars by friends old and new, but were reluctant to take
them lest they be separated from their group and never recon-
nect. The scene was fluid, the mood was gay. Youngsters were
singing, dancing, drumming, and generally entertaining the
visitors as they milled around. At one extraordinary moment, a
small contingent from our group—including Colin Powell and
Congressman Ron Dellums from California—returned the
courtesy to our South African entertainers by singing doo-wop
songs from the 1950s, to the joyous astonishment of our South
African friends as well as our U.S. colleagues. The image of
Colin, Ron, and others, arms around each other's shoulders,
harmonizing to the beat, will remain with me forever.

When our bus finally arrived, we departed for a rural hotel
called the Farm Inn, which was a privately owned country estate of some four hundred acres of wildlife sanctuary and farm
land on the eastern outskirts of Pretoria. The plan was for us to
relax, reflect on the day's events, and prepare for the evening
reception at the U.S. Embassy hosted by the vice president and
Mrs. Gore.

The inn's setting encouraged conversation. Some of us talked,
some napped, some explored the grounds. Eventually several
people found a TV which, in addition to carrying the inaugural events, carried a soccer match between South Africa and

Zambia. The match featured a visit by newly installed President Mandela to the locker room of the South African team, to cheer them on to victory.

Although the reception at the embassy was very well attended and lively, nothing could top what we had witnessed that morning on the grounds of the Union Buildings.

Helping to bring democracy to South Africa was a painstaking effort undertaken by women and men of courage from every segment of that society. The international community, including the Ford Foundation, assisted their efforts. It was always sensitive work, and it had the best chance of success when it was guided by South Africans' articulation of their own values and visions of a just society. This wasn't unlike the principles that held true when I was guiding the Bedford Stuyvesant Restoration Corporation in its community development work. The values and vision of the community needed to play a role in all the work we did in Central Brooklyn. In the case of South Africa, this kind of assistance, done well, could help the nation adopt international norms of behavior and then enable its people to hold the nation to those standards.

Furthering democracy always entails supporting independent analysis and ensuring participation in decision-making by those outside power. It also involves working with established organizations including the judiciary, universities, the private sector, community organizations, and government agencies. This kind of work should hide nothing or fear nothing. Its goal is to create the conditions for advancing human achievement.

I was privileged to know South Africa from several perspectives, my role as president of the Ford Foundation being one of them. At Ford we worked for years in South Africa supporting human rights, legal assistance, education, and community development. We'd also opened our field office in Johannesburg in 1993.

That office allowed us to focus more broadly on the public interest sector, going beyond our long-standing work in public interest law to include programming in rural development, women's issues, community development, and public policy research.

Our work in South Africa was a good investment. We believed it helped the country on its remarkable journey to democracy. We also believed that what could be learned from the South African experience was applicable to many other nations. As Archbishop Desmond Tutu stated, "Once we have got it right, South Africa will be the paradigm for the rest of the world."

23

A Farewell to Ford

I'd been at the Ford Foundation for seventeen years when I announced that I would be resigning as president in December of 1994. The plan was for me to leave in early 1996, with Susan Berresford, who was then vice president of worldwide programs, succeeding me. Susan would be the first woman president of the Ford Foundation. I felt very good about the shape of the foundation when I made the decision, and I knew that post-Ford, I'd have a chance to focus more concretely and discretely on the problems and opportunities in South Africa. I was sixty at the time, feeling that I had many years of active work ahead of me, and the idea of undertaking new endeavors was exciting.

As I contemplated the end of my tenure at Ford, I found myself drawn in two directions. I looked forward to the challenges ahead for philanthropy while asking myself if we had done enough to position Ford as a key player in support of those addressing society's future needs. At the same time, I looked back and marveled at how far we had come in strengthening the foundation's ability to encourage the powerless to speak and the powerful to listen, together fashioning better, more lasting solutions to our shared problems.

When I began at Ford in 1979, the trustees' charge to me, as well as my own vision of the future, was clear:

- Present new program choices and revise existing strategies to help meet the anticipated needs of the world community over the final 20 years of this century.
- Increase the percentage of annual expenditures in support of grantees.
- Stabilize the value of the corpus to provide for current and future needs.
- Find partners—both inside and outside philanthropy—in order to increase the impact of our ideas, work, and money.
- Increase the diversity of people working to solve society's problems, drawing particularly from among those who are most affected by the problems.
- Build into the culture of the Foundation respect for change and renewal as a natural part of a healthy organization's life—not something to be feared and avoided.
- Be more than a good manager. Lead the Foundation in directions that play to its strengths and to my special interests—urban poverty, human rights, and the spread of democracy worldwide, especially in South Africa.

As I began reviewing the foundation's programs in 1979, a senior colleague cautioned me that there were two ways to do my job. One way was to decide which issues I cared most about and direct a substantial percentage of the program budget to those issues. The program staff would then allocate the balance of the budget to existing lines of work, and I could enjoy my presidency from the outset. The other way was to examine every program and ask why it should be continued in the face of other pressing needs. This approach would cause turmoil in a program staff still adjusting to the 50 percent retrenchment of program and staff during the 1974–78 period. It would also, understandably, upset many grantees who would fear losing familiar windows into the foundation. If I pursued that course, I could expect the first years of my presidency to be very difficult. The caution was understandable, but, as I explained, the latter course was the only possible one for me to take, given my own sense of the responsibility of leadership and the trustees' charge to me.

Had I met the charge? One way of measuring that is to review the numbers. In 1979, we were entrusted with $2.2 billion in assets, which we invested in a low-risk, diversified portfolio, both domestically and overseas. When I prepared to leave, those assets were valued at approximately $7.7 billion. Our annual spending had grown from $119 million in 1979 to $420 million in 1995. During that period, a total of $4.2 billion was expended to further the foundation's mission. And the number of people on staff decreased from 800 in 1980 to 550 at the time of my departure.

But, of course, numbers never tell the full story. To arrive at the program agenda we established during the 1980s and 1990s, we consulted widely, both inside and outside the foundation, domestically and internationally. A team of experienced foundation program staff was augmented by outside experts. Their challenge was to discover what had changed in the nature and understanding of persistent problems such as poverty, discrimination, and lack of economic development, and determine if the existing Ford Foundation programs still aimed at the core of these problems. We also wanted to identify the major emerging issues worldwide in order to determine where the foundation should direct its resources, recognizing that we did not have sufficient resources to both continue all of the past agenda and add pressing new items. Finally, it was important to arrive at a responsible way to leave or reduce certain lines of work in order to make room for newer initiatives, without destroying necessary institutions or losing critically needed knowledge.

Some of the findings were encouraging. For example, while Ford was one of only a few foundations working in family planning in the 1950s, by 1980 the topic had attracted larger resources from governments worldwide and from many philanthropies. At the same time, awareness was just emerging about the critical role women's education and women's control of income played in family decisions about contraception and family size, as those facets were not yet documented or understood. Accordingly, we decided to shift our earlier work on population to a women-centered approach that sought to emphasize women's reproductive health, economic advancement, and role in policymaking, as well as child survival.

This work fit well with our growing recognition that a focus on human rights and social justice provided a natural bridge from our earlier separate work on race and gender discrimination and family planning to a social development strategy aimed at removing legal and traditional barriers to full citizenship for groups historically discriminated against. This new formulation was global in scope and encouraged us to think more as one foundation operating worldwide and less as separate units. This was a controversial decision since many doubted that successful program ideas from the developing world could be applied to problems in the United States or that successful U.S. programs could be relevant to problems in the Third World. Experience proved these doubts wrong.

To accomplish the transition to a women-centered approach, we made major grants to several key institutions engaged in population work to help tide them over while they sought new sources of support. We committed funds to continue biomedical research awards for five years and retained our interest in the formulation of family planning policies. In other words, we didn't leave the field of population. Rather, we reconceptualized how we could most effectively advance the objectives of the field. As it turned out, the shift was prescient. The reports of two UN conferences—one on population in 1994 and one on women in 1995—dramatically revealed how the individuals and organizations we supported helped shape the world's understanding of these issues and the importance of the new women-centered approach.

Of comparable impact was our review of work on community-based development. The foundation was an early entrant into this field in the United States, from the Gray Areas program of the early 1960s through support for the first wave of community development corporations in the mid-1960s. Here, too, the importance of a comprehensive view of development and of partnerships was dramatically evident. Similarly evident was the need to build a national system of support for existing and emerging CDCs and a structured way of evaluating their local and societal impact.

In reviewing and reshaping the international affairs program, we focused on the need to combine our interests in democracy, human rights, economic advancement, and the making of U.S. foreign policy with our emphasis on the role and status of women worldwide. We believed that since women constitute more than 50 percent of the world's population, gender was an important additional lens through which many of the world's most pressing issues should be examined.

This awareness was central to our work in all fields during my tenure at Ford. We remained steadfast in our commitment to advancing the principles of democracy and human rights, not only as a shield or prod in dealing with repressive governments, but also as a clear, unshakable standard applicable to all governments. One result is that the Ford Foundation became a resource that contending forces felt comfortable turning to for help as they struggled to find common ground. This was true, for example, in deliberations relating to such pressing issues as the Iran-Iraq War and the transition to democracy in South Africa.

It's not possible to talk about my years at Ford without underscoring the principles that animated and defined that great institution during that time:

- People mattered and it was imperative that they had a central role in deciding how they lived. We respected the dignity and decisions of the people on whose behalf we worked. It was they who had the knowledge, experience, and imagination that created program and policy choices. They had to be active participants in all work related to their well-being.
- Development strategies addressed the totality of the way people lived, worked, and thought.
- The search for pragmatic, innovative, and sustainable approaches to problems involved all sectors of society— governmental, corporate, philanthropic, and community.
- In our own affairs as an institution and in support of the work of others, the Foundation utilized the diverse experiences of all members of society, both for increased effectiveness and for the sake of authenticity.

Those principles reflected the best of Ford at the time, and we hoped they would serve as guideposts for the future, pillars on which to build.

Beyond Ford itself, I'd reflected, during the early 1990s, on the role that philanthropy and the nonprofit sector more generally play in maintaining civil society. There were many world events that occurred during those years that, for me, lent themselves to certain observations. I recall preparing an address I was about to give in 1992 to the Association of Black Foundation Executives in which I planned to observe the crumbling of the Berlin Wall, the independence and free election of the government of Namibia, the freedom of Nelson Mandela and the dismantling of apartheid, and the collapse of the Soviet Union.

My point was that it seemed that history had come down on the side of societies open to change and experiment, and on the side of the way of life that America had expressed so distinctively. I wanted to pose the question whether we as a nation could feel confident about our ability to lead the world in its next crucial stage—creating lasting democratic values and institutions with growing economic prosperity, especially in the face of revived territorial and ethnic disputes in so many of the newly freed nations.

With so much of the world looking to the American example, what could we say when asked, "How do you do it?" How do you translate "Liberty and Justice for All" from a promise into a reality for all of your citizens? How do you draw the best effort out of your diverse population, and provide opportunities for social and economic advancement for all of your people? Could we honestly say that as a society we had faced and answered those questions?

I was in the midst of those reflections when the verdict came in the Rodney King case.

For months Americans had cringed at the televised spectacle of that brutal police beating, only to be stunned by the acquittal of the officers involved—a verdict that lit a spark and ignited violence and destruction in Los Angeles, graphically and dramatically exposing us all to America's unfinished domestic agenda, which was worsening, not improving. Those events in Los Angeles had many effects.

For one, they resulted in the greatest rush to self-examination on the part of Americans in more than a generation, and the lecture I was about to give was no exception. Instead of starting with the global events I'd had on my mind, I decided to begin with LA.

What had happened in Los Angeles presented a chilling metaphor for where the world may have been headed—not toward becoming the peaceful global village that the recent victories of pro-democracy movements around the world had seemed to signal, but a global Los Angeles. The events in Los Angeles also raised to a new level of urgency the question of philanthropy's role in creating and nurturing a civil society.

In one reading, of course, the problems in LA may have seemed the province of those of us concerned specifically with urban poverty. But in a deeper sense, Los Angeles spoke to our nation's, and philanthropy's, need to address a much broader range of issues. At the time, I organized those issues around three themes: voice, vision, and will.

First and foremost, Los Angeles dramatized the need of people to feel that their voices, speaking about their needs and aspirations, are heard, that they have a stake in the system, that they matter to the larger society, that they have some measure of control over the circumstances of their lives, and over the steps they can take to improve those circumstances. It was clear that paying attention to the voices of the people who lived in Los Angeles and who were most directly affected by the unrest, and also to the voices of those who live in similar communities, was essential to finding solutions to the problems that they, and we, as a nation faced.

But Los Angeles also laid bare the new complexities of urban life that had taken shape over the last decade of the twentieth century. Added to the already familiar picture of the city as a place beset by homelessness, drugs, poverty, and crime, there were exacerbated antagonisms within and across groups. It also revealed itself to be a city whose more than ten million inhabitants seemed to share the view that "we are not all in this together."

These realties underscored, first, our need to make sure that as we strengthened the voices of separate communities, we encouraged those communities to begin talking to one another and to search for common ground, and second, our need to also strengthen a common vision of our shared political culture, traditions, and aspirations. Finally, Los Angeles also spoke to the need to marshal the confidence and the political will to try to solve these problems.

In each of the areas—giving voice, forging a common vision, and providing a political will—philanthropy had and has an important and necessary role to play. As I was preparing my address to the Association of Black Foundation Executives and as I was taking stock during my final years at Ford, this was something I firmly believed.

Speaking to the question of voice: How do we make sure that all voices are heard? One way is to support the community-based efforts of disadvantaged people to help themselves. I entered the nonprofit sector twenty-five years earlier as head of the Bedford Stuyvesant Restoration Corporation—during a period fraught with its own sense of terrible urgency—out of a faith in the power of people, no matter what their circumstances, to play a major role in changing the condition of their lives. When I began, it was on the gamble that the energy and spirit that were already there could be harnessed in a new way. I believed that no matter what government did, there was a need for communities to design programs that were rooted in their own needs, abilities, and resources.

I still believed that—with a conviction that was only strengthened over time. When we started, our aim was to put into motion a broad revitalization of the area to give the people of the community the power to play a central role in that work. We believed the process of development, and not just the finished product, should benefit the local people. A key element was substantial and continuing core support from both public and private sources. That helped us test new ideas, develop new programs, and most importantly draw together large numbers of community residents to enlist their ideas and assistance. Our donors trusted us to use these funds creatively and flexibly once we had agreed on major goals.

Those efforts bore fruit in no small part because they were planted in the fertile soil of a long tradition among Blacks of community and of self-help. Scores of other community organizations in New York and other cities were engaged in similar work. What was demonstrated—and what community organizations have continued to assert through their actions—is that the best prospect for healthy communities and for a healthy society is to develop ways for people to exercise some measure of control over their own lives, and to help them develop ways to make effective demands on themselves and on the larger society.

It was important to remember that the basic ideas upon which the community development movement was built were regarded as impossibly optimistic not very long before we were witnessing these positive results. The idea of community empowerment, the idea of public-private partnerships, the idea of the nonprofit sector, the business sector, and government working together— they were at the heart of the success of the community development movement and they had to be the foundation of new efforts that would, in large part, rely on the dedication, expertise, and energy of nonprofit organizations.

There were other ways, too, that the nonprofit sector could help those who are part of a minority to gain a voice. Given the importance of law in securing basic rights, a number of foundations, including the one I worked for at the time, supported the work of minority legal defense organizations. Ford also supported programs that offered legal services to low-income people along with efforts to improve the delivery of those services.

One of the most obvious ways people find a voice in a democratic society is through the vote, and support of nonpartisan voter education and registration is a natural philanthropic activity. So is assistance to programs that monitor compliance with the Voting Rights Act.

In addition to all our other work, we also had (and have) to support efforts to identify and nurture future leaders in the minority community. Much was being written at the time about the problems confronting the nation's Black communities and the need to develop resources to which they can turn for assistance.

But relatively little attention was being paid to the role the Black church played throughout history in supporting the Black community. Partly because of its location within the community, and partly because of the historic respect Black people have for spiritual life and religious institutions, the Black church has provided a safety net for many Black people in both inner cities and rural areas.

Recognizing its key role in providing services and leadership, both locally and nationally, the Ford Foundation had, since 1985, supported Black churches in those activities, mainly focusing on the delivery of social services and training clergy to design and manage those services. Ford also helped establish a national research center to provide the nation's estimated 65,000 Black churches with information on how to develop secular service programs based in churches.

Even as we tried to strengthen the voices of those whose lives and dreams too often went unheard in larger society, we knew that it was important to increase understanding of the hopes and values people hold in common—what it means to be an American, the rights and responsibilities that entails.

Supporting networks of mediating structures within communities as channels for dispute prevention and resolution was essential. We had a foundation task force to consider how we could be most helpful in Los Angeles, and a high priority was placed on broadening and deepening relations among the great mix of people in the area. Forty percent of Los Angeles residents were foreign-born at the time, many whom arrived in the last ten years, and Asians, Latinos, and African Americans made up 60 percent of the population.

There had to be new institutional support to encourage communication and understanding among minority racial and ethnic groups—among the established residents and the newcomers; among traditional leaders and grassroots leaders. And we also had to look for opportunities to help white people to see how their best interests resided in a collaborative, multicultural future—and not to see such a future as something threatening to be resisted.

One of the stories I read in the *L.A. Times* in the aftermath of the Rodney King unrest stands out on this point. It reported on what appeared to be the first signs of another "white flight" from LA, reminiscent of a flight after the 1965 rioting in Watts. It quoted a real estate agent from a northern suburb who had been showing homes to Angelenos. "They're disconcerted about all of the violence that erupted," he said. "They're in fear of not only their own safety, but the safety of the investment they made in the American Dream." That comment caused me to consider just how they were defining the American Dream. It seemed to be limited to their personal material well-being.

The Dream of America is a more generous, a more expansive, and a more noble dream than simply the dream of individual success and security. And we had to remind people of that greater dream.

The America we lived in, then, was created over the course of the last two hundred years through the unceasing demands of women and men in every generation that the promise of America include more and more of its people, that the American identity be rooted in a person's willingness to commit to the ideal of America and to work toward its realization. The commitment to an America that provides opportunity for all its people remains the central principle of our national life and the deepest source of our strength.

Certainly, Black people in America understand—perhaps better than anyone else—that the American Dream isn't complete until it is accessible to everyone. That it is also a dream of community, of people not only making it, but making it together. All sorts of challenges come with leading, but none have been more daunting than those facing the American women and people of color who have led this nation in their demands that America be a just society for all its citizens.

We must work harder and get better at advancing a more generous, more inclusive version of the story of America than the one that has prevailed. Ours is a living, evolving system of government, and each generation's obligation is to protect the positive gains of the past and to take us to new levels of expansiveness and opportunity. This is a civic responsibility we all share.

Much of what was happening in Los Angeles at the time was unprecedented, and it presented an opportunity to take a fresh look at urban life, race relations, poverty, crime, and the kind of world we wanted to create. I remember thinking and saying it was "an opportunity we dare not miss."

It seems we have been presented with this opportunity more times than perhaps we would like over the intervening decades, but when I think about the role of foundations, then and now, I think part of that role is to serve as catalysts in the creation of connections—connections among different groups, classes, and cultures; connections between the public and private sectors; and connections that bridge all the divides and boundaries that limit the capacity to fashion a better future for all people.

24

The Study Group

My last board meeting as president of the Ford Foundation took place in South Africa in the spring of 1996. For me, the choice of location acknowledged the important role South Africa had played in the work of the foundation during my tenure as president, as well as the increased role it would play in the next phase of my life.

During the visit, we spent time with the justices of the Constitutional Court of South Africa, which had been established in 1994 and was formally opened by President Mandela the following year. Later, one of the Ford trustees observed that it felt as though we were sitting with the founders of a nation—that was the level of the quality of the court. There was Arthur Chaskalson, the head of the body, whose earlier work we (the Ford Foundation) had been supporting through the Legal Resources Centre; Richard Goldstone, who had chaired the government-appointed commission of inquiry into the violence that was tearing the country apart in the early 1990s; and Johann Kriegler, a founding trustee of the Legal Resources Centre and chair of the Independent Electoral Commission set up to organize the 1994 election. The other justices, all but two of whom were there, were Tholie Madala, Pius Langa, Yvonne Mokgoro, Ismail Mahomed, Kate O'Regan, Albie Sachs, Laurie Ackermann, and John Didcott.*

---

* Tholie Madala, a human rights lawyer, in 1994 became the first black judge in the Eastern Cape and the fourth black judge in South Africa; Pius Langa

The meeting took place at the Mount Nelson Hotel in Cape Town on April 2. Henry Schacht, chairman of the foundation's board of trustees, was unable to attend the Cape Town meeting, and the acting chair, Dr. M.S. Swaminathan, introduced a proposed resolution of appreciation for me by offering personal reflections about his long association with the Ford Foundation, going back to the opening of its office in India in the 1950s, and with me, starting with a meeting in 1982 with Indira Gandhi. He then read the following resolution:

> Franklin A. Thomas was elected President of the Ford Foundation in 1979 and has served in that capacity longer than any of his predecessors. Before his election, the Trustees had conducted an extensive search for a person who would change the Foundation in its essential aspects—programmatically, fiscally, and administratively; someone who would position the Foundation to address world problems for the balance of the 20th century and beyond.
>
> When the Trustees concluded that Frank was the person best suited for this daunting task, he was already serving on the

---

had been a member of the constitutional committee of the ANC, and in 2005 succeeded Arthur Chaskalson as head of the court; Yvonne Mokgoro was a legal scholar and specialist in human rights; Ismail Mahomed, the single member of the court of Indian descent, built his reputation defending anti-apartheid leaders; Kate O'Regan, a specialist in land and labor law and issues of race and gender equality, had been a lawyer for several anti-apartheid groups and a trustee of the Legal Resources Centre; Albie Sachs, a human rights activist, worked with Oliver Tambo and the ANC in exile, and after 1990 was a member of the National Executive of the ANC; Laurie Ackermann, one of the group of constitutional lawyers who participated in discussions with the ANC in exile about a future South African constitution, in 1994 chaired the Cape Electoral Appeal Tribunal; John Didcott, a human rights advocate, had been on the bench in Natal since 1975, and was a member of the Special Electoral Court for the 1994 election.

Foundation's Board. The inimitable blend of insight, pragmatism and humane values that he brought to the Board's deliberations had also been evident in his earlier career. After graduating from Columbia College and Law School, Frank distinguished himself in the public sector, serving as Assistant U.S. Attorney for the Southern District of New York and as Deputy Police Commissioner in charge of legal matters for the New York City Police Department. He then moved on to service in the non-profit sector as the first President of the Bedford Stuyvesant Restoration Corporation, which became the prime model for much of the later community-based development in the United States. Frank had also become a much sought-after director of business corporations, where he consistently assumed responsibilities in the inner circle of decision-making. In selecting Frank, the Foundation's Trustees also took note of the fact that his talents had come to the attention of the Rockefeller Foundation, which in 1979 made him the Chair of the new Study Commission on U.S. Policy Toward Southern Africa.

At the Foundation, Frank carried out the Trustees' mandate faithfully. In his first two years, he effected sweeping changes by implementing new investment and spending policies; by revamping the program agenda and restructuring the program division; and by streamlining management and reducing staff. In the ensuing years, the Foundation grew and blossomed. Its assets and annual spending more than tripled, and its program agenda and geographic reach expanded. With Frank as president, the Foundation's programs regarding the role and status of women were broadened and deepened. Its work in community development spread throughout the United States, as well as to developing countries, and a new comprehensive national support system was created in the United States. The Foundation created a widely replicated Innovations in Government Awards Program and helped to build the national service move-

ment in the United States. New lines of work related to reproductive health, to sustainable development, and to strengthening
the United Nations were introduced. And the Foundation vig-
orously promoted human rights and democratic and economic
transitions around the world.

As with other institutions in periods of outstanding steward-
ship, the Foundation increasingly reflected Frank's own values
and philosophy. Diverse voices and perspectives were brought into
decision-making at all levels of the institution. Staff worked in
close collaboration with all of society's sectors—business, government, and non-profit. And the Foundation focused on encouraging and supporting people working and living closest to where
problems are located, on the premise that people will solve their
own problems and help create a better society for everybody if
given the opportunity.

During Frank's tenure, there has been an institutional modesty that mirrors his own personal modesty—a sense that the
Foundation's work speaks louder than words. And that has
proved to be the case. Wherever the Foundation is active, there
is clarity about what it stands for and does: strengthening
democratic values; reducing poverty and injustice; and promoting productive cooperation among people and nations.

Frank's vision is truly global and the Foundation under his
direction has touched the lives of millions of people around the
world. It is fitting that we adopt this resolution of appreciation
at a Board meeting in South Africa, for there is perhaps no other
country where Frank individually and the Foundation, through
its programs, contributed so much to peaceful change and a
transition to nonracial democracy. By any measure, Frank's
presidency was a period of extraordinary leadership. He has our
respect, our admiration and our abiding appreciation. We are
especially pleased that after retiring from the Foundation he
will continue to do important work related to the Foundation's

priorities. We thank and salute Frank and extend to him and to Kate our warmest wishes for the years ahead.

The trustees unanimously adopted the resolution.

My reaction to the tribute, and to the ending of this significant phase of my life after seventeen years, was to hug each trustee and staff member.

As the next phase began, there would be some professional continuity. It was always my plan to remain involved in South Africa, and, with the help of the Ford Foundation, we reconstituted and relocated the Study Group, which then became known as the TFF Study Group. Initially created in 1981 to continue the work of the study commission I led on South Africa, the TFF Study Group would now become my base to intensify efforts to help the development process in South Africa, including encouraging local development initiatives that weren't wholly dependent on the government.

Wayne Fredericks and I had also recently accepted President Mandela's invitation to join the board of the Nelson Mandela Children's Fund USA. The fund was established by President Mandela in 1995 to improve the health and education of South Africa's children. The US satellite was set up in 1997. There are now offices in Canada, the Netherlands, and the United Kingdom. Wayne was an adviser to Ford and the Carnegie Corporation on southern and South Africa. He had traveled extensively with the original Study Group and remained an active member when it became the TFF Study Group, with me serving as chair.

At the urging of several leaders of NGOs in South Africa and their U.S. supporters, I agreed, as well, to help the independent sector strengthen its role in the country as a necessary part of the new South African democracy.

Wayne, Milfred Fierce, and I began to travel regularly to South Africa, almost always stopping in the UK to connect with journalists and political and business leaders. We sought their views on progress in South Africa, and discussed ways to convince them that the access of South African products to UK and European markets was crucial for South Africa's economic future.

Milfred was, of course, a key part of the study commission team from the very beginning, and was always an invaluable asset to the work we did in South Africa.

Our group became a resource for consultation on South African development issues generally. As word spread that we were now even more available to provide assistance, requests came from many quarters and often stretched our limited capacity. Yet we seldom declined to help, often reaching out to others more knowledgeable than ourselves to move the process along.

One of the issues the Study Group was able to help with was telecommunications policy. Many South African educators recognized that the policies and systems put in place would affect the cost of Internet access for public and private educational institutions and thus the ability of their students to participate in the exchange of information across the world. On these questions, the Mellon Foundation and its consultants were especially helpful, and shared their suggestions with South African government decision-makers and their advisers.

During this period, our group stayed current on developments in South Africa through our visits to the country, hosting South Africans visiting the U.S., and through information gathering of many kinds. Wayne in particular never let more than a week go by without at least telephone contact with our South African colleagues.

In the summer of 1996, I was invited to join the international advisory board of the Comparative Human Relations Initiative (CHRI), a project examining intergroup relations between people of African and European descent in Brazil, South Africa, and the United States. Started in late 1995, the initiative was a project of the Southern Education Foundation (SEF) of Atlanta, Georgia, in collaboration with the University of Cape Town and the Institute for a Democratic Alternative for South Africa (IDASA), and an informal coalition of groups and individuals in Brazil. Directed by Lynn Walker Huntley of SEF, it was supported by a number of U.S. foundations including Ford, Charles Stewart Mott, the Rockefeller Brothers Fund, Levi Strauss, and Coca-Cola. The initiative explored how racism operates and is maintained, and examined ways to overcome its consequences. It brought together people in each of the three countries to share information and ideas, commissioned research papers, and produced a series of reports and related publications. Members of the advisory group traveled to Brazil and South Africa as well as the United States, and met at regular intervals from October 1996 to October 1998.

The initiative convened three major conferences involving several hundred scholars, activists, government officials, and private-sector representatives, in Atlanta (April 1997), Rio de Janeiro (September 1997), and Cape Town (March 1998). A final international conference in Cape Town in May 2000 launched CHRI's publishing arm under the title "Beyond Racism: Embracing an Interdependent Future."

The final report I was asked to write about the initiative gave me the opportunity to reflect on what the experience meant for me at that particular juncture of my life and career. It came at an important time, as I was stepping down as president of Ford, and still committed to helping South Africa in its remarkable journey to democracy and healthy social and economic development. I was eager to deepen my understanding of the roots and persistence of racial prejudice and racial repression in my own country and elsewhere in the world. The personal and societal costs of the attitudes and behavior associated with racism are enormous, and their destructive and divisive impacts on society were then, and still are, increasingly evident.

By 1996, I had visited both Brazil and South Africa many times over the previous twenty-five years. Each country had special meaning to me: South Africa, with its unique recent history of legally mandated racial discrimination and now a bold push toward equality; Brazil, a country of growing influence in the world, often cited as special because of its high economic potential, extraordinary people, and unique post-slavery policy toward race.

The project was thus a chance to combine my interest in these three societies into a systematic effort to learn more about the common elements of their histories and the specific efforts of each to address the persistent, divisive, and debilitating problem of racial discrimination. The fact that the inquiry would look at the issues through a comparative lens, with colleagues from each of the three countries, was an added attraction. During the process, our work helped me to think about the three countries as partially overlapping circles, with the areas of overlap defining the common aspects of each country's racial history; and the balance of each circle reflecting the unique, culture-specific part of each country—the qualities that make each special and caution us against excessive generalizations across these societies.

Not surprisingly, much of my supplementary learning during this study came from my colleagues. They generously shared experiences from their lives and their reactions to the reports and information we were receiving. In so doing, they helped me see new or deeper dimensions to familiar subjects and reexamine assumptions and other "truths" I thought I knew. All of this confirmed for me the importance of a comparative perspective and a diverse group of commissioners.

In Brazil we were told, and it was evident, that by providing a legitimate forum through which the subject of racial discrimination could get into the public debate, we were performing an important function. By examining that subject in the context of the workplace, education, access to resources and opportunities, we helped Brazilians shed light on attitudes and other obstacles to the realization of the racial democracy they seek and espouse.

In the United States, which had been a beacon for freedom and opportunity for the world for the fifty years prior, our complex history of slavery, emancipation, Jim Crow laws, civil rights struggles, and legal remedies posed a challenge to explain and to understand. So too did the often-expressed American fatigue with affirmative action remedies, coming as it did after less than two decades of sporadic efforts to redress the consequences of more than two centuries of legally sanctioned racial discrimination.

In South Africa, there was great optimism over what was possible under its remarkable new constitution. There was also a growing realism of the enormous tasks it faced to keep faith with the aspirations of the majority of the population that suffered under apartheid and now sought a better life. All of this to be accomplished in the face of a feared worldwide economic slowdown and without alienating the economically powerful white minority. It also had to fashion a multiracial, opportunity-driven society on the heels of centuries of racial discrimination and officially mandated inequality of opportunity.

For me, the commission experience was a powerful reminder that racism takes a toll on all of us, victims as well as others, and that racially discriminatory attitudes and behavior are deeply embedded within our institutions and individual psyches. Often, we are unaware of the existence of race-based assumptions and the subtle but powerful influences they exert upon us. As some have rightly observed, through our policies and practices as a nation, and, most especially, through our individual actions and attitudes, we end up making race every day.

The initiative's activities overlapped with the hearings of South Africa's Truth and Reconciliation Commission (TRC). The TRC began its work in April of 1996, but the groundwork for establishing the commission had been laid over a period of several years. After the unbanning of the African National Congress (ANC) and Nelson Mandela's release from prison, when discussions for a negotiated settlement were underway, it became clear that a way had to be found to deal with South Africa's past as well as its future. After several internal inquiries into human rights violations within the ANC, the ANC's National Executive Committee (NEC) proposed a truth commission as a means of investigating the violations of all the parties in conflict during the period of apartheid, including its own. The NEC put forward a formal proposal for such a commission in 1993.

At the same time, other groups were considering how to deal with South Africa's violent past in the context of a negotiated political settlement. One of these, the Institute for a Democratic Alternative for South Africa (IDASA), was looking at the experiences of countries in Eastern Europe and Latin America for models of societies in transition from authoritarian to democratic regimes, and the ways in which they dealt with the abuses of the past. IDASA organized several conferences, one of which, in February of 1994, brought together leading human rights advocates and activists from those countries around the theme of human rights and transitional justice. The presentations and discussions of the conference made a significant contribution to the evolving concept of the truth commission, and were subsequently published in a volume of proceedings.

Shortly after the February conference, several key members of the ANC asked IDASA's executive director, Dr. Alex Boraine, to draft an outline proposal for a truth commission for Nelson Mandela's consideration. Boraine was a longtime activist in opposition politics in South Africa. He was a member of parliament for the Progressive Party from 1974 to 1986, when he resigned to become a co-founder of IDASA. In March of 1994, Boraine resigned from IDASA to found Justice in Transition, a nongovernmental organization devoted solely to the process of establishing the commission. Boraine's proposal served as the basis for further discussions, and a month after the election, in May of 1994, the new minister of justice, Dullah Omar, announced to parliament the government's decision to establish a commission of truth and reconciliation. If the wounds of the past were to be healed, he said, disclosure of the truth and its acknowledgment were essential: "The fundamental issue for all South Africans is therefore to come to terms with our past on the only moral basis possible, namely that the truth be told and that the truth be acknowledged." The minister made clear from the outset that the commission's emphasis would be on truth and reconciliation, and reparations; there would be provision for amnesty, but amnesty would not be the commission's central thrust. In fact, amnesty already had been written into the final section of the interim constitution that paved the way for the election of 1994; but the detailed procedures and conditions of amnesty were left to be worked out by the new parliament.

Almost exactly one year later, in May of 1995, the Promotion of National Unity and Reconciliation Act establishing the Truth and Reconciliation Commission was introduced in parliament, and in July it became law. According to the terms of the act, the TRC was charged with investigating and documenting gross human rights abuses committed during the apartheid era, from 1960 to 1994. It was also empowered to grant amnesty "to those who make full disclosure of all the relevant facts relating to acts associated with a political objective committed in the course of the conflicts of the past." The TRC was chaired by Archbishop Desmond Tutu; Alex Boraine served as vice-chair. Tutu, an Anglican clergyman and lifelong civil rights activist, became the first Black general secretary of the South African Council of Churches in 1978, and in 1984 received the Nobel Peace Prize for "the courage and heroism shown by black South Africans in their use of peaceful methods in the struggle against apartheid." In 1986 he was elected archbishop of Cape Town and head of the Anglican Church in South Africa. He retired from this position when he was named chair of the TRC.

The TRC began hearings in April of 1996 and finished its work two years later in July of 1998, though ongoing amnesty investigations continued until the following June. It heard testimony from more than 21,000 victims of apartheid and received over seven thousand petitions for amnesty, of which over five thousand were refused and some eight hundred granted. Other petitions were withdrawn or otherwise disposed of. The TRC's findings were published in a five-volume 3,500-page report, and presented to President Mandela at the end of October 1998. Only two hundred copies of the full report were published.

To make the contents of the massive document accessible to as wide an audience as possible, the Independent Newspapers group, in conjunction with IDASA, sponsored the publication of verbatim extracts from the report in five special supplements over five successive days in Independent Newspaper outlets, a group that included dailies in Cape Town, Johannesburg,

Durban, Pretoria, and Kimberley. An editorial note to the first supplement, signed by Shaun Johnson, group editorial director of Independent Newspapers, acknowledged support from the Charles Stewart Mott Foundation, the Ford Foundation, the Rockefeller Brothers Fund, and the Comparative Human Relations Initiative (CHRI) in making the undertaking possible. Lynn Walker Huntley of the Southern Education Foundation, who was project director of CHRI, Peter Bell of CARE, Wilmot James of IDASA, and I were among the individuals mentioned as playing key roles.

CHRI's involvement in the publication project came about through the presence of Shaun Johnson and Wilmot James, then executive director of IDASA, on the initiative's advisory board, together with Peter Bell, then president of CARE, and me. The board met at the beginning of October 1998 at the Pocantico Conference Center in Tarrytown, New York. The TRC's report was due to come out at the end of the month, and Shaun Johnson and Wilmot James were already working on the idea of a special supplement as a means of disseminating its findings. The problem was money. A subsidy was required to underwrite the project, and time was short. Responding to the urgency of the situation, Peter Bell and I and others on the advisory board made calls to foundations and individuals asking for help; that effort raised sufficient funds for the special supplement to go forward.

Wilmot James later wrote that the printing of the five-part series produced a total of nearly three million individual supplements, or over five hundred thousand sets. These were distributed through all Independent Newspaper titles—including the *Star* (Johannesburg), the *Cape Times* and *Cape Argus* (Cape Town), the *Daily News* and the *Mercury* (Durban), the *Pretoria News*, and the *Diamond Fields Advertiser* (Kimberley)—and through IDASA, which placed nearly 75,000 sets in schools throughout the country. James estimated that through these publishing channels, some 1.5 million people gained access to the report. "Considering that only 200 copies of the full report were published," he concluded, "available for R750 (or US$136) for the set of five volumes, this is a stunning achievement in newspaper history, and in the mass distribution of a document in the public interest."

In his foreword to the TRC's report, Bishop Tutu spoke of the justification for the commission and alluded to the controversy surrounding its approach:

> All South Africans know that our recent history is littered with some horrendous occurrences. . . . Our country is soaked in the blood of our children of all races and of all political persuasions. . . . It is this history with which we have had to come to terms. We could not pretend it did not happen. Everyone agrees that South Africa must deal with that history and its legacy. It is how we do this that is in question—a bone of contention throughout the life of the Commission, right up to the time when this report was being written. And I imagine that we can assume that this particular point will remain controversial for a long time.

I visited South Africa more than once during the TRC hearings. On one occasion, in 1997, Wayne Fredericks and I visited the hearing itself, where we were warmly greeted by Bishop Tutu, who read into the record that Wayne and I, two longstanding friends of South Africa, were attending. It was a moving experience for us both. The formal part of the session began with an extensive personal statement by Bishop Tutu regarding his own and his parents' encounters with members of the law enforcement community. He noted that almost all of such contact involved efforts by the police and other authorities to restrict his or his family's freedom of movement or choice. He observed that in light of that history, he understood well how challenging the task was for the nation to change the behavior of law enforcement authorities and to persuade citizens that such a change had occurred.

It was clear that the TRC hearings overall allowed the broad public to see the nature and extent of the brutal governmental repression that characterized the apartheid era. The hearings also offered the opportunity to better understand the difficult challenges the country faced in establishing a rule-of-law culture, where all the governed could rely on the legal system to protect their constitutionally guaranteed rights rather than fear their abuse by that same system. The decision of the TRC to invite testimony from various business and nongovernmental sectors regarding the behavior of those sectors during the apartheid years and to describe any remedial action, proposed or underway, had the potential of broadening the engagement of the entire society in fashioning a new democratic and economically healthy future for South Africa.

Several years after the TRC had finished its work, Mandela and I reflected on the continuing debate about the truth and reconciliation approach versus a Nuremberg-type proceeding. We were discussing a session I had just chaired at a conference in Cape Town, where some university professors and others were taking issue with the TRC, arguing that a Nuremburg-type process would have produced more just punishment for the apartheid regime. The session was part of the final international conference of CHRI in Cape Town in May 2000. Mandela was actively interested in the debate, since the TRC approach fit well with his own personal philosophy. At the same time, he fully understood why some would question it. Mandela reasoned that, unlike the case of the Nuremberg tribunal following World War II, in South Africa there had been no major war, concluding with a clear winner and loser. Instead, there had been a determination to proceed with a negotiated settlement between the ANC and the National Party. That settlement called for a shared transitional government and a new constitution, based on human dignity, that protected all South Africans. In that context, he believed, as did I, that the TRC approach was essential.

As I reflected on it, no one strategy explained the peaceful transition in South Africa. It was a combination of liberation strategies and on-the-ground realities that caused the National Party to see that its long-term interest required a transition to majority rule with protection for minority rights, and that Nelson Mandela represented their best hope of achieving that outcome. Similarly, it was the sophistication of the ANC leadership that enabled it to accept the transitional process, which preserved dignity on all sides and resulted in majority rule under a constitutional democracy.

25

A Call to Action

In December of 1997, Thabo Mbeki was elected president of the African National Congress. At that time, the post-Mandela era was viewed within the country with much less fear than at any other time in the past three years. That development derived in large part from the demonstrated ability of Mbeki. While recognizing that the unique moral authority and leadership style of President Mandela could not be equaled, the country seemed ready to accept the reality that he would not be its elected leader after 1999, and that Thabo Mbeki appeared to be a worthy successor to lead the country during the next phase of its extraordinary journey to embed democracy into its political culture.

Significantly, that point was underscored by a number of Afrikaner leaders as well as in a piece by reporter Raymond Louw that cited an article in the *Financial Mail*, which concluded, "Thabo's middle name—Mvuyelwa—which means a person who people are happy with, was apposite for a man who was essentially a unifier and whose vision for South Africa is the creation of a unifying national consensus." Raymond Louw, an opposition journalist in the apartheid era and a lifelong media freedom activist, was the editor and publisher of the *Southern Africa Report*, a weekly current affairs newsletter. Louw shared his sense of the country's political climate with me during one of my 1997 visits to South Africa, as well as his prediction of the likely direction of the economy and intergroup relations among the various constituencies. He had a careful journalistic eye and his cautious optimism resonated.

The specific purposes of that trip were to update myself on current trends and developments; to consult with the Joint Education Trust on its initiative regarding community service (the trust was a partnership of leaders from the corporate world, the major political parties and labor unions, and representatives of Black business and education organizations whose goal was to restructure the country's segregated education system into one that was more equitable for all South Africans); and to discuss the possibility of a joint SA-U.S. meeting on the role and importance of an independent NGO sector in South Africa with U.S. ambassador James Joseph and Eric Molobi of the Kagiso Trust (a leading NGO). However, the trip coincided with an event to celebrate the legacy of Oliver Tambo on the occasion of his eightieth birthday, which was hosted by the deputy president and Mrs. Mbeki at the deputy president's residence, Over-Vaal, in Pretoria.

The celebration was a joyous occasion. The Tambo family and many of the ANC officials were present, along with representatives of many foreign governments. Thabo Mbeki was the principal speaker, and his expression of deep love, respect, and affection for Tambo was very moving. The afternoon was filled with conversations that deepened my understanding of the political climate in South Africa, and underscored the increasingly high esteem in which Thabo was held. It was one of the high points of the visit, in terms of both substantive content and emotional resonance. In addition, the renaming of the deputy president's house as the Oliver Tambo House assured that the historic contribution Tambo made to the struggle for democracy in South Africa would not be forgotten.

It was nice to see Oliver Tambo acknowledged in this way. I'd always felt that he was the brains of the ANC in exile, the force that virtually kept the organization together for twenty-five years. He was tough as nails but in many ways, he was the easiest to deal with, and with him I felt the deepest connection. Whenever I would go to see him, he was always extremely warm and welcoming.

There were times when Tambo clearly felt frustrated that he didn't have a more active role, despite Mandela's frequent conversations with him. He and I had very candid conversations whenever I visited, and his wife, Adelaide, was quick to tell me how much he looked forward to our meetings, and how important they were to him. They were important to me too.

His generosity of spirit was on full display during a visit I had with him when he was just out of the hospital in London, recovering from a stroke. I spent the afternoon mostly in his backyard, and we talked at length, South Africa being a main topic of conversation. As I was preparing to leave, he asked about my next destination. When I explained that I was returning to New York, he looked surprised and said, "You mean you made this trip just to see me?" When I answered "yes," we embraced and there were tears in his eyes when we disengaged.

Later, when I was visiting Tambo at his house in Johannesburg, Adelaide told me that IFP leader Gatsha Buthelezi also had come to London to visit Tambo around that same time. But she wouldn't let Buthelezi see Tambo, and she hadn't told him that Buthelezi had come until that moment. Tambo was visibly upset. He told Adelaide she should have let Buthelezi visit and that she had made a mistake.

I remember talking with Tambo once about doing the difficult work of getting in front of large groups of people and saying things you knew that at least half of them didn't want to hear. We could have been talking about a number of things, as I'd spent a great deal of time in the course of my working life listening to and talking with people about difficult topics, often trying to help them find some common ground or get to a place where they were able to hear one another. On that occasion we might have been discussing the contentious debate over divestment, particularly, about a time, in the mid-1980s, when I spent two days as a visiting scholar on the Columbia University campus, giving talks and meeting with people about U.S. policy toward South Africa regarding divestment.

It was a charged atmosphere with some stressful moments, especially since there were many politically active students who were skeptical about anything that questioned the kind of orthodoxy that was then popular on campus. Some were conflicted because there I was—an African American, a graduate of the college and the law school, well known for working in Black communities, and the head of a major foundation that was doing good work in South Africa—and I was asking them to think more broadly about some of their positions. They both respected and were disappointed in me for questioning them.

Recognizing this, I said at the beginning that I hadn't come to try to persuade them to think differently about what constituted appropriate U.S. policy toward South Africa. That, I thought, was something they each had to decide for themselves. What had brought me there was to talk, to share information, to say to those who had doubts with respect to policy and practices that were then flourishing on campus, that there were others of us who had spent a lot of time on this subject who had doubts too, that it's okay to have doubts and to raise those doubts, whatever the outcome.

As our talks proceeded, I noted that I was especially curious about why this particular group had refused to give Buthelezi an audience. I reasoned that they didn't have to agree with him, but that he lived and operated in South Africa, and thus represented millions of people there. I said that the core of their interest in South Africa was a belief in and support of the people in that country, and I didn't understand how they could deny a legitimate representative of some of those people to come and talk to them about his views and why he held them, to identify the differences of view, if they exist, and find out what those differences are based on, to form their own opinion.

I wasn't there to try to convince them of anything and I made that clear. I just wanted to open up the discussion and to share my own thinking on how the situation had evolved, where I thought it was leading, and what its implications were for the policy choices of universities and similar institutions. In the end, we had a good discussion. The kids were smart and they had sharp questions. They also had the ability to be very certain and narrow-minded.

I gave many lectures at universities and other venues, and I always took questions from the floor. Perhaps my being head of a major foundation encouraged people to listen more closely to what was being said, even when they disagreed. And through-out my working life I found myself in situations where I was attempting to create space for dialogue, or collaboration, or sometimes even just a space for listening. It was never easy work, and I remember Oliver, who understood this approach, at the end of that story, saying to me in his quiet and persistent way, "Keep at it, Frank!"

Keeping at it. He knew that's what had to be done. But you often got bloodied and battered in the process. There was never an end to it. You seldom saw light, and when something posi-tive did evolve later on, it was rare that anyone would make the connection back to the many roles played by people along the way.

Just a week before he died, in 1993, Adelaide told me that Oliver had wanted to talk to me. I didn't know if he was reach-ing out for a particular purpose or just wanted to talk, but by the time I got to South Africa he had died.

Oliver and Adelaide Tambo (who passed away in 2007) were two tenacious warriors on behalf of justice, freedom, and opportunity for all South Africans. They were also among the most humane and gentle people I have ever met.

I made frequent trips to South Africa in the later part of the 1990s, Milfred Fierce and Wayne Fredericks often accompanying me. One of the most memorable was in June of 1999, when Thabo Mbeki succeeded Nelson Mandela as the second democratically elected president of South Africa (with the ANC receiving more than 66 percent of the vote and carrying all but two of the nine provinces). Wayne Fredericks and I attended his inauguration.

Thabo was well known and widely respected. As deputy president to Mandela for five years, he had quietly overseen much of the government's strategy development and implementation. In his inaugural address and in his subsequent speech at the opening of parliament, he made clear his understanding of the urgent need to acccelerate the pace of economic growth so that more good jobs would be created for the people of South Africa, and to devolve more equity ownership to people of color so that their stake in the future health of the economy would be deepened.

He knew that accomplishing these goals would require more direct foreign investment, a systematic dismantling of many of the government-owned and -controlled entities, and the patience and support of the majority of Black South Africans, who naturally and understandably equated political power with economic advancement. He also recognized that the decades of economic and social mismanagement of the country by the National Party under apartheid could not instantly be reversed.

Thabo was acutely aware that patience was growing thin among the masses and that challenges from the labor movement and others in the ANC coalition were rising. He acted swiftly.

The Central Bank and the Ministries of Commerce and Finance were charged with leading the fight against inflation, which had been at double digits before the transition in 1994, and remained a significant problem. At the same time, the need to show demonstrable progress in the short term remained urgent.

Thabo organized advisory groups of international bankers and financiers to advise him and his cabinet, and went out among the people to explain the development strategy and the milestones they could expect to reach during the upcoming years. He also pledged an open and accountable administration that saw its mission rooted in the historic mission and values of the ANC.

While Mbeki was assuming the presidency, Nelson Mandela was rallying those around him for post-presidential work he was assuming for himself. This is how, in 1999, the Nelson Mandela Foundation was established, primarily as a vehicle for his active engagement with South African and world affairs. Its programs were designed to promote his vision and values and included work on HIV/AIDS, improving the quality of rural education, and peace and reconciliation interventions. Five years later, the Nelson Mandela Centre of Memory and Dialogue was established as an archival and documentation project and to promote dialogue around critical social issues. That center would later become the main focus of the foundation's work.

It was during the final international conference of the Comparative Human Relations Initiative (CHRI) in Cape Town, where we had all gathered for the official release of the initiative's reports after our four years of work, that I had the chance to talk in depth with Mandela about the foundation, both while seated next to him at the opening dinner and then later at a private meeting. He'd asked me to lend a helping hand to Khehla Shubane, who was acting executive director of the foundation and a member of the CHRI's advisory board, in his efforts to shape the organization's program agenda. I agreed and kept my word through extended conversations for several years with both Khehla and Jakes Gerwel, who was the foundation's chairman of the board.

My work with the Study Group kept me very busy in those years, and the majority of my time and energy was focused on South Africa. Quite unexpectedly, however, I was called upon to shift gears after the tragic events of September 11, 2001.

When nineteen militants associated with the Islamic extremist group Al-Qaeda hijacked four airplanes, carrying out suicide attacks against targets in the United States, two of the planes were flown into the twin towers of the World Trade Center in downtown Manhattan in New York City.

On that clear Tuesday morning, at 8:46 a.m., an American Airlines Boeing 767 crashed into the north tower of the World Trade Center, leaving a gaping hole near the 80th floor of the 110-story building. Television cameras were broadcasting live images of the horrific scene when, seventeen minutes later, another Boeing 767, United Airlines Flight 175, appeared in the sky and crashed into the south tower near the sixtieth floor.

By 10:30 a.m. both towers had collapsed in massive clouds of smoke as the world watched the unimaginable events in New York City unfold, along with simultaneous attacks at the Pentagon and in western Pennsylvania.

Close to three thousand people were killed in the September 11th attacks, most of them at the World Trade Center, including the first responders who rushed to the site in an attempt to evacuate the workers trapped in the building before the towers fell. Countless lives were affected by this act of terrorism that was unlike anything our country had experienced before. And New York City, specifically lower Manhattan, was Ground Zero.

The city rallied in the wake of the tragedy, showing its resilience and resolve amid the devastation and loss. And the philanthropic community immediately sprang into action.

Lorie Slutsky of the New York Community Trust immediately joined forces with the United Way to find a way to respond. Within a day they'd established an entity they called the September 11th Fund for New Yorkers, Americans, and the world to have a way to contribute to the enormous needs that would result from the attacks. Lorie was in touch with many philanthropic leaders in this effort, including my predecessor at Ford, Susan Berresford. There were many things to be figured out, and with each day that passed the need for this fund and the massive challenges it would face in terms of meeting the needs of those affected became more pronounced. Within a week more than $100 million was raised.

Lorie and I knew each other from my days at Ford when we'd done some work together on inequities in New York state education, primarily as it related to funding formulas. At the time of the September 11th attacks she was president of the New York Community Trust, and she knew immediately that the work required of the September 11th Fund was well beyond what her staff or the staff of the United Way (who were already managing full workloads) could do. It was decided that a new organization would be formed, which wouldn't be permanent but would have its own dedicated staff and leader, ideally a person who understood New York in a way that would allow the organization to distribute the enormous resources in a timely and smart way, and who could bring together a distinguished board. Little did I know that in her conversations with various stakeholders, she said on more than one occasion that it "had to be someone like Frank Thomas."

In the heat of all of this, I was having dinner with Kate in a restaurant on Thirty-Fourth Street, and Lorie happened to come in with some of her staff members whom she was taking out to dinner after a late night working on the September 11th project.

She told me a bit about what she was up to and asked if I might have some time to talk to her about it in the next day or two. I was eager to offer whatever advice I could and we met.

We talked at great length about the fund, the possibilities for board appointments, the distribution of monies, and a host of other details, and then Lorie said she couldn't think of anyone who would be better suited to chair the effort than I. By that time, I'd been deep into thinking about the workings of this entity and, of course, the importance of it, but taking on such a position, especially in light of how busy I already was with my Study Group efforts, didn't seem possible. I told her I would think about it, though, and we left it at that.

I spent a couple of days thinking of all the reasons why I couldn't or shouldn't do it, but I kept coming back to how important New York was, and had always been, to me. I realized that I wanted to do it. Like so many other positions I'd held in my life, it was completely unplanned and unexpected, but something about it felt right. I accepted the offer and became the chairman of the board of the September 11th Fund. Joshua Gotbaum, former executive associate director and controller of the U.S. Office of Management and Budget, was named executive director and CEO, and the board was drawn from the governing bodies of the United Way of New York City and the New York Community Trust. As a group, we would be responsible for establishing guidelines for the effective and fair distribution of the donations to help victims' families and the communities affected by the disaster.

We faced difficult choices about whom to help and how best to provide aid. We had to find ways to reach victims from both the metropolitan area and the rest of the country, even those from other countries. There were immediate and longer-term needs to be met, and in addition to the people most immediately and directly affected, we wanted to meet the needs of larger affected communities and to be sure we were reaching all the victims, including those who might not have spoken English and who may have been reluctant to seek assistance. The task was daunting and there was no model in place to follow.

From September 2001 through December 2004, the fund awarded grants totaling almost $528 million. The money provided financial assistance, services to individuals and families, services to assist businesses and communities in rebuilding efforts, and help with rescue and recovery.

Almost everyone living in New York had personal connections to the tragedy as well. My friend and former colleague from the Bedford Stuyvesant Restoration Corporation, Ben Glascoe, lost his son, Keith, in the towers that day. Keith perished along with six other New York City firefighters from Ladder Company 21, leaving behind two children and his wife, who was pregnant at the time. I attended Keith's funeral and saw firsthand the loss and pain of the families affected. It felt extremely worthwhile to do anything I could to begin to address the needs of the countless victims of the attacks while putting to use my knowledge of city government, politics, and philanthropic operations.

When all was said and done, I took some degree of comfort knowing that the September 11th Fund helped as many people who were affected by the September 11th attacks as we possibly could have, and that we helped them in the wide variety of ways that people need help when they are rebuilding their lives in the wake of tragedy.

26

Full Circle

I consider myself a fortunate person who has lived a fulfilling and rewarding life. I've worked hard and have seized the opportunities presented to me, even though many of them came with significant challenges, and even though many were completely unexpected.

Talking about myself and what I've done throughout my life is not something I ever find myself wanting to do. The work is there and what it represents speaks for itself. It did become clear, however, that documentation could be useful and would also honor the people who worked with me and the values, ideals, and principles that form the foundation of everything I've done. For this reason, I accepted the offer to sit down with Julieanna Richardson for hours of interviews that would serve as the basis for one of her HistoryMakers live events. The HistoryMakers project records the oral histories of African Americans to provide a more inclusive record of American history and to "educate and enlighten millions worldwide." It also interviews people who have been a part of the subject's life. All of this culminates in a televised event that weaves the stories and experiences together seamlessly.

No stone was left unturned in the many, many hours of interviews Julieanna conducted. From my high school and college classmates to my Bedford Stuyvesant Restoration team, to my Ford Foundation colleagues, to the many people who worked with me on projects associated with South Africa, every part of my life was represented.

On the evening that the live event was recorded—a Saturday evening in November 2017—most of these people were in attendance, as were dear friends and family. Darren Walker, current president of the Ford Foundation (and the second African American to hold the position), chaired the event and provided reflections that were meaningful to me as he and I have spent a lot of time sharing experiences, discussing his work and mine, and, of course, Ford. Vernon Jordan and Gloria Steinem hosted the event, and having such close friends at the reins set the tone for a lovely and very memorable evening.

Hearing my story told through the eyes of people who've played important roles in my life, from my boyhood to the present day, was an experience that I felt quite fortunate to have, even as the spotlight is not always a comfortable place for me.

When I was called up to sit with Gloria and Vernon, I remarked that "I even got a little excited about this," which is somewhat of a rarity, as those who know me can attest. I commented that I had a sense of fulfillment, not about the end of things but about the continuation of things that matter. I also thought about my friendships and just how much each person, and what they were doing in their lives, meant to me. And, of course, I was flooded with thoughts of my sisters, who were all older than I was, and who nurtured and supported me in a way that made me know what was possible in my life. And thoughts of my mother, who instructed me that getting the best education I could and using that education—along with whatever talent, knowledge, and capacity I possessed—to help not just myself, but other people, would lead to a life filled with important and meaningful work.

As I listened to Al Vann and George Patterson reminisce about my drum and bugle corps days and high school basketball, and Stephen Kaufman, Pierre Leval, and Robert Morgenthau talking about my time in the U.S. attorney's office, and Jim Shipp and Charles Shorter discussing our work at the Bedford Stuyvesant Restoration Corporation, and Darren Walker and Buzz Tenny reflecting on my Ford experience, and Henry Schacht and Sandy Weill reflecting on my work on corporate boards, and Albie Sachs, Mamphela Ramphele, and Gay McDougall sharing about my efforts on behalf of South Africa, I was reminded of so much impactful work, for which I could only partly take credit since so many others were also involved. On my journey I always recognized the importance of finding smart and dedicated people and using whatever talent and skills I had to nurture theirs.

Less than a month after the HistoryMakers evening, with the event, the people who turned up for it, and the flood of memories it unleashed still fresh in my mind, I traveled to South Africa, accompanied by Kate and my daughter Hillary. I've said on numerous occasions that South Africa would always be a special part of my life, and this trip was just another reminder to me of why.

The catalyst for my visit was that the University of the Witwatersrand in Johannesburg was awarding me an honorary doctorate of laws degree and wanted me to be present for the honor. We'd decided that the degree would be conferred on December 5 during a graduation ceremony of the Faculty of Commerce, Law and Management.

It was wonderful to be back in South Africa with Kate. And traveling with Hillary was also quite meaningful. Hillary had spent time in South Africa, as had I, and it was special that now we would be sharing the experience for the first time.

In the days leading up to the degree ceremony, I attended a roundtable hosted by Nicolette Naylor, the regional director of the Ford Foundation's Southern Africa office in Johannesburg. It was a lively conversation that included Ford staff, which allowed me to share both professional and personal observations and stories. Hillary and Kate were present and were also included in the discussion. Someone raised the question of what inspired the work I'd done throughout my life—a question I'd been asked before and will probably be asked again. So often this question brings to mind my mother and the values instilled in me at a young age. I always knew the strength of my own willpower as well as the transformative possibilities that existed when it was combined with the willpower of others. It is important to be conscious at all times that you are just one part of a larger picture. Along with this, however, I was always mindful that individual work could have a big impact on the greater good and that we all had a responsibility to contribute to something greater.

We also had the opportunity that week to visit with Justice Edwin Cameron of the Constitutional Court of South Africa, along with some members of his staff. Cameron was appointed to the bench by President Mandela in 1994, and before serving as a justice of the Constitutional Court (from 2009 to 2019), he was a judge of the Supreme Court of Appeal and of the High Court. Cameron was hailed by Mandela as "one of South Africa's heroes," and he was a fierce advocate for human rights, gay rights, and HIV/AIDS awareness and policy.

I had a deep connection to the law and to those practicing it in South Africa, including the ongoing Franklin Thomas fellowships, funded by the Ford Foundation, that were awarded annually by the Constitutional Court Trust to promising young Black South Africans who have clerked at the Constitutional Court. The fellowship provided them with an opportunity to study toward a one-year master of laws degree at a law school in the U.S. The discussion with Justice Cameron and his staff allowed me to listen and learn about the ongoing processes of the legal profession and the creation and interpretation of new laws in South Africa and reflect on the country as a dynamic, ever-evolving entity. It was also a good opportunity to acknowledge the similarities between the U.S. and South Africa, and how at that moment in time, nearing the end of Trump's first year as president, human rights in the U.S. were being trampled.

The primary reason for my trip, the awarding of the honorary degree, took place on December 5, a notable date in South African history as it was the birth date of Robert Mangaliso Sobukwe, the founding president of the Pan Africanist Congress, and the date that Nelson Mandela passed away, exactly four years earlier, in 2013.

During the degree ceremony, Vice-Chancellor Adam Habib offered remarks to a wonderfully diverse audience that included the families of local students who were graduating. He called me a friend of South Africa and discussed the role I'd played in mobilizing support for the oppressed during apartheid rule. He also talked about the role the Ford Foundation played in strengthening support for social justice programs in South Africa and for enabling large numbers of Black South Africans to study for degrees that would help them fight for and support a free South Africa.

When I addressed the audience that day, once again, I thought back to my childhood, as the son of immigrants who could easily have been discounted for many reasons. But through the support of my family, and hard work, I was able to secure a law degree that I put to use for the collective good. I wanted the students there that day to know they, too, had this power and were able to make change happen in the world around them.

This wasn't the first honorary degree I'd been awarded but it was a special one. From the moment I became involved with South Africa, I could never remove myself, or it from my life. I was grateful for the work I was able to do there and the friendships I built through it, including with Nelson Mandela, and for having the ongoing privilege of supporting the blueprint he left for the entire world.

There was a dinner that same evening at the vice-chancellor's home that Hillary, Kate, and I attended along with numerous people associated with the university. It was a lively evening with good discussion about the role of the U.S. and organizations like Ford in South Africa, as well as the part that younger people have played in creating change in the country. Almost every conversation included questions about President Trump and the state of things in the U.S., which from the outside was, I'm sure, a source of confusion and fascination. It was a period when the country's collective conscience seemed satisfied to turn a blind eye toward the many assaults on basic human rights that were occurring because Americans were comfortable with the health of the economy. It was concerning, to say the least.

Our trip culminated with a visit to the Nelson Mandela Children's Hospital, an institution that had been a dream of Mandela's for a very long time, and which treated its first patients in June of 2017. The idea began in 2005 when Mandela expressed his desire for improved medical care for children and asked the Nelson Mandela Children's Fund to perform a study of pediatric care in the country. When the need for the hospital was identified, the fund began a massive fundraising effort to make it a reality. I was very involved in the fund's U.S. office and knew the importance of this facility to Mandela's vision for South Africa. Visiting the hospital on that December day was a joyous occasion. It was an impressive state-of-the-art facility and a beautiful tribute to Mandela's commitment to the health and welfare of South African children.

We were shown around the very large facility by a number of staff, as well as Sibongile Mkhabela, the CEO of the Nelson Mandela Children's Fund and the Nelson Mandela Children's Hospital Trust. Mkhabela was instrumental in growing the endowment of the fund and in navigating its strategic direction. The hospital itself was very welcoming, designed with bright colors and inviting reception areas and lounges. There were gardens and play areas for children and art throughout, created by children and artists from around the world. The hospital housed multiple wards, including an ICU and a nephrology unit, as well as ten operating rooms. In keeping with Mandela's vision and spirit, the philosophy behind the hospital's medical care was infused with care and hope. I think I was beaming with happiness and pride throughout the entire three-hour visit.

The time I'd spent in South Africa over the years always motivated me; and my commitment to and passion for the place, which had developed on my very first trip with Vernon in the mid-1970s, never waned. I was struck by this during my visit in 2017, as I reflected on the changes that had taken place in those forty years, and the life of Nelson Mandela, whose perseverance, patience, and resolve, as well as his willingness to risk and sacrifice everything to stand on principle, helped propel me in my own life and work. I wasn't sure when, or if, I'd travel to South Africa again, but it would continue to be a part of me nonetheless.

I've often used the word "unplanned" when talking about my life. Some of the most satisfying professional experiences I've had came knocking at my door and took me in directions I'm not sure I ever imagined. They usually had one thing in common, though: the fact that after careful consideration, I thought I could make a difference and was energized by the work before me, even when it promised to be difficult. But any difference I've made must also be attributed to the tremendous peers and colleagues I've had along the way, as our collective impact was far greater than anything I could have accomplished alone.

Acknowledgments

To all of you who have encouraged me to write it all down—
thank you!

Index

About the Author

Franklin A. Thomas's career spanned many civic roles, from assistant U.S. attorney to president and CEO of the Bedford Stuyvesant Restoration Corporation. In 1979, he was named president of the Ford Foundation, where he served until 1996.

Publishing in the Public Interest

Thank you for reading this book published by The New Press. The New Press is a nonprofit, public interest publisher. New Press books and authors play a crucial role in sparking conversations about the key political and social issues of our day.

We hope you enjoyed this book and that you will stay in touch with The New Press. Here are a few ways to stay up to date with our books, events, and the issues we cover:

- Sign up at www.thenewpress.com/subscribe to receive updates on New Press authors and issues and to be notified about local events
- www.facebook.com/newpressbooks
- www.twitter.com/thenewpress
- www.instagram.com/thenewpress

Please consider buying New Press books for yourself; for friends and family; or to donate to schools, libraries, community centers, prison libraries, and other organizations involved with the issues our authors write about.

The New Press is a 501(c)(3) nonprofit organization. You can also support our work with a tax-deductible gift by visiting www.thenewpress.com/donate.